THE CONCEPT OF RUDRA-ŚIVA THROUGH THE AGES

THE CONCEPT OF RUDRA-ŚIVA THROUGH THE AGES

MAHADEV CHAKRAVARTI

MOTILAL BANARSIDASS
Delhi Varanasi Patna Madras

The publication was financially supported by the Indian Council of Historical Research, New Delhi. The responsibility for the facts stated, opinions expressed or conclusions reached is entirely that of the author and Indian Council of Historical Research accepts no responsibility for them.

Head Office: Bungalow Road, Delhi 110 007
Branches: Chowk, Varanasi 221 001
Ashok Rajpath, Patna 800 004
6 Appar Swamy Koil Street, Mylapore,
Madras 600 004

First Edition: Delhi, 1986

ISBN: 81–208–0053–2

Printed in India by Narendra Prakash Jain at Shri Jainendra Press, A-45 Naraina, Phase I, New Delhi 110 028 and published by Shantilal Jain for Motilal Banarsidass, Delhi 110 007.

To my mentor
Professor D. C. SIRCAR

CONTENTS

PREFACE

The present work is an attempt to throw light, with the help of literary and archaeological data, on the gradual development of the concept of Rudra-Śiva in his theriomorphic, anthropomorphic and phallic forms since the days of the Harappa civilization. The approach to the subject is mainly historical.

In the first chapter, an attempt has been made to congregate the flakes of ideas about Rudra as found in the Vedic literature, then to identify the Vedic Rudra with a host of pre- and post-Vedic deities and finally to show how this composite Aryan-non-Aryan divinity was not only admitted but was ultimately crowned with an exalted position in the Brāhmaṇical pantheon.

The second chapter deals with the theriomorphic representation of Śiva as bull. It has been shown how Śiva in this form has so many counterparts in the other religions of the world. Stress has been laid on the fact that in course of time the bull, though once identical with the deity, was relegated to the position of the mount of Śiva.

In the third chapter, there is the interesting story of the phallic cult which has to be regarded as a part of the general evolution of the religious thoughts of man in various parts of the world. A part of the discussion refers to the relation between Śaivism and Phallicism and the different representations of the phallic god in early Indian literature.

In the final chapter, I have discussed the different anthropomorphic images of Śiva since the Harappa civilization. Owing to paucity of sculptural specimens, numismatic and glyptic data have been particularly examined to determine the human and phallic forms of Śiva in early Indian art. The last two sections in this chapter on art are : 'Śiva and the *Liṅga* in Further India', and 'Śiva's Bull in Art'.

The present work is the outcome of years of research under the supervision of Professor D. C. Sircar who introduced me to the world of traditional scholarship in letter and spirit which made it possible for me to go through the original Sanskrit texts. The original title of the work was *Rudra-Śiva in Ancient India—His Theriomorphic, Anthropomorphic and Phallic Forms* and it was submitted as a thesis for the degree of Doctor of Philosophy at the Department of Ancient Indian History and Culture, Calcutta University in 1976. The eminent scholars of Ancient Indian History, Professor B. Mukherjee of Calcutta University, Professor T. V. Mahalingam of Madras University, Professor B. P. Sinha of Patna University were kind enough to go through the manuscript and all of them offered many valuable suggestions, inspiring comments and urged its early publication. As per the suggestion of the Editor of M/s Motilal Banarsidass, I have also consulted all the available publications which have come out after my thesis was written and referred to the same at relevant places in the present book.

I express my unfeigned gratitude and thanks to all those from whom I have taken the photos for illustration and to the authors and publishers of the books which I have consulted in the present work. I offer my thanks to the Indian Council of Historical Research and to M/s Motilal Banarsidass for the publication of this book. My friends and colleagues, particularly Dr. Biswapati Roy, have put me under a debt of gratitude by their words of encouragement. No word is enough to express my gratitude to my wife, Smt. Tapati Chakravarti, Assistant Professor of Economics.

I shall feel amply rewarded if the present work stimulates any thinking along the lines of my approach.

Mahadev Chakravarti

Calcutta University
Post Graduate Centre,
Agartala, Tripura-799004

LIST OF ABBREVIATIONS

ABORI	*Annals of the Bhandarkar Oriental Research Institute*
ĀGS	*Āśvalāyana Gṛhyasūtra*
AICFE	*Ancient Indian Colonies in the Far East,* by Majumdar, R.C.
AIHT	*Ancient Indian Historical Tradition*, by Pargiter, F.E.
ARASI / *ASIAR*	*Annual Report of the Archaeological Survey of India*
ASR	*Archaeological Survey Report*
AU	*Atharvaśiras Upaniṣad*
AV	*Atharvaveda*
BEFEO	*Bulletin de l'École Française d'Extême*
BG	*Bombay Gazetteer*
BMC / *BMCCGSKI*	*British Museum Catalogue of Coins of the Greek and Scythic Kings of India*, by Gardner, P.
CAI	*Coins of Ancient India*, by Cunningham, A.
CBIMA	*A Catalogue of the Brāhmaṇical Images in Mathurā Art,* by Agrawala, V.S.
CCAI	*Catalogue of Coins of Ancient India*, by Allan, J.
CCAWKTB	*Catalogue of Coins of the Andhra, Western Kṣatrapa, Traikūṭaka and Bodhi Dynasties*, by Rapson, E.J.
CCGDBM	*Catalogue of Coins of the Gupta Dynasty in the British Museum*, by Allan, J.
CCIM	*Catalogue of Coins in the Indian Museum*, by Smith, V.A.
CHI	*Cambridge History of India*
CII	*Corpus Inscriptionum Indicarum*
CIK	*Coins of the Indo-Scythians and Kuṣāṇas*, by Cunningham, A.
CR	*Calcutta Review*

DHI	*Development of Hindu Iconography*, by Banerjea, J.N.
EI / *Ep. Ind.*	*Epigraphia Indica*
EHI	*Elements of Hindu Iconography*, by Gopinatha Rao, T.A.
ERE	*Encyclopaedia of Religion and Ethics*
EWA	*Encyclopaedia of World Art*
GI	*Gupta Inscriptions*, by Fleet, J.F.
GB	*The Golden Bough*, by Frazer, J.G.
HG	*Hiraṇyakeśī Gṛhyasūtra*
HIIA	*History of Indian and Indonesian Art*, by Coomaraswamy, A.K.
HIL	*History of Indian Literature*, by Winternitz, M.
IA	*Indian Antiquary*
IC	*Indian Culture*
IHQ	*Indian Historical Quarterly*
IMC	*Indian Museum Catalogue*
Ind. Stud.	*Indische Studien*
JAOS	*Journal of the American Oriental Society*
JAS	*Journal of the Asiatic Society*
JASB / *JRASB*	*Journal of the Asiatic Society* (or *Royal Asiatic Society*) *of Bengal*
JBBRAS	*Journal of the Bombay Branch of the Royal Asiatic Society*
JBRS	*Journal of the Bihar Research Society*
JBORS	*Journal of the Bihar and Orissa Research Society*
JDL	*Journal of the Department of Letters* (Calcutta University)
JGIS	*Journal of the Greater India Society*
JIH	*Journal of Indian History*
JISOA	*Journal of the Indian Society of Orienta Art*
JNSI	*Journal of the Numismatic Society of India*
JOR	*Journal of the Oriental Research*
JUPHS	*Journal of the U.P. Historical Society*
KU	*Kaṭhopaniṣad*
MASI	*Memoir of the Archaeological Society of India.*
Mbh	*Mahābhārata.*

MIC	*Mohenjodaro and the Indus Civilisation*, by Marshall, J.
NC	*Numismatic Chronicle*
ORLI	*Outlines of the Religious Literature of India*, by Farquhar, J.N.
OST	*Original Sanskrit Texts*, by Muir, J.
P	*Purāṇa*
PHAI	*Political History of Ancient India*, by Raychaudhuri, H.C.
PMC	*Punjab Museum Catalogue of Coins*, by Whitehead, R.B.
PR	*Popular Ṛeligion and Folk-lore of Northern India*, by Crooke, W.
PTR	*Paurāṇic and Tāntric Religion,* by Banerjea, J.N.
QJMS	*Quarterly Journal of the Mythic Society*
RAA	*Religion in Art and Archaeology*, by Banerjea, J.N.
Ram.	*Rāmāyaṇa*
RPVU	*Religion and Philosophy of the Vedas and Upaniṣads*, by Keith, A.B.
RV	*Ṛgveda*
SB	*Śatapatha Brāhmaṇa*
SBE	*Sacred Books of the East*
SI	*Select Inscriptions*, by Sircar, D.C.
SU	*Śvetāśvatara Upaniṣad*
SV	*Sāmaveda*
TA	*Taittirīya Āraṇyaka*
TS	*Taittirīya Saṁhitā*
VM	*Vedic Mythology*, by Macdonell, A.A.
VS / Vaj. Sam.	*Vājasaneyī Saṁhitā*
VSMRS	*Vaiṣṇavism, Śaivism and Minor Religious Systems*, by Bhandarkar, R.G.
YV	*Yajurveda*
ZM	*Zoological Mythology*, by Gubernatis, A.D.

CHAPTER I

RUDRA AND RUDRA-ŚIVA

(i) Concept of Rudra in the Vedic Literature

Rudra is comparatively a minor, though physically attractive, atmospheric god in the *Ṛgveda* with only three entire hymns to him and about seventy-five casual references in all.[1] But in course of ages this minor deity has developed, as a result of fusion with a number of non-Aryan divinities, into the great and powerful god Rudra-Śiva, the third deity of the Hindu triad. The concept of Śiva is not built up by the Vedic faith and tradition alone, for we have already a prototype of *trimukha yogīśvara paśupati ūrdhvaliṅga* Śiva in the pre-Vedic Harappa civilization. However, we shall here examine the gradual development of the concept of Rudra as found in the Vedic Literature.

By Vedic literature of the earlier stratum we mean the *Saṁhitās*, the *Brāhmaṇas*, the *Āraṇyakas* and the *Upaniṣads*, falling respectively under Mantra, Vidhi, Arthavāda and Vedānta. The last stage of Vedic literature is represented by the *Sūtras* which are compendious treatises dealing with Vedic ritual on the one hand, and with customary law on the other.[2] In the present section, we first propose to cite the texts of the *Ṛgveda*, in which the word 'Rudra' occurs as the name of a deity.

In the *Ṛgveda*, Rudra is described as fierce[3] and destructive like a terrible wild beast,[4] the swift,[5] the red boar of the sky,[6]

1. Macdonell, A.A., *Vedic Mythology*, Strassburg, 1897, p. 74.
2. Macdonell, A.A., *A History of Sanskrit Literature*, 1965, p. 29.
3. II. 33. 9.
4. II. 33. 11.
5. I. 114. 4.
6. I. 114. 5.

the cow-slayer,[7] the man-slayer,[8] the lord of animal sacrifices,[9] the father of the Rudras or Maruts,[10] and one who bears swift arrows[11] and strong bow.[12]. Although no distinct cosmical function is ascribed to him,[13] he is, in a vague and uncertain anthropomorphic form, of the dreadful and destructive powers of nature—of storms, lightning and forest fires.[14] In a passage of the *Ṛgveda*[15] he is also identified with Agni who had his abode in the sky as the sun, in the atmosphere as lightning and on the earth as fire.[16] The crackling flame of the fire as of the unbridled fury of the raging storm, its roaring, its tearing up of heaven and earth;[17] the dark masses of clouds pierced only by the quivering gleams of lightning and thunderbolt must have produced a strong and overpowering impact upon the minds of the old Aryans of India or the Vedic bards who saw Rudra as the cause of all these shuddering and fearful phenomena and naturally connected everything terrible and horrible with him. Many are the occasions in the life of man which excite fear and the sentiment of fear is at the bottom for many of the hymns addressed to Rudra in the *Ṛgveda*. But human beings do not believe in a purely malignant power or a malevolent deity reigning in the universe;[18] necessarily, the characters ascribed to Rudra in the *Ṛgveda* are the most heterogeneous, frequently indefinite and of rather incompatible qualities,[19] and numerous opposite functions are constantly assigned to him.

7. I.114.10.
8. I.114.10.
9. I. 43. 4.
10. I. 114, II. 33.
11. II. 33. 10.
12. VII. 46. 1.
13. *ERE*, Vol. II, p. 812.
14. *Ibid.*, Vol. XI, p. 91.
15. II. 1.
16. Rao, T.A.G., *Elements of Hindu Iconography*, Madras, 1914, Vol. II, p. 41.
17. According to Weber (*Indische Studien*, I, 1853, p. 272) Rudra is called 'red boar of the sky' in the *RV* (I. 114. 5) as the storm-clouds are elsewhere conceived under the same image.
18. Bhandarkar, R.G., *Vaiṣṇavism, Śaivism and Minor Religious Systems*, Strassburg ed., 1913, p. 102.
19. Wilson, H.H., *Rig-Veda-Saṁhitā*, Vol. II, Poona, 1925, p.v.

We have also some picturesque epithets applied to Rudra in the *Ṛgveda*. He is fair-lipped,[20] youthful,[21] tawny,[22] dazzling,[23] shining like the bright sun,[24] arrayed with golden ornaments,[25] the wise,[26] the intelligent,[27] the most liberal,[28] the most powerful,[29] the lord of songs,[30] the possessor of healing medicines,[31] or the physician of physicians.[32] He is the god with braided hair,[33] is decked with brilliant golden ornaments,[34] sits on a chariot,[35] the unconquered conqueror[36] and the universal ruler.[37]

True, Rudra in the *Ṛgveda* represented the ruthlessness of nature, the storm and the pestilential wind—the only god who is feared and held in awe by the Vedic bards. But side by side, the healing aspect of the deity is reflected in the 'beneficent rains loosened by the storm'[38] which is a very important feature of Rudra's character and without which he could hardly have been accepted as a god in the Ṛgvedic religion.[39] He combines in himself the malevolent and benevolent, the terrific and pacific, the demoniac and angelic features. These are the germs which afterwards developed into Rudra-Śiva. Rudra in the *Ṛgveda* is implored to 'slacken his bow'[40], and not to do any harm, in his

20. II. 33.
21. II. 33. 11.
22. II. 33.
23. I. 114.
24. I. 43. 5.
25. II. 33.
26. I. 43. 1.
27. VII. 46. 1.
28. I. 43. 1.
29. I. 43. 1.
30. I. 43. 4.
31. I. 43. 4., *Jalāṣa-bheṣaja*, II. 33.7; VII. 35.6.
32. II. 4. 4, 4.
33. I. 114. 1, 5.
34. II. 33. 9.
35. II. 33. 11.
36. VII. 46. 1.
37. VII. 46. 2.
38. Keith, A.B., *The Religion and Philosophy of the Veda and Upaniṣads*, Harvard University, 1925, p. 147.
39. *Loc. cit.*
40. Sitaramiah, G., 'Rudra in the Ṛgveda' in *Quarterly Journal of the Mythic Society*, Bangalore, Vol. 32, 1941, October, p. 146.

anger, to his worshippers. The Vedic bard flatters this malevolent deity with fair words to deprecate his wrath, eulogises in superlatives to pacify his anger, and tries in every way to render him gracious or auspicious, that is, Śiva. Let us quote some hymns of the *Ṛgveda* in this context :

"We implore Rudra,...for health, wealth, and his favour."[41]

"We offer these prayers to Rudra, the strong, whose hair is braided, who rules over heroes, that he may be a blessing to man and beast, that everything in this our village may be prosperous and free from disease."[42]

"Be gracious to us, O Rudra, and give us joy, and we shall honour thee, the ruler of heroes, with worship."[43]

"We call down for our help the fierce Rudra, who fulfils our sacrifice, the swift, the wise; may he drive far away from us the anger of the gods; we desire his goodwill only."[44]

"Do not slay our great or our small ones, our growing or our grown ones, our father or our mother, and do not hurt our own bodies, O Rudra."[45]

"O Rudra, hurt us not in our kith and kin, nor in our own life, not in our cows, nor in our horses ! Do not slay our men in thy wrath : carrying libations, we call on thee always."[46]

"Let thy cow-slaying and thy man-slaying be far away, and let thy favour be with us, O ruler of heroes ! Be gracious to us, and bless us O god, and then give us twofold protection."[47]

The etymology of the word *rudra* is also somewhat uncertain as regards the meaning. It is usually derived from the root *rud* (to cry), and interpreted as the 'howler'.[48] By Grassmann[49] *rudra* is connected with a root *rud* having the conjectural meaning of 'to shine', or according to Pischel,[50] 'to be ruddy'. We have

41. I. 43. 4.
42. I. 114. 1.
43. I. 114. 2.
44. I. 114. 4.
45. I. 114. 7.
46. I. 114. 8.
47. I. 114. 10.
48. Macdonell, A.A., *Vedic Mythology*, p. 77.
49. cf. *loc. cit.*; Keith, *op. cit.*, 146.
50. *cf. loc. cit.*

another etymology in which Rudra is associated with Rodasī, the meaning of which is Heaven and Earth,[51] implying the male and female aspects of Rudra,[52] and this conception of Vedic Rodasī becomes ultimately *Ardhanārīśvara* in Purāṇic formulation.[53] A clear proof of the obscurity of the exact basis of Rudra is that Sāyaṇa[54] suggests no fewer than six derivations of the word.[55]

51. Dikshitar, V.R.R., The *Purāṇa Index*, Vol. III, Madras, 1955, p. 102.

52. According to Yāska, Rodasī is the wife of Rudra. See Wilson, H.H., *Rig-Veda-Saṁhitā*, Vol. III, p. 411n.

See also Bhattacharji, S., *The Indian Theogony*; *a comparative study of Indian mythology from the Vedas to the Puranas*, Cambridge, 1970, p. 158. Bhattacharji in her article 'Rudra from the Vedas to the Mahabharata' in *ABORI*, 41 (1960), pp. 85-128, also discusses in detail the concept of Rudra and the names of the consort of Rudra as they appear in the original texts.

53. Agrawala, V.S., *Śiva-Mahādeva*, 1st ed., p. 9.

54. *cf.* Muir, J., *Original Sanskrit Texts*, Vol. IV, London, 1873, p. 303, n. 9.

55. "*Rodayati sarvam antakāle iti Rudraḥ* /
yadvā rut saṁsārākhyaṁ duḥkham /
tad drāvayaty apagamayati vināśayati iti Rudraḥ /
yadvā rutaḥ śabda-rūpāḥ upanishadaḥ /
tābhir drūyate gamyate pratipādyate iti Rudraḥ /
yadvā rut śabdātmikā vāṇī tat-pratipādyātma-vidyāvā /
tam upāsakebhyo rāti dadāti iti Rudraḥ /
yadvā ruṇaddhy āvṛiṇoti iti rud andhakārādi /
tad dṛiṇāti vidārayati iti Rudraḥ /
yadvā kadāchid devāsura-sangrāme 'gny-ātmako
Rudro devair nikshiptam dhanaṁ apahṛitya niragāt /
asurān jitvā devāḥ enam anvishya dṛishṭvā dhanam apāharam /
tadānīm arudat /
tasmād Rudraḥ ity ākhyāyate //"

"He is called Rudra(1)because he makes everyone weep (*'rodayati'*) at the destruction of the world; or(2) 'rut' means the suffering called the world. He drives away (*'drāvayati'*), removes, destroys that : therefore he is named Rudra; or (3) 'rut' in the plural means the Upanishads, which are composed of words: by them he is attained, expounded (*'drūyate'*):therefore he is termed Rudra; as (4) 'rut' signifies language composed of words, or the science of soul which is to be explained by it : this he gives (*'rāti'*) to his worshippers: hence he is denominated Rudra; or (5) the root 'rudh' means to shut, cover; and therefore, 'rut' means darkness, etc. : he tears (*'dṛiṇāti'*), rends, it : therefore he is designated Rudra; or (6) when on one occasion there was a battle between the gods and Asuras, Rudra having the nature of Agni carried off the

Arbman[56] sees in Rudra a primitive popular deity, the prototype of Śiva. Oldenberg[57] traces the nature of Rudra in its essence to a mountain and forest god. Hillebrandt[58] finds in him a god of the horrors of the tropical climate. Schroeder[59] insists that Rudra is nothing more than the elevation to the rank of a high god of the chief of the souls of the dead. But the main defects of the above theories are that they are not based upon the characteristics of Rudra as found in the Vedas; as Keith[60] rightly points out, they depend too exclusively upon the later accounts of the nature of Rudra-Śiva.

The Ṛgvedic Rudra remains the same in the *Sāmaveda*, but in the *Yajurveda* he appears in a much more developed form.[61] True, many of the epithets applied to Rudra in the *Ṛgveda* occur here again, namely, 'brown' or 'tawny'[62] 'fierce',[63] 'gracious',[64] the god with 'spirally-braided hair'[65] etc.; but in place of the young, unassailable, fair-lipped Ṛgvedic Rudra, we have in the *Yajurveda* a dwarf Rudra,[66] 'clad in a skin',[67] 'dweller in the mountains',[68] 'aged',[69] 'thousand-eyed'[70] etc. In the words of Muir[71] the imagination of the *ṛṣi* of the Vedic hymns "runs riot in the invention of these epithets". Ambikā is mentioned here[72]

---

treasures which had been thrown down by the gods and went away. But the gods, after conquering the Asuras, sought him, saw him, and took the treasures from him : then he wept ('*arudat*') and from that he is called Rudra."

56. *cf.* Winternitz, M., *A History of Indian Literature*, Vol. I, Calcutta, 1959, p. 66, n.2.
57. *cf. loc. cit.*; Macdonell, *Ved. Myth.*, p. 77.
58. *cf. loc. cit.*; *Vedische Mythologie*, II, p. 14ff.
59. *cf.* Keith, *op. cit.*, p. 146; *VOJ*, IX, pp. 233-52.
60. *op. cit.*, p. 147.
61. Bhandarkar, R.G., *op. cit.*, 103.
62. *YV*, XVI. 6.
63. *Ibid.*, XVI. 40.
64. *Ibid.*, XVI. 51.
65. *Ibid.*, XVI. 10.
66. *Ibid.*, X. 20 ('*krivi*').
67. *Ibid.*, III. 61; XVI. 51.
68. *Ibid.*, XVI. 2. 3, 4.
69. *Ibid.*, XVI. 36.
70. *Ibid.*, XVI. 7.
71. *Op. cit.*, Vol. IV, p. 402.
72. *Vāj. Saṁ.*, III. 57.

for the first time[73] and is described not as the wife, but as the sister of Rudra.

In the *Yajurveda*, Rudra's benign or auspicious (*śiva*) form is distinguished from his malignant or terrific (*rudra*) appearance and the two contrary sets of attributes are telescoped here in such a way that we are now in a position to conclude that all the basic elements which created the complex Rudra-Śiva cult of later ages are to be found here.[74]

In the *Śatarudriya* section of the *Yajurveda*,[75] where Rudra is invoked by one hundred names, all the floating conceptions regarding him of the early Vedic times are drawn together. In fact, the *Śatarudriya* provides a fresh starting point for new developments, adds various disgraceful attributes to Rudra, introduces some dark and malevolent associations, and furnishes the transition to the terrific and repulsive characteristics of Rudra-Śiva of Hindu mythology. He is painted here as Paśupati[76] (lord of beasts), Nīlagrīva (blue-necked), Śitikaṇṭha (white-throated), Giriśaya.[77] The range of Rudra in the *Śatarudriya* becomes so wide that he is everywhere[78]—in the stream and on the road, in the pool and the ditch, in the lake and the river, in the pond and the well, in the abyss and the bank, in the cloud and the lightning, in the rain and the drought, in the wind and the house, in the barren land and on the beaten track, in the cowpen and the cattle-shed, in the heart and the whirl-pool, in what is dried up and what is green, in the dust and the mist, in the copse and the gully. From a minor atmospheric god of the *Ṛgveda*, he now becomes the lord of all quarters[79]—of forests and fields, of trees and plants, of food and of moving creatures. Herein lies the reason which rendered him in later times the omnipresent supreme lord of the universe.[80] He is propitiated in a variety of ways in the *Śatarudriya* hymns. To quote one :

73. Muir, J., *op. cit.*, Vol. IV, p. 403.

74. Bhattacharji, S., 'Rudra from the Vedas to the Mahabharata' in *ABORI*, Vol. XLI, p. 90.

75. *Tattirīya Saṁhitā*, IV. 5; *Vājasaneyī Saṁhitā*, XVI.

76. *Vāj. Saṁ.*, XVI. 28.

77. *Ibid.*, XVI. 29.

78. *Ibid.*, XVI. 37-39, 43-45.

79. *Ibid.*, 18.

80. Bhandarkar, R.G., *op. cit.*, 106.

"Neither to our children, and our children's children, nor to our life, neither to our kine nor to our horses do thou injury ! Smite not our shining warriors : with offering we ever invoke thee, O Rudra !"[81]

Rudra is thus regarded with a kind of cringing fear, as a deity whose wrath is to be deprecated and whose favour curried.

Regarding the derogatory attributes of Rudra in the *Śatarudriya* hymns,[82] he is styled the lord of wanderers and thieves, the prowling rover, the tricking arch-trickster, the lord of pilferers, robbers, pillagers, and the cut-throats, and is in Yama's (death's) power. Although the commentators usually advance some apologetic remarks that Rudra in sport assumes the forms of thieves[83] etc., still, the various epithets occurring here, approximate to the fierce, terrific, impure, and repulsive nature of post-Vedic Rudra-Śiva.[84]

Among several new gentle names ascribed to Rudra in the *Yajurveda*, Bhava[85] is notable. 'Bhava' is explained n various ways, sometimes as the 'existent' or 'eternal', sometimes as the 'creator', the exact opposite of 'śarva', the 'archer' or 'destroyer'.[86] The term Bhava, according to Weber,[87] has been formed with the view of propitiating the terrible god by a favourable name. In the *Śatarudriya*, grace is sought from the benevolent (aspect of the) god : "Reverence be to the gentle and the friendly one ! reverence be to the peaceful and pleasing one ! reverence be to the kindly and the kindliest."[88]

In the *Ṛgveda*, Rudra is the father of the Maruts or Rudras, but he is never associated, like, Indra, with the warlike exploits of the Rudras.[89] The *Śatarudriya* rendered homage to a plurality

81. *SBE*, Vol. XLIII, p. 151 (*Vāj. Saṁ.*, XVI. 16).
82. *Vāj. Saṁ.*, XVI. 19-21.
For a free translation of the entire Śatarudriya hymn, See Sivaramamurti, C., *Śatarudriya: Vibhuti of Śiva's Iconography*, New Delhi, 1976, pp. 13-32.
83. Muir, J., *OST*, Vol. IV, p. 327, n. 60.
84. Macdonell, A.A., *Ved. Myth.*, p. 76.
85. *Vāj. Saṁ.*, XVI. 18, 28.
86. Muir, J., *OST*, IV, p. 328, n. 61; *ERE*, XI, p. 90.
87. *Ind. Stud.*, II., p. 37, *cf. OST*, IV, p. 328.
88. *Vāj. Saṁ.*, XVI. 41.
89. Macdonell, A.A., *Ved. Myth.*, p. 74.

of Rudras,[90] as *gaṇapatis*, or leaders or lords of tribes, to the non-Vedic carpenters, potters, blacksmiths, fishermen, huntsmen[91] and the *Niṣādas* who belonged to the proto-Australoid forest tribes.[92] Rudra thus appears here as the leader of troops, called his *gaṇas* and *pramathas*, of beings greatly inferior, yet similar, to himself; and sometimes the host of Rudras have been blended in the conception of one Rudra.[93] He also appears here as the representative of a particular class of people and the followers of different professions found in him their own god. It might often happen that their own peculiar gods were identified with the Aryan Rudra. In his absolute form Rudra is spoken of as 'one' in the Vedas, though in his immanent form he is 'eleven'.[94] The earliest representation of the *Ekādaśa Rudras* in a group is to be found in the Varāha cave facade at Udayagiri near Bhilsa, where, interestingly enough, all the eleven are ithyphallic in nature.[95] The number 'eleven' seems to have attained a sanctity of its own. With the passing of time, 'eleven' became 'eleven-hundred' and Śiva became its best form.[96]

Rudra is further elevated to a higher platform in the *Atharvaveda*[97] which represents a transitional stage between the conception of Rudra in the *Ṛgveda* and the systematic philosophy of Śaivism in the *Śvetāśvatara Upaniṣad*. The religion of the *Atharvaveda* is an amalgam of Aryan and non-Aryan ideals.[98] While the *Ṛgveda* records the conflict between the fair com-

90. *Vāj. Saṁ.*, XVI. 53-66.
91. *Vāj. Saṁ.*, XVI. 27.
92. Sircar, D.C., 'The Śākta Pīṭhas' in *JRASB*, Vol. XIV, No. 1, 1948, p. 102.

The mention of various castes indicates that the Indian caste system and polity were already fully developed.

93. *ERE*, Vol. II, p. 812.
94. Hopkins, E.W., *Epic Mythology*, 1968, p. 172.
95. Banerjea, J.N., *Paurāṇic and Tāntric Religion*, 1966, p. 67.
96. Hopkins, E.W., *Epic Myth.*, p. 173.

The words of Kṛṣṇa: "Of Rudras I am Śaṁkara" in the *Bhagavadgītā* is notable in this context.

97. The *Atharvaveda*, at first was not regarded strictly as one of the Vedas. The *RV*, *SV*, *YV*, were the *Traividyā*.

The oldest name of the *AV* is *Atharvāṅgirasaḥ*, that is, the *atharvan* ('holy magic bringing happiness') and the *aṅgiras* ('hostile or black magic').

98. Radhakrishnan, S., *Indian Philosophy*, Vol. I, 1958, p. 120.

plexioned (*śvitnya*) Aryans and the dark-skinned, 'noseless' (*anāsa*) aboriginals called *Dāsa* or *Dasyu*,[99] the *Atharvaveda* speaks to us of the period when the conflict is more or less settled and the two are trying to live in harmony by mutual give and take.[100] As a result of admixture of Aryan and non-Aryan blood to a very considerable degree, the spirit of accommodation, sorcery, magic, witchcraft, which the *Ṛgveda* did neither encourage nor recognise, crept into the religion of the *Atharvaveda*. In fact, the *Atharvaveda* is a collection of the most popular spells current among the masses,[101] who out of their helplessness against the catastrophic natural forces saw a weird repulsive world full of imps and hobgoblins, darkly scowling demons, death and disease.

With this background it becomes easy to understand Book XV of the Saṁhitā, where the Brahman is conceived of as the Vrātya and Rudra is exalted as *Eka-vrātya*, the vrātya *par excellence*, and this epithet characterises in a very interesting manner the association of elements in his composite character, not derived from the orthodox Vedic order.[102] The *Atharvaveda*[103] speaks of the seven attendants of *Eka-vrātya* as Bhava in the intermediate space of the eastern region, Śarva of the southern region, Paśupati of the western region, Ugra of the northern region, Rudra of the lower region, Mahādeva of the upper region and Īśāna of all the intermediate regions. Although they appear as seven distinct deities, still they were allied to and were looked upon as different manifestations of *Eka-vrātya*[104] who is represented to have been fond of the strong *surā*[105] and is brought into very special relation to the *puṁścalī* or harlot and the *māgadha*.[106] Owing to the obscurity of the vrātya book, the

99. Macdonell and Keith, *Vedic Index*, Vol. I, 1958, p. 356.
100. Radhakrishnan, S., *op. cit.*, p. 118.
101. Macdonell, *History of Sanskrit Literature*, 1965, p. 156.
102. Banerjea, J.N., *The Development of Hindu Iconography*, 1956, p. 448n.
103. XV. 5. 1-7.
104. Bhandarkar, D.R., *Some Aspects of Ancient Indian Culture*, Madras, 1940, p. 41.
105. *AV*, XV, 9. 2.
106. *Ibid.*, XV, 2. 1-4.

proper meaning of this term *māgadha* is not clear, and scholars[107] differ on this point. D.R. Bhandarkar[108] puts forward a theory that *Māgadha*, connected with Eka-vrātya, was a priest of the Māgadha tribe who emigrated from Śākadvīpa to India. Further, the vrātya cult which afterwards developed into Śaivism, originally came to the Indus valley with the immigration of the Māgadhas to India.[109]

Charpentier[110] considers the vrātyas to be the early worshippers of Rudra-Śiva. In the *Yajurveda*[111] the vrātyas are included in the list of victims at the Puruṣamedha ('human sacrifice'), where, however, no further explanation of the name is given.[112] The vrātyas were an obscure non-sacrificing ethnic group of people[113]—whether Aryan,[114] either fallen or uninitiated, or non-Aryan[115]—

107. It has been generally translated by 'a panegyrist, a bard'. See Bhandarkar, D.R., *op. cit.*, p. 47.

Māgadha of the Vrātya book is an heretical teacher. *cf.* Weber, A., *The History of Indian Literature*, Varanasi, 1961, p. 112.

It is tempting to connect this *Māgadha* with Magadha, South Bihar, which was known as Kīkaṭa in the time of the *RV* and Prācya in the Brāhmaṇa period. See Bhandarkar, D.R., *op. cit.*, p. 47.

The *Māgadha*—explained by Sāyaṇa as *Magadhadeśotpanno brahmacārī*—is contemptuously introduced by the Sūtrakāra to *TS*, VII. 5. 9. 4, in association with a *puṁścalī*; see Weber, *Ind. St.*, XII, p. 330; *cf.* Weber, *Hist. of Ind. Lit.*, p. 112, n. 126.

108. *op. cit.*, p. 48.

109. This curiously agrees with the fact that the associates of Śiva, the Maruts, have been called Śāka in two *Rks* (V. 30.10 and VI. 1.9.4).

110. *WZKM*, 23, pp. 151ff.; *cf.* Winternitz, *op. cit.*, Vol. I, p. 135n; *JRAS*, 1913, p. 155.

111. *Vāj. Saṁ.*, XXX. 8; *Taitt. Brāh.*, III. 4, 5, 1.

112. Macdonell and Keith, *Vedic Index*, Vol. II, 1958, p. 342.

113. For the vrātyas, see also Mayrhofer, M., *Etymological Sanskrit Dictionary*, vol. III, Heidelberg, 1976, *s.v.* 'Vrātaḥ'; J.C. Heesterman, 'Vrātya and Sacrifice' in *IIJ*, 6 (1962), p. 18; Walker, B., *Hindu World*, Vol. II, London, 1968, p. 583.

114. According to *Viṣṇu-sūtra* (*SBE*, Vol. VII, p. 115) the youths belonging to any of the three castes— namely, Brāhmaṇa, Kṣatriya and Vaiśya,— who have not been initiated at the proper time, are excluded from initiation, and condemned by the twice-born, and are called vrātyas.

The vrātyas, though uninitiated, spoke like the Aryan the speech of the initiated.

115. *cf.* *Pañcaviṁśa Brāhmaṇa*, XVI. 1-4.

Roth, Whitney, Bloomfield, Chanda and R.R. Bhāgavat regard the vrātyas as non-Aryans.

belonging to a roving band (*vrāta*)[116] and were swallowers of poison.[117] Roth[118] considers the praise of the vrātya in the *Atharvaveda* as an idealising of the devout vagrant or mendicant (*parivrājaka*) who is the benefactor of human society. The extravagant respect paid to the vrātyas in this Veda either shows that they themselves, through their representatives, compiled these hymns after gaining victory over the Aryan, or it indicates "the lofty spirituality of the Aryan culture which sublimated the lewd and repulsive features of the vrātya cult before it was absorbed into Brāhmaṇism and developed into Śaivism."[119]

Bhava and Śarva[120]—two of the well-known forms of the thousand-eyed[121] Rudra—are implored by virtue of their cosmogonic powers to afford protection against calamity,[122] and with the familiar Atharvanic specialisation, to destroy the sorcerer who prepares a spell or manipulates the roots (of plants) against his worshippers. In another verse[123] Bhava is said to rule over the sky and the earth, and to fill the vast atmosphere. In the *Atharvaveda* reference is made to the therapeutic character of Rudra and he is invoked, in his various aspects not to assail his worshippers with celestial fire, nor to contaminate with fever, cough or poison[124] and to cause the lightning to descend elsewhere.[125] The Rudra of the *Yajur-* and *Atharvavedas* is not Brāhmaṇic, not a deity of the priests and orderly ritual, but of the ordinary pre-Aryan people and places. Though a destroyer

116. Whitney, *Translation of the AV*, 770ff.

117. Chaudhuri, R., 'The Cult of the Vrātyas' in *IHQ*, vol. 38, 1958, p. 267.

118. *The St. Petersburg Dictionary, s.v.*

119. Bhandarkar, D.R., *op. cit.*, p. 48.

120. Venkataramanayya (*Rudra-Śiva*, p. 33) has tried to show that Śarva was originally an Iranian god and Bhava a god of the nearby region, somewhere in the north outside the Aryan world beyond the Muñjavat. But the theory requires still more corroboration.

121. *AV.*, XI. 2. 3.

122. *Ibid.*, IV. 28.

123. *Ibid.*, XI. 2. 27.

124. Though Rudra here (*AV.*, XI. 2) threatens men with poison, he is elsewhere reported as himself drinking it. *cf. SBE*, XLIII, p. 621.

125. *AV*, XI. 2. 22 and 26.

he is not opposed to creation, rather he is recognised as the Lord and Law of all living things.[126]

We may now turn to the second part of the Vedic literature, the *Brāhmaṇas*. The period of the *Brāhmaṇas*, as Aufrecht[127] observes, was one when "the old polytheism was in a condition of decline and the new faith which presents itself in Indian religious history as Śaivism was gaining ground." In fact, we see the power of Rudra in the *Brāhmaṇas* at its height,[128] because the gods are even afraid of him. The main subject of theosophical speculation in the *Brāhmaṇas* centred round Prajāpati, but he is not a god of the people as Rudra is and this is indicated by the attention devoted to him in the *Aitareya*, *Kauṣītaki* and the *Śatapatha Brāhmaṇas*. The *Brāhmaṇas* embody several stories ragarding the birth of Rudra.

According to the *Aitareya Brāhmaṇa*,[129] in order to punish Prajāpati, who committed incest with his own daughter, the gods out of their most fearful forms fashioned a divine being called Bhūtavat (that is, Rudra), who pierced the father god and thus asserted outraged morality. After piercing the incarnation of Prajāpati's sin, Rudra in the *Aitareya Brāhmaṇa*, asked, and obtained, the boon that he should henceforth be the ruler of the dominion of Prajāpati over all cattle.

The *Tāṇḍya*[130] and the *Śatapatha*[131] *Brāhmaṇas* present other versions of this legend about Prajāpati's illicit passion for his daughter, which, as Muir[132] suggests, probably refers to some atmospheric phenomenon. To Hillebrandt also the story has some astronomical signification.[133]

126. Eliot, C., *Hinduism and Buddhism*, Vol. II, London, 1957, p. 142.

127. *cf.* Keith, A.B., *Ṛgveda Brāhmaṇas*, p. 26.

128. Keith, A.B., *Religion and Philosophy of the Veda and Upaniṣads*, Harvard University, 1925, p. 144.

129. III. 33. 1.

130. VIII. 2. 10.

131. I. 7. 4. 1; II. 1. 2. 9.

132. *OST*, IV, p. 45; I, p. 107.

133. *Ved. Myth.*, ii, pp. 164-5; *cf.* Keith, *Rel. and Philo. of the Veda and Upan.*, p. 146.

Prajāpati in his form as a deer became the constellation called Mṛga (i.e. Mṛgaśīrṣa), while his daughter became the asterism Rohiṇī. The arrow,

According to another story in the *Aitareya Brāhmaṇa*[134] Rudra appears on the place of sacrifice in black raiment and claims all that is over as his own. The *Aitareya*[135] also furnishes another sign of the greatness of Rudra when it is prescribed that a formula must be altered from the form in which it occurs in the *Ṛgveda* in order to avoid the direct mention of the name of this terrible god by referring simply to 'the god here'; and the same practice is also to be seen in the *Śatapatha Brāhmaṇa*[136] and elsewhere. This, as Keith[137] points out, is a clear proof of advance in the conception of Rudra since the days of the *Ṛgveda*.

Let us now have a look into the *Śatapatha Brāhmaṇa* which belongs to the white *Yajurveda*, as this *Brāhmaṇa* is, next to the *Ṛgveda*, the most important production in the whole range of Vedic literature.[138]

In the *Śatapatha*[139] and *Kauṣītaki*[140] *Brāhmaṇas*, Kumāra (that is, Rudra) is described as the son of Uṣas and Prajāpati. As soon as he was born the boy wept. The father asked why he wept. He replied, 'I am not freed from (guarded against) evil; I have no name given to me: give me a name'.[141] Prajāpati gave him eight names one by one, seven of which are the same as those given above from the *Atharvaveda* and the eighth is Aśani. Of the eight names Rudra, Śarva, Ugra and Aśani are descriptive of his terrific aspect, the other four, Bhava, Paśupati, Mahādeva and Īśāna, indicating the pacific one.[142] As such passages

on the other hand, with which Prajāpati was pierced, became the constellation called 'the three-knotted arrow [perhaps the girdle of Orion]'.

cf. SBE, XII, p. 284n.

134. V. 14; cf. *AV*, II. 27.6; XI. 2.18.
135. III. 33; III. 34.7.
136. I. 7. 4. 3.
137. *Rel. and Philo. of the V. and U.*, p. 145.
138. Macdonell, A.A., *A History of Sanskrit Literature*, p. 180.
The '*Brāhmaṇa* of the hundred paths', so called becuase it consists of one hundred *adhyāyas* or 'lessons'.
139. VI. 1. 3. 7-8.
140. VI. 1. 9.
141. *SB*, VI. 1. 3. 9.
142. Banerjea, J.N., *Paurāṇic and Tāntric Rel.*, p. 67.

are of considerable interest, which show, on the one hand, the tendency towards identifying and blending originally distinct and apparently local Vedic gods with one another, and, on the other hand, the origin of the conception of Rudra-Śiva in the pantheistic system of the post-Vedic period,[143] let us recount the story as found in the *Śatapatha Brāhmaṇa*.[144]

Prajāpati said to him, 'Thou art Rudra'. And because he gave him that name, Agni became such-like (or, that form), for Rudra is Agni: because he cried (*rud*) therefore he is Rudra. He said, 'surely, I am mightier than that: give me yet a name'.

He said to him, 'Thou art Śarva'. And because he gave him that name, the waters became such-like for Śarva is the waters, inasmuch as from the water everything (Śarva) here is produced. He said, 'Surely, I am mightier than that: give me yet a name!'.

He said to him, 'Thou art Paśupati'. And because he gave him that name, the plants became such-like, for Paśupati is the plants: hence when cattle (*paśu*) gets plants, then they play the master (*pati*). He said, 'surely, I am mightier than that: give me yet a name!'.

He said to him, 'Thou art Ugra'. And because he gave him that name, Vāyu (the wind) became such-like, for Ugra is Vāyu: hence when it blows strongly, they say 'Ugra is blowing'. He said, 'Surely, I am mightier than that: give me yet a name !'.

He said to him, 'Thou art Aśani'. And because he gave him that name, the lightning became such-like for Aśani is the lightning: hence they say of him whom the lightning strikes, 'Aśani has smitten him'. He said, 'surely, I am mightier than that: give me yet a name !'.

He said to him, 'Thou art Bhava'. And because he gave him that name, Parjanya (the rain-god) became such-like; for Bhava is Parjanya, since everything here comes (*bhavati*) from the rain-cloud. He said, 'surely, I am mightier than that: give me yet a name !'.

He said to him, 'Thou art Mahān Devaḥ (the Great God)'. And because he gave him that name, the moon became such-

143. *SBE*, Vol. XII, p. 201n.
144. VI. 1. 3.

like, for the moon is Prajāpati, and Prajāpati is the Great God. He said, 'surely, I am mightier than that: give me yet a name!'.

He said to him, 'Thou art Īśāna'. And because he gave him that name, the Sun became such-like, for Īśāna is the Sun, since the Sun rules over this All. He said, 'So great indeed I am: give me no other name after that.!'[145]

The same story appears in somewhat different form in the *Śāṅkhāyana*[146] and the *Kauṣītaki*[147] *Brāhmaṇas*. This passage of the *Śatapatha Brāhmaṇa* appears to be the original, from which the legend of the birth of Rudra in the *Mārkaṇḍeya* and *Viṣṇu Purāṇas* is perhaps borrowed. The *Śatapatha Brāhmaṇa*[148] gives also anotner version in regard to the birth of Rudra.

The isolated position of Rudra, owing to his formidable characteristics, is emphasized by a myth in the same *Brāhmaṇa*[149], according to which he remained behind when the other gods attained heaven by ritual means. Rudra cried aloud: 'I have been left behind: they are excluding me from the sacrifice!'.

We have some other interesting points in the *Śatapatha Brāhmaṇa*.

Rudra, in the *Śatapatha Brāhmaṇa*,[150] receives oblations on a cross-road, for the cross-road is known to be his favourite haunt. What is injured in the sacrifice, belongs to him.[151] The north is his region[152] and the mole[153] is his animal (victim). He is also requested in the same *Brāhmaṇa* to depart beyond the Muñjavat with his 'bow unstrung and muffled up'.[154]

145. *SBE*, Vol. XLI, pp. 159-'60.
146. VI. 1.ff.
147. VI. 1. 9.
148. IX. 1. 1. 6.
149. *SB*, I. 7. 3. 1.
150. II. 6. 2. 7.
151. I. 7. 4. 9.
152. V. 4.2.10; I. 7.3.20.
153. II. 6. 2. 10.

According to *Taitt. Brāh.* (I. 1. 3. 3), Agni at one time concealed himself from the gods, and having become a mole, dug himself into the earth; so that the mole-hills thrown up by him, have some of Agni's nature attaching to them. *SBE*, Vol. XII, pp. 278-79, note 3.

154. *SB*, II. 6. 2. 17.

Ambikā, who first appears in the *Vājasaneyī Saṁhitā*[155] as the sister of Rudra, is still now his sister in the *Śatapatha Brāhmaṇa*[156] where it is said: "Ambikā, indeed, is the name of his (Rudra's) sister; and this share belongs to him conjointly with her; and because that share belongs to him conjointly with a woman (*strī*) therefore (these oblations) are called Tryambakāḥ."[157] She is given the same identity in the *Taittirīya Brāhmaṇa*,[158] where she appears as *śarat* (autumn) and helps Rudra when he carried out his work of killing. As a matter of fact, the *śarat* (autumn) has been looked upon as the most dangerous part of the year since the early Vedic period.[159]

Finally, the *Śatapatha Brāhmaṇa*[160] enlightens us with the following information:

From the place of sacrifice, they (the sacrificer and the priests) then return without looking back. Having returned thither, they touch water; for they have been performing a ceremony relating to Rudra, and water is (a means of) purification. According to the general rule given in the *Kātyāyana Śrauta Sūtra*,[161] the same purificatory act has to be performed whenever, in the course of ceremonial performances, a sacrificial formula or prayer has been used, which is addressed to, or directed against, Rudra, the Rākṣasas, the Asuras, and the Manes.

An important factor in the process of Rudra's growth is his identification with Agni in the Vedic literature and this identification contributed much to the transformation of his character as Rudra-Śiva.

Next to Indra, Agni is the most frequently invoked of the Vedic gods, being celebrated in about one-fifth of the hymns of

155. III. 57.
Eṣa te Rudra bhāgaḥ saha svasrā Ambikayā
156. II. 6. 2. 9.
157. *SBE*, XII, p. 440.
158. I.6, 10, 4-5.
159. *RV*, I. 72. 3; II. 27. 10.
AV, I. 10. 2; II. 13. 3.
Vāj. Saṁ., XXV. 22.
160. II. 6. 2. 18.
161. I. 10. 14.

the *Ṛgveda* and is designated Rudra in a number of hymns.[162] The principle of express and complete identification of Rudra with Agni which is 'first found only incidentally in the *Ṛgveda*'[163] is widely extended in the rest of the Vedic literature and Rudra now shared not only the names of Agni but also the features of his nature. In the crackling flame of the fire, to put the whole idea in the words of Weber,[164] the Vedic people heard again the wrathful voice of the storm, that in the consuming fierceness of the former, they perceived once more the destructive fury of the latter.

Muir[165] thinks that in the *Ṛgveda* the two deities were not completely identified as the distinctive epithets applied to Rudra prove that he was generally discriminated from Agni by his early worshippers. However, the *Śatarudriya* suggests a complete blending of the two destructive deities (storm and fire); and the epithets which are there assigned to Rudra lead us back partly to himself and partly to Agni.[166] Rudra's epithets Nīlagrīva, Śitikaṇṭha, Hiraṇyabāhu, Vilohita, Sahasrākṣa and Paśupati—which occur already in the *Śatarudriya* section of the *Yajurveda*—belong to fire, and designate some forms of a fire-god merged in Rudra[167]. R.G. Bhandarkar[168] thinks that the epithet Kapardin or 'the wearer of matted hair', is probably due to his being identical with Agni, the fumes of fire looking like matted hair.

We have already seen that Sāyaṇa gives six explanations of the name 'Rudra', of which the last is as follows: "When on one occasion there was a battle between the gods and Asuras, Rudra having the nature of Agni carried off the treasures which had been thrown down by the gods and went away. But the gods, after conquering the Asuras, sought him, saw him, and took the treasures from him: then he wept (*arudat*) and from that he is called Rudra."[169] We have also seen how in the

162. *RV*, I. 27.10; II. 1.6; III. 2.5; VIII. 72.3.
163. Keith, A.B., *Rel. and Philo. of the V. and U.*, p. 144.
164. *Ind. Stud.*, ii, p. 20; cf. Muir, *OST*, Vol. IV, p. 397.
165. *Op. cit.*, Vol. IV, p. 404.
166. Weber, *Ind. Stud.*, ii, p. 20; cf. Muir, *op. cit.*, IV, p. 397.
167. *ERE*, Vol. II, p. 81. 2.
168. *Op. cit.*, p. 103.
169. *OST*, IV, p. 303.

Śatapatha Brāhmaṇa[170] Prajāpati gave him the name Rudra, for Rudra is Agni and because he cried (*rud*) therefore he is Rudra. A story, like the one given by Sāyaṇa, is to be found in the *Taittirīya Saṁhitā*[171] also.

As early as the *Yajurveda*, Bhava and Śarva occur as names of Rudra, and in classical literature they are common synonyms of Śiva. In the *Śatapatha Brāhmaṇa*,[172] Agni is declared to be the gentle (*śānta*) name of Rudra whom the eastern people call Śarva and the Bāhlikas[173] call Bhava. This *Brāhmaṇa*[174] also suggests a fanciful etymology of *Śatarudriya*, as if it were *śānta* (propitiated) and *rudriya*, instead of 'that which relates to a hundred Rudras'. We have some other references in the *Śatapatha Brāhmaṇa* wherein Rudra is the newly kindled fire[175] or Agni is created as the hundred-headed Rudra.[176]

Thus we see how in the *Brāhmaṇas* all those ideas were already in the making which attained their full development in the later Vedic literature. The *Āraṇyakas*, composed by the Vānaprasthas and yatis in their forest homes, attempt at allegorical interpretation of the inner significance of the elaborate rituals to the common people who could not perform such expensive sacrifices.[177] But this intellectual approach to religious problems reached its pinnacle in the Upaniṣads which are rightly adjudged as the Vedānta, the acme of the Vedas.[178]

In the age of the Upaniṣads, when the old Ṛgvedic belief in the existence of a variety of personal gods of a henotheistic or kathenotheistic character gave place to the faith in the impersonal Brahman, when the sacrificial ceremonial became useless and speculative knowledge all important, we have some metrical

170. VI. 1. 3. 10.
171. I. 5. 1. 1.
172. I. 7. 3. 8.
173. Inhabitants of the present Balkh in Afghanistan.
174. *SB*, IX. 1. 1. 2 and 7.
175. *Ibid.*, II. 3. 2. 9.
176. *Ibid.*, IX. 2. 3. 32.
177. Banerjea, J.N., *PTR*, p. 4.
178. The *Upaniṣads*, in the words of Keith (*Religion and Philosophy of the Veda and Upaniṣads*, Vol. II, p. 497), "represent the outcome of the reflections of a people whose blood was mixed. We may, if we desire, call the *Upaniṣads* the product of Aryo-Dravidian thought."

Upaniṣads, which are chronologically later in point of date, where pantheism of the early *Bṛhadāraṇyaka, Aitareya, Chāndogya*, etc., is supplemented by theism, and the concept of the one god given different names is clearly personalised.[179] The *Śvetāśvatara* is one such metrical Upaniṣad—'a monument of theism', as Deussen[180] calls it—where Brahman is occasionally identified with Rudra.

R.G. Bhandarkar[181] opines that this Upaniṣad is 'not a sectarian treatise'. With due deference to the great historian, we venture to quote some passage from the *Śvetāśvatara Upaniṣad* which clearly shows the cult of Rudra as some sort of a sectarian god.

In one passage[182] Rudra is represented as the Maheśvara (Great God) among the gods (*Īśvaras*) and as the Supreme Deity among the divinities.

In another passage[183] Rudra is mentioned as one who created Brahman and delivered the Vedas to him.

In the third one we have the following: "He, the creator and supporter of the gods, Rudra, the great seer, the lord of all, he who formerly gave birth to Hiraṇyagarbha, may he endow us with good thoughts."[184]

In a fourth passage it is said that "this whole universe is filled by this person (*puruṣa*), to whom there is nothing superior."[185]

Again, Rudra appears as the creator, preserver and destroyer when this Upaniṣad says that "there is one Rudra only, they do not allow a second, who rules all the worlds by his powers. He stands behind all persons, and after having created all worlds he, the protector, rolls it up at the end of time."[186]

179. Banerjea, J.N., *PTR*, pp. 5-6.
180. Radhakrishnan, S., *Indian Philosophy*, Vol. I, 1958, p. 511.
181. *Op. cit.*, p. 110.
182. *ŚU*, VI. 7.
tam īśvarāṇāṁ paramaṁ Maheśvaraṁ
taṁ devatānāṁ paramaṁ ca daivatam
183. *ŚU*, VI. 18.
yo Brahmāṇaṁ vidadhāti pūrvaṁ
yo vai vedāṁśca prahiṇoti tasmai
184. *Ibid.*, III. 4; IV. 12.
185. *Ibid.*, III. 9.
186. *Ibid.*, III. 2.

True, the Upaniṣadic Brahman-Ātman is sometimes referred to by the 'non-sectarian general name Deva'.[187] But in later times Hiuen Tsang[188] refers to Śiva as Deva or Īśvara-Deva. The epithet *devavrata* applied to Gondophares on his coins may be significant; it is likely that deva here does not simply mean 'god' but the god Śiva. Early Buddhist works like the *Chullavagga* and *Saṁyuttanikāya* describe Śiva as *deva* or *devaputra*.[189] In a passage of the *Niddesa*,[190] we do not find Śiva but Deva along with those of Vāsudeva, Baladeva and others and it is presumable that the Deva and Deva-worshippers there are Śiva and his votaries. The *Śvetāśvatara Upaniṣad* also assigns the name Deva to Rudra.

In the *Śvetāśvatara Upaniṣad*, Rudra is endowed with a number of names, such as Hara,[191] Mahādeva,[192] Īśa,[193] Īśāna,[194] Maheśvara,[195] and Bhagavat.[196] Weber[197] suggested long ago that such epithets like Mahādeva and Īśāna, involving quite a prominence of this deity as compared with the other gods, indicates a sectarian worship; but this observation is too far-reaching. The word *śiva*, in the Vedic hymn,[198] was mostly used as an adjective, and was attributed to more than one deity. In the *Śvetāśvatara Upaniṣad*,[199] the name Śiva occurs

Eko hi Rudro na dvitīyāya tasthurya imān lokānīśata īśanībhiḥ /
Pratyaṅ janāṁstishṭhate sañchukopāntakāle saṁsṛjya viśvā bhuvanāni goptā /

187. Bhandarkar, R.G., *op. cit.*, p. 110.
188. Watters, *On Yuan Chwang*; I, p. 214.
"Outside the west gate of the city of Pushkalāvatī was a Deva temple and a marvel-working image of the Deva." The word *deva* here refers to Śiva.
189. Banerjea, J.N., *PTR*, p. 70.
190. *cf.* Bhandarkar, R.G., *op. cit.*, p. 3;
Banerjea, J.N., *PTR*, p. 70.
191. I. 10.
192. III. 12.
193. III. 17; III. 20.
194. III. 15.
195. IV. 7.
196. III. 11.
197. *Ind. Stud.*, ii. p. 302; *cf.* Banerjea, *DHI*, p. 448.
198. *RV*, X. 124. 2.
199. *ŚU*, III. 11; V. 14.
Jñātvā śivaṁ sarvabhūteṣu gūḍham—IV. 16.

in several passages mainly as an attributive of Rudra, and the process of transforming the 'adjective' into 'noun' for designating the cult god has already begun in the Vedic literature. He is here the great lord—the Māyin—with Māyā[200] as his Prakṛti (nature) and invoked as both woman and man[201]. The word *liṅga* is also used in one verse,[202] but 'perhaps in the Nyāya sense'.[203] R.G. Bhandarkar,[204] however, does not deny the possibility that when the *Śvetāśvatara Upaniṣad* speaks of the lord Īśāna as presiding over every *yoni*[205] and of the lord as presiding over all forms and *yonis*,[206] "an allusion to the physical fact of the *Liṅga* and *yoni* connected together may have been meant as typifying the philosophical doctrine of gods presiding over every creative cause."

Regarding the other epithets ascribed to Rudra in this *Upaniṣad* we may note the following: he is the 'dweller in the mountains',[207] 'lord of the mountains',[208] 'thousand-headed', 'thousand-eyed',[209] who 'stands alone, fixed like a tree in the sky (*sthāṇu*),'[210] and rules over all 'two-footed and four-footed beings'.[211]

The *Śvetāśvatara Upaniṣad* declares that the reality of god cannot be proved by logic; it can only be realised by faith, love, *bhakti*, meditation and *Yoga*.[212] There is evidence in this *Upaniṣad* that Śvetāśvatara, the supposed author-sage, absolutely surrendered himself to Rudra as Arjuna did to

200. *Ibid.*, IV. 10.
Māyāntu prakṛtiṁ vidyān māyinantu Maheśvaram
201. *Ibid.*, IV. 3.
202. *Ibid.*, VI. 9.
203. Radhakrishnan, S., *op. cit.*, p. 511.
204. *Op. cit.*, p. 114n.
205. *ŚU.*, IV. 11.
206. *Ibid.*, V. 2.
207. *Ibid.*, III. 5.
208. *Ibid.*, III. 6.
209. *Ibid.*, III. 14.
210. *Ibid.*, III. 9. For *Sthāṇu*, the Pillar, see also Kramrisch, S., *The Presence of Śiva*, Princeton Univ. Press, 1981, pp. 117-122.
211. *Ibid.*, IV. 13.
212. *Ibid.*, III. 20; I. 10; IV. 4-6;
yasya deve parā bhaktiryathā deve tathā gurau |
Tasyaite kathitā hyarthāḥ prakāśante mahātmanaḥ || VI. 23;

Kṛṣṇa.[213] R.G. Bhandarkar[214] truly observes that the *Śvetāśvatara Upaniṣad* 'stands at the door of the Bhakti school and pours its loving adoration on Rudra-Śiva'. Incidentally, we should note that the roots of *Yoga* and *Bhakti* are traceable to the beliefs and practices of the pre-Aryan inhabitants of India.[215] This vast mass of un-Aryan people appear to have been believers in a kind of religion which was totally different from the religion of the higher section of Indo-Aryans as found in the *Ṛgveda* and other early *Saṁhitās* and *Brāhmaṇas.* The *Śvetāśvatara Upaniṣad* therefore points to the non-Aryan contribution to the development of *Bhakti,*[216] and the influence of Śiva, worshipped by the pre-Aryans, upon the Vedic Rudra.

Reference should also be made in this context to the two well-known seals from the Indus Valley representing the proto-Śiva in a Mahāyogin posture, with a kneeling human being to either side of him with hands uplifted in prayer.[217] Sircar[218] suggests that the existence of a class of sectarian devotees of the proto-Śiva as early as the days of the Mohenjodaro civilization is proved by the kneeling human figures.

However, after the *Śvetāśvatara Upaniṣad,* the theistic ideas of Śaivism are further developed in the *Atharvaśiras Upaniṣad,* a later sectarian work. Here Rudra is not only identified with other deities, but also shown as transcending each of them individually and collectively.[219] The gods asked Rudra who he was. Rudra replied: "He alone was, is, or will be, and nothing else. He is in all quarters."[220] For the attainment of true knowledge of Rudra one should take moderate food, forsake greed (*lobha*)

Tat kāraṇaṁ sāṅkhyayogādhigamyaṁ jñātvā
devaṁ mucyate sarvapāśaiḥ—VI. 13.

213. Banerjea, J. N., *PTR*, p. 69.

214. *Op. cit.*, p. 110.

215. Marshall, J., *MIC*, Vol. I, p. 54.

216. Sircar, D.C., *Studies in the Religious Life of Ancient and Medieval India*, 1971, p. 13n.

217. Marshall, J, *op. cit.*, Vol. I, pp. 54, 68ff.; Vol. III. Pls. cxvi, 29 and cxviii, 11.

218. *Studies in the Rel. Life.*, p. 11.

219. Banerjea, J.N., *PTR*, p. 69.

220. *cf.* Bhandarkar, R.G., *op. cit.*, p. 111.

and anger (*krodha*), practise meditation (*dhyāna*), devote oneself to reading or listening (*śravaṇa*) to prescribed texts, thinking (*manana*) on their real meaning, undertaking to perform the Pāśupata vow (*vrata*) and thus becoming a *Paramahaṁsa*. or 'a single-minded devotee'.[221]

The *Pāśupatavrata* is described in the *Atharvaśiras Upaniṣad* as consisting of besmearing the initiate's body with ashes in conjunction with the muttering of a mantra which is calculated to effect a deliverance from the trammels of life.[222] The expression *Paśupāśa-vimokṣaṇa*—one of the principal *vidhis* or characteristics of the Pāśupata school of later days—means that by performing this *vrata*, the worshipper of Rudra-Śiva has his bonds (*pāśa*) loosened, and he is delivered from the fetters of his individual (*paśu*) existence.[223] The Śiva-bhāgavatas of Patañjali's *Mahābhāṣya*[224] were apparently followers of the *Pāśupata-vrata* mentioned in the *Atharvaśiras Upaniṣad*.

The next stage in Vedic literature is represented by the *Sūtras*. Extending our inquiries to this branch of Vedic literature we find that Rudra was still a violent hostile deity, who had to be appeased. The *Āśvalāyana Gṛhyasūtra*,[225] the *Śāṅkhāyana Gṛhyasūtra*,[226] the *Pāraskara Gṛhyasūtra*[227] and the *Gṛhyasūtra* of Hiraṇyakeśin[228] describe in details the *śūlagava* or spit-ox sacirfice to Rudra. That some traits of non-Aryan aboriginal religion have gone into the make-up of Śiva of later days is proved by the fact that this ceremony is to be performed at the outskirts of a village, and its remains should not be brought into it, for, 'this god will do harm to (human) creatures'.[229] Again, the red colour of the god was interpreted

221. *cf. Ibid.*, p. 112.

222. 'The ash is fire, the ash is wind, the ash is water, the ash is earth, the ether is ash, everything is ash, the mind, the eyes and other senses are ashes'.—*cf.* Banerjea, J.N., *PTR*, p. 70; Bhandarkar, R. G., *op. cit.*, p. 112.

223. Radhakrishnan, S., *Indian Philosophy*, Vol. I, 1958, p. 448; Banerjea, J.N., *DHI*, p. 451.

224. Comment on Pāṇini's *Sūtra*, V. 2. 76.

225. IV. 8.

226. III. 11.

227. III. 8.

228. II. 3. 8.

229. *ĀGS*, IV. 8. 32.

as the colour of blood and fire.[230] In the ritual Rudra is marked out emphatically from the other gods. The *Gobhila Gṛhyasūtra*[231] prescribes that at the end of a sacrifice the worshipper should besprinkle a handful of grass with water and should throw it into the fire with the verse: 'Thou who art the lord of cattle, Rudra, who walkest with the lines [of cattle], the manly one: do no harm to our cattle; let this be offered to thee.'

We have already seen how, in the *Śatapatha Brāhmaṇa*,[232] the abode of Rudra is in the north, while the abode of the other gods is in the east, the place of the rising Sun. According to the *Āpastamba Dharmasūtra*,[233] any food left over after meal is placed in a spot to the north for Rudra to take. The *Śāṅkhāyana Gṛhyasūtra*[234] prescribes the sick persons to worship Rudra, and purification, by touching water, is required after prayers or making offerings to him. All these show that though in the period of the *Sūtras* Rudra was perhaps not exactly within the orthodox pantheon apparently due to his gradual association with the non-Aryan customs and deities, still he was accepted by some but not by others.

The *Āśvalāyana Gṛhyasūtra*[235] mentions twelve names of Rudra, viz., Hara, Mṛḍa, Śarva, Śiva, Bhava, Mahādeva, Ugra, Bhīma, Paśupati, Śaṅkara and Īśāna. In the *Āpastamba*[236] and *Hiraṇyakeśin*[237] *Gṛhyasūtras* he is Kṣetrapati. In the *Hiraṇyakeśin*[238] a *mantra* is prescribed for the consort of Rudra, Śarva, Īśāna, Paśupati, Ugra and Bhīma; and Rudra is also invoked against evil demons and enemies: "Rudra with the dark hair-lock ! Hero ! At every contest strike down this my adversary, as a tree [is struck down] by a thunderbolt."[239]

230. Keith, A.B., *Rel. and Philo. of the V. and U.*, p. 145.
231. I. 8. 28.
232. *SBE*, Vol. XII, p. 438; Vol. XLIII, p. 158; Vol. XLIV, p. 488.
233. II. 24. 23.
234. I. 10. 9; V. 6. 1-2.
235. IV. 8. 19.
236. VII. 20. 12-18.
237. II. 3. 9. 7-12.
238. II. 3. 8. 7.
239. *Ibid.*, I. 4, 15. 6.

Directions are given in *Pāraskara Gṛhyasūtra*[240] to adore Rudra at the time of traversing a path for he dwells on the path, coming to a crossing of four roads for he dwells at the cross-roads, swimming across a river, or getting into a ship for he dwells in the waters, entering a forest for he dwells in the forests, ascending a mountain for he dwells on the mountains, passing by a burial ground for he dwells among the fathers, or by a cow-stable for he dwells among the dung-heaps and such other places for 'Rudra is this universe'. The *Hiraṇya-keśi-gṛhyasūtra*[241] similarly directs one to adore Rudra and repeat a specific formula, when one comes to a cross-road or to a heap of cattle-dung, when serpents creep for Rudra dwells among the serpents, or when one is overtaken by a tornado or plunged into a river, or when one approaches a beautiful place, a sacrificial site, or a big old tree for Rudra dwells there. Thus in the *Gṛhyasūtras* adoration to Rudra was necessary in each and every walk of life; for, he could only protect man from fear and danger—of which he may be the originator—that threaten life at every moment. The tendency to adopt this deity by emphasizing his benevolent aspects continues in these *Sūtras*. "Herein lies the reason", in the words of Bhandarkar,[242] "which rendered him in later times the omnipresent supreme lord of the universe to the exclusion of all other Vedic gods excepts Viṣṇu."

In closing this survey of Vedic literature relating to Rudra, we have lastly to call attention to the fact that the essence of Rudra was, in the minds of the Vedic bards, 'the power of the uncultivated, and unconquered, dangerous, unreliable and unpredictable',[243]—hence, much to be feared from him. This sentiment of fear was at the bottom.[244] The adoration to Rudra in the Vedic literature was not sincere, but, utilitarian. The Epic and Purāṇic Rudra-Śiva represents the 'fusion' or 'syncretism'[245] of more than one deity. It is not the gradual develop-

240. III. 15. 7-16.
241. I. 5. 16. 8-13.
242. *Op. cit.*, p. 106.
243. Gonda, J., *Viṣṇuism and Śivaism*, London, 1970, p. 5.
244. Bhandarkar, R.G., *op. cit.*, p. 106.
245. Keith, *Rel. & Philo. of the V. and Up.*, p. 148.

ment of a Vedic deity along lines chalked out in the *Ṛgveda*, but the metamorphosis of an Aryan god into a god who has both Aryan and pre-Aryan features. The Ṛgvedic atmospheric god became in course of time the lord of various professions. In fact, the cosmopolitan nature of Rudra enables him to absorb local gods. The conception of Śiva from its opposite Rudra resulted partially from an attempt at 'appeasement by flattery'[246] and partially perhaps from his gradual amalgamation with the Pre-Aryan Father-god.

(ii) Identification of Rudra and Śiva

Between the Vedic Literature and the Epic and Purāṇic texts relating to Rudra, a wide chasm intervenes. What was merely a sketch in the Vedic literature has now new dimensions and details. On the figure of Rudra-Śiva having taken a definite shape, attributes and epithets are lavished in profusion.[1] The precise relation between Rudra and Śiva is not yet satisfactorily traced out. The introduction of an entirely new divinity of the north has been thought of. A popular deity of the pre-Aryan people has also been supposed to have been engrafted upon the ancient religion by being identified with Rudra;[2] and again a blending of some features of Agni with Rudra has been supposed to originate a new development. Barth[3] regards Rudra in the *Ṛgveda* as mainly and distinctly beneficent, and concludes that the more terrible aspect of his nature does not come into

246. Sircar, D.C., *The Śākta-Pīṭhas*, p. 102.

Based on original Sanskrit texts, Stella Kramrisch (*The Presence of Śiva*, Princeton University Press, 1981) ponders the metaphysics, ontology, and myths of Rudra and Śiva from the Vedas to the Purāṇas in her above monumental work. For the birth of Rudra see pp. 98-116.

See also Bhattacharji, S., *The Indian Theogony: a comparative study of Indian mythology from the Vedas to the Puranas*, Cambridge, 1970.

1. Eliot, C., *Hinduism and Buddhism*, Vol. II, London, 1957, p. 145.
2. Whitney, W.D., in *Journal of the American Oriental Society*, Vol. III, 1853, p. 318f.
3. *The Religions of India*, London, 1882, pp. 160-63.

prominence until we reach the *Atharvaveda*, when his cult had already coalesced with the cult of Śiva.

The name Śiva

The name Śiva is euphemistic and is used as an attributive epithet not particularly of Rudra, but of several other Vedic deities. One of the earliest uses of Śiva as a proper name of Rudra is found in the *Śvetāśvatara Upaniṣad*,[4] in which beginning of the cult of Rudra-Śiva was traced.

All the uncanny and baleful traits of Rudra-Śiva start from the conception of a deity of mountain and forest. Even his wife is the daughter of the mountains. Is there any couple of deified hunters at the back of this concept ? The custom of deifying human beings of supernatural powers and worshipping them as gods was very probably non-Vedic[5] and arose with the warrior tribes who were often denounced for their irreverent attitude towards Brāhmaṇism.[6] But it is really very difficult to define the career of Śiva and we have only some stray legends about him in different sacred texts although the germs of these myths and legends are to be traced to pre-Aryan antiquity. Regarding non-Aryan influence, some even go to the extent of suggesting that 'Śiva' came from the Tamil word *śivaṇ* (*chivaṇ*) meaning red, the word *rudra* also often seems to mean 'red',[7] and the metamorphosis from Rudra to Śiva was facilitated by this resemblance.[8]

Śiva as the name of a people occurs in the *Ṛgveda*[9] in the *Dāśarājña* ('Battle of the Ten kings') context. According to

4. III. 11; V. 14.

5. Hazra, R.C., 'Further Light on the God of the Famous Mohenzo-daro Seals' in *Our Heritage*, Vol. XVII, Part I, Jan-June 1969, p. 23.

6. *ERE*, Vol. VI, pp. 658ff.

7. Barnett, L.D., *Linguistic Survey of India*, 'Munda and Dravidian Languages', Vol. IV, p. 279; *Śambhu* has also been compared with the Tamil *Chempu* or *Śembu* meaning 'copper', i.e. 'red metal'.—see *Vedic Age*, 1957, p. 162.

8. Walker, B., *Hindu World*, s.v. 'Śiva', p. 406.

9. VII. 18. 17.

Dandekar[10], Śiva was the chief god of these Śivas, while Banerjea[11] points out that Patañjali in his *Mahābhāṣya*[12] mentioned Śiva twice as a god and once he is classified as one of the folk divinities (*laukika-devatā*), distinct from the gods of the Vaidika order. The *Mahāmāyūrī*, one of the five great *mantra*-formulas of northern Buddhists (composed before the 4th century A.D.), writes about Śiva and Śivabhadra, the tutelary deities of the towns of Śivapura and Bhīṣaṇa.[13] Sylvain Levi[14] connects this Śivapura with *Udīcya-grāma* (a village of the north) of Patañjali.[15] Scholars have identified Śivapura, 'the city of the Śivas', with modern Shorkot in the Jhang District of present Pakistan.[16]

The exclusive worshippers of Śiva are described by Patañjali as Śiva-bhāgavata[17] who were *āyaḥśūlika* (endowed with an iron lance) and a *daṇḍājinaka* (holder of a staff and wearer of the animal hide). This description of the Śiva-bhāgavatas partially tallies with that of the Siboi, one of the tribes of the Punjab, subdued by Alexander. Curtius, Diodorus, Arrian and some other classical writers describe the Siboi people as dressed in skins, carrying a cudgel and branding on the backs of their oxen the representation of a club, wherein the Macedonians recognised a memorial of Herakles.[18] Megasthenes describes the Indian Dionysios (Śiva) as the god of hills and mountains.[19]

10. *Some Aspects of the History of Hinduism*, First ed., p. 5.
11. *DHI*, pp. 337-38; *PTR*, pp. 73-74, 147.
A.K. Chandra (*The Rig-Vedic Culture and The Indus-Civilisation*, Calcutta, 1980, p. 48) thinks that "Śiva's dogma was anti-Vedic or anti-sacrificial, and not 'non-Arya' as supposed by many."
12. Once in the course of his comment on *Vārttika* 2 on Pāṇini's *Sūtra* VI. 3. 26; and the other in his comment on V. 3. 99.
13. Banerjea, J.N., *DHI*, p. 450.
14. *Journal Asiatique*, 1915, pp. 37, 70.
15. Patañjali while commenting on the Vārttikas on Pāṇini's *Sūtra* IV. 2. 104.
16. *Political History of Ancient India*, 1938, p. 204.
17. Commenting on Pāṇini's *Sūtra*, V. 2. 76.
18. Arrian, *Indica*, V. 12.
cf. McCrindle, J.W., *Ancient India as described by Megasthenes and Arrian*, 1960, pp. 34-37.
19. McCrindle, J.W., *op. cit.*, pp. 34ff.; 110-12.

It is interesting to note in this connection that Dionysios, in Greek mythology, is described, just like Śiva, as a healing god, specially associated with vegetation rites, snakes and phallic emblem.[20]

In Sibae, Lassen[21] has recognised the Śibis or Uśīnaras of Indian literature. Pargitar[22] suggests that Śibi (Śivi) Auśīnara (son of Uśīnara), ruled from Śivapur, over the whole of the Punjab except the north-west corner. Vogel,[23] while editing an inscription found at Shorkot—palaeographically assignable to the fifth century A.D., observes that the mound of Shorkot, the findspot of the inscription, represents the site of the city of the Śibis. In the list of the sixteen *mahājanapadas* of the early Pāli texts, as found in the *Mahāvastu*,[24] we have Śibi and Daśārṇa, in place of Gandhāra and Kāmboja. In the *Mahābhārata*,[25] Nakula, the fourth of the five Pāṇḍavas, overcame the Śibis along with other tribes. In the episode of Jayadratha's attempt to carry off Draupadī, the Śibis are clearly mentioned as a tribe dependent on Sindhu.[26]

We have some coins of the Śibis[27] which reveal that Madhyamikā (modern Nagarī near Chitor) was the capital of a branch of the Śibi people that settled there at a later period.

From all these data we can safely conclude that the cult of Śiva had developed in parts of Northern India even long before the time of Patañjali and an early effort was made to cause an amalgam between the Vedic Rudra and Śiva as the Aryan invaders gradually imbibed blood and ideas of the pre-Aryan population.[28]

In the *Mahābhārata* we have two lauds of Śiva, one giving him a thousand and the other a thousand and eight names,

20. *ERE*, Vol. VI, pp. 402, 417, 548.
21. *Epigraphia Indica*, Vol. XVI, 1921-22, p. 16.
22. *Ancient Indian Historical Tradition*, 1962, p. 264.
23. *Epigraphia Indica*, Vol. XVI, 1921-22, pp. 15ff.
24. I. 34.
25. II. 1189; Bombay ed., II. 32.7.
26. *Mbh.*, III. 15626, Bombay ed., III. 266; *cf. Ep. Ind.*, Vol. XVI, p. 16.
27. *ARASI*, 1915-16, Pt. I, p. 15; *Prinsep's Essays on Indian Antiquities*, Vol. I, London, 1858, pp. 112-14.
28. Eliot, C., *op. cit.*, Vol. II, p. 141.

both marked by late Purāṇic elements.[29] We have now a god clad in an animal hide (deer, tiger, or elephant), with matted hair and crescent on his head, bearing serpents, carrying a trident and having a bull for his ensign. Gopinatha Rao[30] quotes the following story from the *Suprabhedāgama* : When Śiva was passing by the slopes of the mountain Meru without any garments the wives of the Ṛṣis fell in love with him. In their rage, the Ṛṣis performed incantations to kill Śiva and from their ceremonial ground sent snakes, a *kṛṣṇa-mṛga*, and *Apasmārapuruṣa*, a *paraśu,* a bull, a tiger, a lion and several other things. But Śiva smilingly took into his hands for his sports the black-deer, the snakes and the *paraśu*; the *Apasmārapuruṣa* was trampled under his feet and is always serving him as a foot stool; the lion and the tiger were killed by him and their skins worn by him as his garments, while the skull and the digit of the moon were placed on his *jaṭāmukuṭa* as ornaments.

As a bestower of gifts

The Epico-Paurāṇic Rudra-Śiva is a "powerful, wrathful and impetuous god but generous and bountiful and spared nothing when he was propitiated".[31] To show him as a bestower of gifts to supplicants stories are invented or adapted and he now got the supreme position. Kṛṣṇa, Arjuna, Upamanyu, Drupada, Vyāsa, Vālmīki, Viśvāmitra, Parāśara, Paraśurāma, Jāmadagnya, Jayadratha, Jarāsandhya, Aśvatthāman and Garga—all received boons from this great god. The various boon-bestowing aspects of Śiva are called Anugrahamūrtis in Indian iconography : for example, he is called Caṇḍeśānugrahamūrti, as he conferred on Caṇḍeśvara the boon of being the steward of his household; Viṣṇvanugrahamūrti (as Cakradānamūrti), because he restored an eye to Viṣṇu which the latter offered to Śiva and also presented Viṣṇu with the *cakra* or discus; Nandīśānugrahamūrti, as he granted Nandikeśvara the prayer of complete exemption from old age and pain and also the mastery over a section of his *gaṇas*; Vighneśvarānugrahamūrti, as Vighneśvara was blessed

29. Hopkins, E.W., *Epic Mythology*, 1968, p. 222; *Mbh.*, Bombay ed., XII. 285; XIII. 17. 130.

30. *Elements of Hindu Iconography* Vol. II, Part I, 1916, pp. 113-14.

31. Bhandarkar, R.G., *op. cit.*, p. 114.

by Śiva by restoring him to life by placing on his shoulder the head of an elephant; Rāvaṇānugrahamūrti, because he presented Rāvaṇa with a sword at his request, when the latter first made a futile attempt to raise the Kailāsa mountain and then sang hymns in praise of Śiva.

As a holy comforter, he gave Vyāsa, after the death of his son Śuka, a shadow like his son, never leaving him to console the bereaved father.[32] Gālava, going to his widowed mother, by the grace of Śiva, saw his father alive again.[33] The moral of all this is that even after committing all crimes, as Hopkins[34] points out, men are freed from sin by (mental) worship of Śiva.

The Yogin

The pre-Aryan proto-Śiva of the Harappa civilization is an arch *yogīn* with the eyes fixed on the tip of the nose, with feet drawn up beneath him, toes turned down and hands extended above the knees.[35] Marshall[36] points out that like Śiva and Śaivism, *yoga* also had its origin among the pre-Aryan population and this explains why it was not before the Epic period that it came to play an important part in Indo-Aryan religion. The Vedic religion is conceived chiefly in terms of the sacrifice. But in the Epic period it had been supplanted by *tapas*, *yoga* or asceticism. The Rudra-Śiva of later days, unlike the Vedic Rudra, is himself an ascetic sitting in philosophical isolation. He is *Mahāyogin*, *Mahātapāḥ*, *Taponitya*, *Yati* and *Yogīśvara*. Incidentally, we should also remember that the *Ekavrātya*, in the *Atharvaveda*, is said to know the process of Yoga.

The association of munis with Rudra may be traced to the Keśi-Sūkta of the *Ṛgveda*[37] where the Keśin (people having long or matted hair) are characterised as half-naked, wearing (short) garment of brown colour soiled with dust and frenzied by the

32. *Mbh.*, Bombay ed., XII. 334. 38; Hopkins, E.W., *op. cit.*, p. 225.
33. *Mbh.*, Bombay ed., XIII, 18. 58; cf. Hopkins, E.W., *op. cit.*, p. 225.
34. *Op. cit.*, p. 225.
35. Marshall, J., *MIC*, Vol. I, p. 53.
36. *Ibid.*, p. 54.
37. X. 136.

performance of austerities.[38] Although Sāyaṇa has found in this a reference to the Sun-god[39] (Keśi-muni with long hair is like Sūrya with his spreading rays), still, this Sūkta reminds us of the sectarian Pāśupata devotees of later date and suggests that these people recited or sang the *Śatarudriya* hymns incorporated in the *Yajurveda.*[40] Keith[41] regards this Sūkta as curiously isolated as it belongs to the last stratum of the *Saṁhitā*. In the *Atharvaveda*[42] we have the reference of the chariot of the Keśin, that is, Rudra. In the *Śatapatha Brāhmaṇa*[43] Keśin is the name of a tribe—perhaps a branch of the Pañcālas[44]—which is probably the reason why they are not approved of by the Vedic bards.[45]

In the temples of Salsette, Elephanta and Ellora, the principal figure is in most cases, Śiva, decorated with ear-rings, such as are still worn by the Kanphaṭā Yogins;[46] the walls are covered with ascetics in the various *āsanas*, and the cells attached to some of the temples are also indicative of a yogin's residence, and one of the caves at Salsette is named that of Yogīśvara.

We have seen that, in the *Śvetāśvatara Upaniṣad,*[47] one of the epithets of Rudra is *Sthāṇu*. In the *Vāyu Purāṇa*[48] the god practised severe austerities standing on one foot for a whole heavenly year without taking any food. In the *Matsya Purāṇa*[49] he is *Sthāṇu* because of his standing motionless like the trunk of tree till the dissolution of the world, or because of his refusal

38. Banerjea, J.N., *PTR*, p. 73.
39. *cf. Loc. cit.*
40. Sircar, D.C., *Studies in the Religious Life of Ancient and Medieval India*, 1971, p. 10.
41. *RPVU*, p. 402.
42. XI. 2. 18.
43. XI. 8. 46.
44. Bhandarkar, D.R., *Some Aspects of Ancient Indian Culture*, Madras, 1940, p. 3.
45. In the epic literature, Keśin is a demon slain by Kṛṣṇa. *cf. SBE*, Vol. XLII, p. 620.
46. Wilson, H.H., *Religious Sects of the Hindus*, Calcutta, 1958, p. 119, n. 123.
47. III. 9.
48. 77. 81.
49. *Matsya Purāṇa*, VII. 181. 4; 182. 4.

to move with the act of creation of mortal beings as per the instruction from Brahman.[50] In the *Mahābhārata*[51] he is *Sthāṇu* because he is *Sthitaliṅga*. Since, standing aloft, he consumes the lives of men, and since he is fixed, and since his *liṅga* is perpetually fixed, he is called *Sthāṇu*[52] in the same work. In the *Vikramorvaśīya*,[53] Kālidāsa described Śiva as *Sthāṇu*.

Nīlakaṇṭha and Śitikaṇṭha

The references in the Keśisūkta of the *Ṛgveda* to the Keśin (Muni) drinking *viṣa* (the meaning of which is both 'water' and 'poison') with Rudra may have given rise to the Epico-Paurāṇic story of Śiva's drinking poison. The *Śatarudriya* section of the *Yajurveda*[54] alludes to Rudra's blue-neck (*Nīlagrīva*). But the linking of the two facts, namely, drinking of poison and blue-neck, is post-Vedic. The story is well known to the students of Indian mythology, namely, how Vāsuki, the serpent king, at the time of the churning of the milk ocean for ambrosia (*amṛta*), vomited *halāhala*, the deadly poison, which enveloped the world in a destructive conflagration, and how Śiva, at the request of the gods, swallowed the poison and kept it in his gullet which turned his throat blue, whereupon he is known as Nīlakaṇṭha.[55]

The *Pañcaviṁśa Brāhmaṇa*[56] refers to a class of non-Aryan ascetics who swallowed poison and this naturally reminds us the Nīlakaṇṭha aspect of Śiva. Even to this day we have some votaries of Śiva, who take delight in showing indifference to worldly objects, by eating and drinking not only ordure and carrion but also poisonous acids and nails.[57] In the Kālañjara hill

50. *Ibid.*, 4. 32; *Brahmāṇḍa Purāṇa*, Pūrva Bhāga, 10. 82-99.
51. VII. 124f., 202.
52. *cf.* Rao, T.A.G., *EHI*, Vol. II, Pt. I, p. 60.

Heras (*Studies in Proto-Indo-Mediterranean Culture*, Vol. I, Bombay, 1953, p. 284n.) thinks that *Sthāṇu* is a compound word, the elements of which are *Sthā* and *Anu* or *An*, evidently meaning 'Anu who is standing'. Among the well known tribes in the *Ṛgveda*, we have the reference of Anus in the *Dāśarājña* context. In the *Mahābhārata*, Anu is the name of Śiva and, according to Heras, those who worshipped him were Anus.

53. I. 1.
54. *Vāj. Saṁ.*, XVI. 28.
55. *Brahmāṇḍa Purāṇa*, Pūrvabhāga, Adh. 25; *Vāyu P.*, Adh. 54; *Mbh.*, I. 18. 42. See also Kramrisch, S., *The Presence of Śiva*, pp. 145-52.
56. XVII. 1. 2.
57. Wilson, H.H., *op. cit.*, p. 131.

Nīlakaṇṭha is enshrined.[58] At Paharpur (now in Bangladesh) a sculpture representing the offering of *halāhala* to Śiva was found.[59]

We have seen that in the *Śatarudriya* section of the *Yajurveda*[60] Rudra is painted as Śitikaṇṭha (white-throated) and in it we may find the nucleus of the following Epic story. Śiva at the time of destroying the sacrifice of Dakṣa, as the story runs in the *Mahābhārata*,[61] hurled his flaring trident repeatedly at Dakṣa and the assembled gods. Nārāyaṇa repelled the trident, which returned to its owner howling. Śaṅkara in anger ran up to Nārāyaṇa, when the latter in defence seized the former by his throat. Hence Śiva is designated Śitikaṇṭha or Śrīkaṇṭha.

Paśupati

The pre-Aryan Śiva is not only the prince of Yogins, but also the lord of the beasts, and according to Marshall,[62] it is seemingly in reference to this aspect of his nature that the animals are grouped about him in the Mohenjodaro seals. In the *Ṛgveda*[63] an interesting epithet of Rudra is *Paśupa* and this may conceivably have been one of the reasons for identifying Rudra with Śiva.[64] Although the expression Paśupati is free and common occurrence in the case of many other deities in the Vedic literature, still, gradually it became a distinctive epithet for Rudra.

58. Ramachandra Dikshitar, V.R., *The Purāṇa Index*, Vol. III, 1955 p. 258.

59. *ARASI*, 1926-27, pl. XXXIII(b).

60. *Vāj. Saṁ.*, XVI. 28.

61. *Harivaṁśa*, 3. 31. 43ff.

62. *Op. cit.*, p. 54. For the bovine legs of Proto-Śiva, see also Srinivasan, D., 'The so-called Proto-Śiva seal from Mohenjo-Daro : An iconological Assessment' in *Archives of Asian Art*, 29, p. 55.

To Heras ('Plastic Representation of God Amongst the Proto-Indians' in *Sardesai Com. Volume*, p. 224) this image or a similar one may certainly have originated the idea of Paśupati at a later period, but it cannot be called Paśupati; for, it is the representation of Śiva (the lord of various tribes) surrounded by the *lāñchanas* (containing the figures of animals) of the various proto-Indian tribes.

63. I.114.9.

64. Marshall, J., *op. cit.*, p. 54.

In the *Yajurveda*,[65] *Atharvaveda*,[66] *Śatapatha Brāhmaṇa*[67] and *Āśvalāyana Gṛhyasūtra*,[68] Paśupati is a form of Rudra. This epithet also seems to point to his rapproachement with the pre-Aryan deity worshipped at the Indus Valley even as early as the later Ṛgvedic age.

With the exaltation of Rudra-Śiva as the supreme lord of the universe in the post-Vedic age, his authority is necessarily extended and the term 'Paśupati' is given a new interpretation. From the lord of cattle he became the lord of all creatures. The adherents of Śiva-Paśupati appear to have been mainly Pāśupata at first, and then Śaiva.[69] Although the *Rāmāyaṇa* does not connect Śiva with the Pāśupata sect, in the *Mahābhārata*.[70] Śiva not only appears on many occasions as Paśupati, but also claims to have himself declared the Pāśupata religion.

Varāhamihira[71] describes the Pāśupatas as *Sabhasmadvijas*, while Hiuen Tsang refers to the same sect as 'the ash-besmeared tīrthikas'. Bāṇabhaṭṭa's[72] description of the Pāśupatas as dressed in 'red garments' (*raktapaṭa*) may be compared with Bhavabhūti's[73] description of the Kāpālika Aghoraghaṇṭa. The *Pāśupata-Sūtras*[74] and the commentary on it by Kauṇḍinya incorporate some Pāśupata practices of outlandish character.

65. *Vāj. Saṁ.*, XVI. 28.
66. VII. 11.2; VII. 11. 6. 9.
67. I. 7. 3. 8; VI. 1. 3. 12.
68. IV. 8. 19.
69. Banerjea, J.N., *PTR*, p. 87.

Chennakesavan, S., (*A Critical Study of Hinduism*, Delhi, 1980, p. 81) points out how Mādhavācārya in his *Sarvadarśana Saṁgraha*, explains Śaivism under the name of Nākuliśa Pāśupata; and how the early worshippers of Śiva claimed the Āgamas as their source-books. In the words of Chennakesavan: "The Pāśupata system is not a living religion today and its interest for us is that, historically, it is the fore-runner of the Śaivism of today." (p. 81).

Dehejia, V., (*Early Stone-Temples of Orissa*, New Delhi, 1979, p. 11) observes : "The early Śiva temples of Orissa display affiliation to this Pasupata Sect, and all of them are embellished with carvings of Lakulin."

70. XII. 284. 195; XII. 349. 67; De, S.K., 'Sects and Sectarian Worship in the Mahābhārata' in *Our Heritage*, Vol. I, 1953, p. 6.
71. *Bṛhatsaṁhitā*, S. Dvivedi's ed., Ch. 59, V. 19.
72. *Kādambarī*, *cf. DHI*, p. 451.
73. *Mālatīmādhava*, Act V.
74. About the authorship of the Pāśupata-Sūtras, nothing is known. Śaivism is not only a cult of worship but a philosophy of life. As the

Tryambaka

Many of the names of Śiva are easily intelligible; but there has been controversy on the original meaning of the term 'tryambaka' which occurs in the *Ṛgveda,*[75] *Yajurveda,*[76] *Śatapatha Brāhmaṇa*[77] and in other branches of Vedic literature a number of times. Roth and Böhtlingk[78] as well as Keith[79] interpret it as 'having three wives or sisters'. Max Müller[80] and Macdonell[81] take it to mean 'having three mothers'. Hillebrandt[82] suggests that '*tri*' is equal to '*strī*', as we have in a passage of the *Śatapatha Brāhmaṇa*[83]*:* "because that share belongs to him (Rudra) with a *strī* or female, he is called Tryambaka". However, Rudra is *Ambikāpati* or husband of Ambikā only in the late *Taittirīya Āraṇyaka.*[84]

In the post-Vedic literature, also Tryambaka is a common epithet of Rudra-Śiva. In classical Sanskrit *ambaka* denotes 'an eye'. In the *Mahābhārata*[85] he is painted as 'three-eyed'. The story runs that the third eye—as luminous as the sun—

Pāśupata system (On Self : Paśu; On Bond : Pāśa; On Lord : Pati) lost its importance, the most important of Śaiva schools are the Śaiva Siddhānta, the Vīraśaiva or the Liṅgāyata sect and Śaivism as practised in Kashmir. See Chennakesavan, S., *A Critical Study of Hinduism*, Delhi, 1980, pp. 81-82.

For a research work on Śaiva Siddhānta, see Sivaraman, K., *Śaivism in Philosophical Perspective*, Delhi, 1973 (A Thesis for the Ph.D. Degree of the Banaras Hindu University).

Jash, Pranabananda, in his *History of Śaivism*, (Calcutta, 1974, Ph.D. dissertation of the Visva Bharati University) deals exhaustively with the history of the Siddhānta School, along with the Pāśupatas, the Liṅgāyatas, the Śaiva āchāryas of Kashmir, the Kāpālikas, the Kālāmukhas, the Harihara sub-sect and Śaiva sects of the Far South.

75. VII. 59. 12.
76. *Vāj. Saṁ.*, III. 58.
77. II. 6. 2. 9.
78. *Sanskrit-Worterbuch*, Vol. III, pp. 456-59; *cf.* Venkataramanayya, N., *Rudra-Śiva*, 1941, p. 16n.
79. *Rel. and Philosophy of the V. and U.*, p. 143.
80. *SBE*, Vol. XXXII, p. 389.
81. *Vedic Mythology*, p. 74.
82. *Ved. Myth.*, II, p. 188; *cf.* Keith, *op. cit.*, p. 149.
83. II. 6. 2. 9.
84. X. 18.
85. XIII. 140. 34.

breaks out on his forehead when Umā covers his two eyes in sport because of which the whole universe was submerged in cosmic darkness.[86]

Again, *ambaka* is also a synonym of *śṛṅga* so that Tryambaka is the same as *Triśṛṅga*, that is, the 'three peaked mountain'. In the *Rāmāyaṇa*, according to Hopkins,[87] *parvatas Tryambakaḥ* (triyambaka being a metrical form) is originally the god itself.

Ambā or *ambikā* is a Vedic word meaning 'mother' and Tryambaka may mean '[the god] born of three mothers', though it appears physically impossible to us. The case is not unlike the myth of the birth of his son Skanda or Kumāra or Kārttikeya and Jarāsandha as found in the Epics and the Purāṇas.[88]

As no three mothers of either Rudra of Śiva are known to us, Hopkins[89] suggests that Tryambaka Śiva has not three mothers but three Mother-goddesses (Gaurī, Kāli and Umā), who are the Ambikās, each originally an Ambā or Mother. Some scholars[90] invent three Ambās from among the figurines of the Mother-goddesses found in the Mohenjodaro to account for Rudra being called Tryambaka. If the connection of Rudra with the cult of the Mothers were real, we might then see in the Rudra of the *Ṛgveda* a figure 'already complicated by contamination'[91] with an aboriginal or pre-Aryan deity; for, we have very little evidence or probability of Mother worship as an Aryan or Indo-European custom.

86. *cf.* Rao, T.A.G., *op. cit.*, Vol. II, p. 49.

87. *Epic Mythology*, p. 220.

88. *Rāmāyaṇa* (Bombay ed.), XXXVII, V. 5ff. I, 36ff.; *Mbh.*, III. 225ff., IX. 44ff.; XIII. 84ff.; Wilson, *Viṣṇu P.*, 1865, II, 118 note.

The story is as follows: Śiva's energy being dissipated fell on fire but merely enhanced Agni's power, who flung it as seed into the Gaṅgā. But the latter could not retain it, and threw it on the slope of the Himālaya into a thicket of reeds (*Śaravaṇa*). There it was transformed into a fine boy, and the Six Kṛttikās (like the Greek Pleiades) nursed the child. As each of them desired him to be her son, he assumed six faces (*Ṣaḍānana*) and sucked their breasts simultaneoulsy.

89. *Op. cit.*, p. 220n.

90. *cf.* Bhandarkar, D.R., *op. cit.*, p. 43.

91. Keith, A.B., *op. cit.*, p. 149.

Keith[92] believes that the epithet *tryambaka* refers to the god as connected either with three seasons, or with the three worlds; namely, heaven, air and earth, which is natural in a god closely connected with Agni of whom nothing is more assured than his triple nature. Moreover, the allusions of the three mothers of Agni are to be found in the *Ṛgveda.*[93]

Association with Mountains

A non-Aryan mountain deity has definitely lent some of his characteristics to Rudra, the earlier counterpart of Śiva, from the very beginning. The relation with hill tribes is indicated by his epithets *Giriśanta*, *Girīśa*, *Giritra*, etc., as found in the *Śatarudriya* section of the *Yajurveda*[94] and the *Śvetāśvatara Upaniṣad,*[95] these being regular names of Śiva in post-Vedic mythology. The residence of the Paurāṇic Śiva is situated upon Mount Kailāsa round which a real cycle of myth has grown in the course of centuries. The cult of mountains is usually regarded as purely non-Aryan. But in the *Ṛgveda*[96] there is a direct appeal to mountains : 'May the mountains be propitious to us'. With the exception of Muñjavat no individual peak of the Himālaya (like Kailāsa) is mentioned. In the *Ṛgveda*[97] soma is described, according to the interpretation of Yāska,[98] as coming from Mount Muñjavat. In the *Atharvaveda*[99] Muñjavat is the name of a people who, along with the Mahāvṛṣas and others are mentioned as dwelling far away and to whom fever is banished. In the *Taittirīya,*[100] *Vājasaneyī*[101] *Saṁhitās* and the *Śatapatha Brāhmaṇa,*[102] the name Muñjavat, however, is typical for a region far distant, and Rudra, with his destructive force,

92. *Loc. cit.*
93. III. 56.5; cf. Hopkins, *op. cit.*, p. 220,
94. *Vāj. Saṁ.*, XVI. 29; *Tait. Saṁ.*, IV. 5. 1.
95. III. 6.
96. VII. 35. 8.
97. X. 34. 1.
98. *Nirukta*, IX. 8.
99. V. 22.5, 7, 8, 14. *cf. Baudhāyana Śrautasūtra*, II. 5.
100. I. 8. 6. 2.
101. III. 61.
102. II. 6. 2. 17.

is entreated to depart beyond it. In fact, Muñjavat was a hill from which the people took their name and Rudra was associated with it in the Vedic literature.

Jacobi[103] thinks that the character of Rudra-Śiva as god of the mountains may have made him the favourite god of southern India. The Tamil work *Aruṇācala Purāṇam*[104] records how on one occasion Śiva himself appeared as a mountain. Tirumalai, one of the popular names of Śiva in southern India, is a sacred mountain.[105] In fact, the cosmopolitan character of the great Rudra-Śiva enabled him to absorb a number of anonymous mountain-deities born of the imagination of many hill tribes in India and elsewhere.[106]

Śiva and Umā

As Śiva is Girīśa, so is his spouse Giriśā, Śailasutā, Pārvatī, Giriputrī, Girirājaputrī, Śailarājaputrī, irijā, Parvatarājakanyā etc., in the Epics.[107] Her old name is Umā, and we find her first described as the daughter of Himavat (Umā Haimavatī) in the *Kena Upaniṣad*.[108] Apparently she appears here as an independent goddess conversant with Brahman. The earliest reference of Umā as the consort of Rudra is to be found in the *Taittirīya-Āraṇyaka*.[109] Although the name of Rudrāṇī (the consort of Rudra) is to be found in some early Saṁhitā texts along with those of Indrāṇī, Varuṇānī and others, these had no part to play.[110] Pāṇini[111] also mentions Bhavānī, Śarvāṇī, Rudrāṇī and Mṛḍānī—all wives of Śiva under his different appellations of Bhava, Śarva, Rudra and Mṛḍa. But it does

103. 'Brahmanism' in *ERE*, Vol. II, p. 812.

104. Ch. II, *cf.* Heras, H., *Studies in Proto-Indo-Mediterranean Culture*, Vol. I, Bombay, 1953, p. 280.

105. Thurston, *Castes and Tribes of Southern India*, Vol. III, p. 423.

106. *ERE*, Vol. II, p. 812.

107. *Ram.*, III. 16. 43; *cf.* Hopkins, E.W., *op. cit.*, p. 224; *Mbh.*, S. Indian ed., I. 172. 28; I. 187, 4; Hopkins, *op. cit.*, p. 224.

108. III. 25.

109. X. 18.

110. Banerjea, J.N., *PTR*, p. 114.

111. IV. 1. 49.

not follow that these goddesses had risen to any importance in Pāṇini's time.[112]

In the *Rāmāyaṇa*[113] Umā was the younger sister of Gaṅgā. According to the *Harivaṁśa*[114] (where she is called Aparṇā), she was the eldest daughter of Himavat by Menakā or Menā. She had two sisters, Ekaparṇā and Ekapāṭalā. Umā is derived in late tradition from "O don't", as her mother Menā thus addressed Aparṇā to dissuade her from the path of severe austerities. Aparṇā-Umā was given in marriage to Śiva, and the latter is known in the *Mahābhārata* as Umādhava, Umāsahāya, Umāpati, etc.[115] The *Amarakośa*[116] endorses the tradition recorded in the *Harivaṁśa*.[117]

Umā, due to her peculiar name and her association with mountains, seems to be the counterpart of the Babylonian mother-goddess Ummu or Umma, the Arcadian Ummi, the Dravidian amma, the Scythian Ommo and the Cappadocian Mā—the consort of Teshub who has considerable resemblance with Rudra-Śiva.[118] In a quarter stater of Huviṣka, in the collection of the Punjab Museum, we have two figures, one male and the other female, standing facing each other, the former being described as Oesho (Bhaveśa) and the latter as Nana (Umā).[119] The figure of Umā is also to be found on the reverse side of a gold coin of the same Kuṣāṇa ruler, in the British Museum collection, where the goddess was correctly described by the die-cutter in four Greek letters as OMMO[120] (Umā).

From the testimonies adduced, it seems certain that towards the end of the Vedic period, several female deities of non-Vedic origin began to be associated with the Vedic Rudra in various ways. Vindhyavāsinī, a similar mountain-goddess of the Vindhyas, is also identified with the wife of Śiva.

112. Muir, J., *OST*, IV, p. 405, f.n. 175.
113. I. 35. 14.
114. I. 18. 15ff.
115. Hopkins, E.W., *op. cit.*, p. 224.
116. I. 36ff.
117. Sircar, D.C., *Studies in the Religious Life*, p. 102.
118. Raychaudhuri, H.C., *Studies in Indian Antiquities*, 1958, pp. 201-02.
119. Banerjea, J.N., *DHI*, p. 126.
120. *Loc. cit.*

Turning now to Śiva's wedlock with Umā or Pārvatī as found in the *Mahābhārata*[121] and the different *Purāṇas*[122] and in the *Kumārasambhava* of Kālidāsa, we cannot but subscribe to Keith's appreciation of the whole theme in Kālidāsa when he said: "Their nuptials and their love serve as the prototype for human marriage and human love and sancitfy with divine precedent the forces which make the home and carry on the race of men."[123] The fact that Umā is the daughter of the mountain Himālayas stirs up the imaginative power of the poet to describe vividly both the beauty of the daughter and the grandeur and serene atmosphere of the mountain. The union of this primordial pair is immortalised in Indian art by the *Kalyāṇasundara*, *Vaivāhika* or *Śivavivāha mūrtis*, the most outstanding specimens of which being the Elephanta and the Ellora reliefs. However, the husband-wife relation between Śiva and Pārvatī later on received philosophical sublimation as Puruṣa and Prakṛti of the Sāṁkhya or Brahman and Māyā of the *Vedānta* systems.[124]

The Epic and Paurāṇic Śiva, unlike the Vedic Rudra, sometimes appears in his androgynous form as Ardhanārīśvara, with a hermaphrodite body, uniting in himself the principles of male and female generation. According to the *Mahābhārata*[125] all creatures bear the male or female sign and as such all of

121. Hopkins, *op. cit.*, p. 226; *Mbh.*, XIII. 84.71.

122. *Śiva P.*; *Skanda P.*, Śiva-rahasya; *Vāmana P.*, Adh. 51ff.

123. Keith, A.B., *A Hist. of Sansk. Lit.*, Oxford, 1920, p. 57;

Is the marriage of Śiva with Umā a later event when marriage in human society had become a recognised institution? See, Kosambi, D.D., *Myth and Reality*, Bombay, 1962, p. 10.

Hogarth ('Aegean Religion' in *ERE*, Vol. I, p. 147) and Briffault (*The Mother*, New York, 1927, pp. 590ff.) have shown how the Mother Goddess in the ancient world was everywhere unwed. See also Letourneau, C.F., *Evolution of Marriage*, New York, 1891).

124. Hazra, R.C., *Studies in the Upapurāṇas*, Vol. II, p. 24.

125. XIII. 14. 33-35; cf. Hopkins, *op. cit.*, p. 223;

Kosambi (*The Culture and Civilization of Ancient India*, London, 1965, pp. 204ff.) thinks that the Syncretic Ardhanārīśvara image, unlike Hari-Hara, lasted because this fusion meant a more productive society where the differences between the matriarchal and patriarchal forms of property were reconciled.

them belong either to Śiva or to his female counterpart Devī. Like the Hari-Hara, Mārttaṇḍa-Bhairava (Sūrya-Śiva), Śiva-Lokeśvara, Trimūrti and many other syncretistic icons, Ardha-nārīśvara emphasizes the mental approach of reconciliation of the principal cult deities of Śaivism and Śāktism.

This model of conjugal inseparability[126] has given rise to many mythological tales. Gopinatha Rao[127] relates a story from the Purāṇas in this way: On one occasion the Devas and Ṛṣis circumambulated both Śiva and Pārvatī at Kailāsa and bowed to both. But Ṛṣi Bhṛṅgin, being an exclusive worshipper of Śiva, went round Śiva alone. To save Pārvatī's honour, as she grew angry at this insult, Śiva united his body with hers with the hope that Bhṛṅgin would thus be compelled to pay homage to his spouse, while paying respect to him. It is stated in the *Śiva Purāṇa*[128] that when Brahman asked Śiva to divide himself, the latter became divided into male and female forms. In the *Liṅga*[129] and *Padma*[130] *Purāṇas*, this Ardhanārīśvara form is referred to. The *Prapañcasāra Tantra*[131] dedicates a whole chapter[132] on Ardhanārīśvara, where Śiva in the right

126. Somadeva, *Kathā-Sarit-Sāgara*, pp. 31-32.

Upadhyaya, Padma, in her *Female Images in the Museums of U.P. and their Social Background*, (Varanasi, 1978) has painted the domesticity of the gods which has found portrayal many a time at the hands of the Indian sculptors. Regarding Śiva-Pārvatī images as the model of conjugal insepar-ability, Upadhyaya observes:"The closeness of the couple has been so much the subject of attraction for the Hindu domesticity that the devotee and the artist could not be satisfied by even a composite proximity of them and did not stop until they had conceived the dual unity of an *Ardhanārīśvara* figure, thus achieving a veritable oneness between the masculine and feminine entities. The idea of this particular figure of *Ardhanārīśvara* is to locate the man in the woman as also the woman in the man and to create a perfect homogeneity in domestic affairs. This is the completion of the idea which started with the *Pārvatī Pariṇaya* figures in which Śiva and Pārvatī stand shoulder to shoulder to get into marital sanctum." (pp. 145-146).

127. *Op. cit.*, Vol. II, pp. 322-23. Gopinatha Rao has not given the source of this story.

128. *cf. ibid.*, p. 321.

129. XIX. 8.

130. Book I, Sṛṣṭikhaṇḍa.

131. Vidyāratna, Tārānātha, ed. in *Tantrik Texts*, Vol. III, 1914.

132. Chap. XXVIII; cf. Winternitz, M., *op. cit.*, Vol. I, Part II, p. 528.

half is represented as a wild-looking man, and Śakti in the left half is painted as a voluptuous woman. The *Matsya Purāṇa*[133] states how Śiva manifested his Ardhanārīśvara form at Kṛta-śauca after Andhaka was killed. Kālidāsa's *Mālavikāgnimitra* also refers to this form.[134]

But the cosmogonic motif of a bisexual or androgynous primeval being like Ardhanārīśvara is very old and may be traced in the Vedic literature. It may be traced in the notion of the Ṛgvedic twins, Yama and Yamī.[135] In the *Kaṭha Upaniṣad*[136] Prajāpati is said to have assumed a bisexual form for the purpose of creation and did not have any other being for pairing. The *Bṛhadāraṇyaka Upaniṣad*[137] says that the *Ātman*, the original Puruṣa, was bisexual and divided himself into male and female, and multiplied. Some scholars[138] find a prototype of Ardhanārīśvara amongst the proto-Indian specimens.

The numismatic and glyptic representations of Ardhanārīśvara go back to a fairly early date, long before the explanatory myths came to be fabricated. V.S. Agrawala[139] has drawn our attention to a miniature relief of the Kuṣāṇa period depicting the theme. The Greek author Stobaeus quotes a passage from Bardasanes (c. 154-222 A.D.) who learnt about the Ardhanārīśvaramūrti from an Indian embassy visiting Syria.[140] Among the outstanding specimens of later date the fine panel in the rock-cut temple at Bādāmi, at the Bṛhadīśvara temple at Thanjavur and at Dārāśuram may be noted.

Opposite Functions

It may appear strange that, from the very beginning, Vedic literature attributes to Rudra opposite functions, namely, good

133. 179. 87ff.
134. I. 1.
135. *RV*, I. 66. 8. Dandekar, R.N., 'Yama in the Veda' in the *B.C. Law Vol.*, I, p. 203.
136. XIII. 7.
137. I. 4.
138. *cf.* Karmarkar, A.P., *The Religions of India*, Vol. I, 1950, pp. 42, 73.
139. *JISOA*, 1937, p. 124, pl. XLIV, 2.
140. Sircar, D.C., ed. *Prācyavidyā-taraṅginī*, pp. 218ff.; *JAS*, Vol. IX, 1967, p. 181.

and bad, benevolent and malevolent—though appearing as contraries. Kṛṣṇa in the *Mahābhārata*[141] praises the two bodies of Rudra-Śiva, one awful and the other auspicious. The Epico-Paurāṇic Rudra-Śiva is both the god of procreation and destruction. He impersonates the generating power worshipped in the *liṅga*; similarly he reduces to ashes the god of 'desire' or sexual love, Kāma (known as Manmatha, Madana, Kandarpa, Anaṅga, Smara, etc.) for the latter's audacity in attempting to arouse in his mind feelings of love for Umā when he was performing austerity.[142] The Chola artist of the Śiva temple at Gangaikondacholapuram has illustrated the Kāmāntakamūrti in a very striking manner.

Śiva is symbolized both as the god of death, *Mahākāla*, playing the dance of destruction and also the vanquisher of death as *Mṛtyuñjaya*. All these epithets indicate, as Jacobi[143] rightly holds, that Śiva was regarded first as the ruler, and then the representative of the vast and various classes of demonic beings who were created in the imagination of the superstitious, due to fear and awe, inspired by everything relating to death, the dead and destruction. Here, we have the explanation of the Purāṇic Śiva's predilection for *Śmaśānas* or his wearing of the garland of skulls.

Yama, a deified hero in the *Ṛgveda*, has become in Brāhmaṇical mythology the dreaded god of the nether world, the sovereign of the dead.[144] In the *Ṛgveda*,[145] Rudra is also the man-killer. In the *Śatarudriya* hymns,[146] Rudra is said to have in his

141. *Dve tanū tasya devasya vedajñāḥ brāhmaṇāḥ viduḥ |*
Ghorām anyāṃ Śivam anyāṃ te tanū bahudhā punaḥ ||
—Anuśāsana Parvan.

142. *Rāmāyaṇa* (Bombay ed.), I, 23. 10ff.; *Harivaṁśa*, 9263ff.; *Kumārasambhava*, IV. 42; *Liṅga P.*, cf. *EHI*, Vol. II, p. 147; Hopkins, *op. cit.*, pp. 164-67.

143. 'Brahmanism' in *ERE*, Vol. II, p. 813.

144. Ibid., p. 806.

Long, J.G., in his Ph.D. dissertation, University of Chicago, *Visions of Terror and Bliss*, Chicago, 1970, has also pointed out the opposite functions of Śiva.

145. IV. 3. 6.

146. *Vāj. Saṁ.*, XVI. 33; see *SBE*, Vol. XLIII, p. 153.

possession Yama's power. The account of Jarāsandha in the *Mahābhārata* shows how innumerable kings were conquered and imprisoned by him at Girivraja, as elephants by a lion in the cave of a great mountain, to sacrifice to the glorious Mahādeva.[147] Again, like the dogs—the regular messengers of Yama[148]—Rudra in the *Yajurveda*[149] is described as *Śvapati* ('lord of dogs') and in the *Atharvaveda*[150] as having 'howling dogs'. It is of interest to note that the invariable concomitant of the later Vaṭuka-Bhairava image is his dog-companion. According to the orthodox Hindus, the dog is an unclean quadruped, and this attendant of Śiva as Vaṭuka-Bhairava emphasizes his unorthodox character.[151]

But it is difficult not to recognize the differences between a real death god Yama and Rudra, which indicate the basic difference of origin.[152] Yama is the regent of the south, but Rudra is of the north. The usual mount of Yama is the buffalo, but the mount of the later Rudra-Śiva is the bull. On the basis of the noose in the hand of Śiva on some Kuṣāṇa coins, Cunningham[153] describes 'Śiva as Yama'. But the intimate connection of Śiva with noose (*pāśa*) is old.[154]

Terrific forms

Rudra-Śiva is a complex figure, combining in himself clear traits of multifarious elements, as is natural in a god formed by the syncretism of different beliefs.[155] It is as destructive rather than reproductive energy that Rudra-Śiva is famed in the *Mahābhārata*; hence the battle-ground of death is his playground.[156] In the Epics and the Purāṇas he is said to have

147. *cf.* Muir, *OST*, IV, pp. 244ff.
148. *RV*, X. 14.11; *AV*, XVIII. 2.12.
149. *Vāj. Saṁ.*, XVI. 28; *Kāṭhaka Saṁ.*, XVII. 13; *Mait. Saṁ.*, II. 9. 5.
150. XI. 2. 30.
151. Banerjea, J.N., *Rel. in Art and Architecture*, p. 73.
152. Keith, A.B., *Rel. and Philo. of the V. and Up.*, 146.
153. *Coins of the Indo-Scythians and Kushans*, Pt. III, pp. 74ff.; *cf.* Banerjea, J.N., DHI, p. 127.
154. Banerjea, J.N., *DHI*, pp. 127-28.
155. Keith, A.B., *Rel. and Philo. of V. and Up.*, pp. 148-49.
156. Hopkins, E.W., *op. cit.*, p. 221.

destroyed not only demons like Gajāsura, Andhakāsura, Tripurāsura and Jālandhara, but also punished such gods as Yama, Kâma, Narasiṁha and others. All these themes are depicted in Indian art as the *Saṁhāramūrtis* of Śiva.

Rudra in the Vedic literature, especially in the *Śatarudriya* section,[157] is given the epithet *Kṛttivāsa* which means one that has a skin for his garment. Being represented as roaming in forests and other lonely places, it was natural for the later Vedic bards to depict him with a skin-clothing and was compared with the Niṣāda. In Rudra's epithet *Kṛttivāsa*, we have the nucleus of the elaborate mythology underlying the Gajāsurasaṁhāramūrti, as found in the *Kūrma* and the *Varāha Purāṇas*, where Śiva is shown as using the hide of the elephant as his outer covering after slaying the elephant-demon (Gajāsura) when the latter came near the Śivaliṅga to disturb the meditations of the worshippers.[158] The notable specimens of the *Gajāsurasaṁhāramūrti* in Indian art are to be found in the ornamented facade of the Amṛteśvara temple at Amṛtapura in Mysore,[159] in the temple at Valuvūr where the Gajāsura is supposed to have been destroyed, and the Dārāśuram[160] sculpture (Thanjavur District).

A thousand-headed demon named Andhaka (because he walked like a blind man) in the Epics and the Purāṇas is a victim of Śiva, who is styled Andhakaghâtin in the *Mahābhārata*.[161] The seed of this story is to be found in the *Atharvaveda*[162] where the thousand-eyed powerful Rudra is the slayer of Andhaka. The much mutilated Ellora and Elephanta panels, depicting the Andhakāsuravadhamūrti of Śiva, is a notable specimen of sculptural art.

On one occasion Śiva destroyed the three castles (*tripura*) of the demons. The story, as related in the *Mahābhārata*,[163] runs

157. See *SBE*, Vol. XLIII, pp. 150f. See also Sivaramamurti, C., *Śatarudriya : Vibhūti of Śiva's Iconography*, pp. 13-32.

158. The *Varāha P.* gives a different account.

159. Rao, T.A.G., *op. cit.*, Vol. II, pp. 152-53, pl. XXXI.

160. *Ibid.*, pp. 154-55, pl. XXXII.

161. XII. 10356; *Harivaṁśa*, Andhyakāvadha Adh.

162. XI. 2.

163. VIII. 24.

thus: Tārakākṣa, Kamalākṣa and Vidyunmālin, the three insolent sons of Tārakāsura, after pleasing Brahman by severe austerities obtained the boons through the influence of which the three brothers got three invincible castles of gold, silver and iron, constructed by Mayadānava, in heaven, air and earth respectively and after a thousand years the castles should unite into one and should only be destructible with a mighty single arrow. Being frightened at the unbounded strength of the demons and disappointed at the same time at his inability to overthrow them, Indra, followed by other depressed gods, approached Śiva through the creator Brahman and succeeded in inducing Śiva to undertake the task and parted with a half of their strength. Mahādeva fulfilled the desire of the gods by destroying the demons outright in a manner as previously demanded by them.

This Epic mythology also seems to have had a Vedic basis. In the *Bṛhadāraṇyaka*[164] and *Chāndogya*[165] *Upaniṣads* and the *Śatapatha Brāhmaṇa*[166] the struggles between the Devas and the Asuras are referred to though both the groups were born of the same father, Prajāpati.[167] In the commentary of the *Vājasaneyī Saṁhitā* of the *Yajurveda*[168] it is said that the three castles of the Asuras were destroyed by Agni. The *Taittirīya Saṁhitā*[169] somewhat amplifies the story. In the Epics and the Purāṇas this story was employed with modifications to enhance the greatness of Śiva. Tripurāntakamūrti of Śiva in the Bṛhadīśvara temple at Thanjavur,[170] the Daśāvatāra cave in Ellora[171] and the Kailāsanātha temple at Kāñcīpuram[172] are notable in this respect.

164. I. 3. 1.
165. I. 2. 1.
166. I. 2. 4. 8; I. 2. 5. 1-4, etc.
167. *ŚB*, I. 5.3.2; I. 7.2.22; IX, 5.1.12; XIV. 8.2.1; *Ait. Br.*, III. 36.
168. *cf.* Rao, T.A.G., *EHI*, Vol. II, p. 165.
169. *cf. Ibid.*, p. 166.

For the different versions of the Tripura myth, as found in the Purāṇas, see O'Flaherty, W.D., *The Origins of Evil in Hindu Mythology*, Berkeley, 1976, pp. 180-89. Kramrisch, S., *The Presence of Śiva*, Princeton Univ. Press, 1981, pp. 405-408.

170. Banerjea, J.N., *DHI*, p. 487, pl. XXXII, fig. 3.
171. *Loc. cit.*
172. Rao, T.A.G., *op. cit.*, Vol. II, pp. 170-71, Pls. XXXVII-XXXVIII.

The *Śiva Purāṇa* gives the details of the story how Śiva killed an eponymous demon Jalandhara when the latter, at the instigation of Nārada, proceeded to ravish Pārvatī. The name of modern Jalandhara (in Punjab) is associated with the name of this demon, on whose back the town is supposed to be built while Hiuen Tsang mentions it as a holy place of pilgrimages.[173]

The Paurāṇic theme how Śiva saved the life of the young devotee Mārkaṇḍeya from the hands of Yama by administering a kick on the chest of Yama is depicted in a characteristic manner in a Bṛhadīśvara temple relief at Thanjavur.[174]

The mythology of Śiva having incarnated himself in the composite form of man, bird and beast as Śarabha for the chastisement of Viṣṇu in his hybrid form of Narasiṁha that killed Hiraṇyakaśipu—an ardent devotee of Śiva—for his bitter denunciation of his own son who was an exclusive worshipper of Viṣṇu, is illustrated by the peculiar image of Śarabheśamūrti in the *Liṅga*[175] and *Kālikā*[176] *Purāṇas* and the best specimen of which is in a Dārāśuram temple relief.[177] The legend is once alluded to in the late *Taittirīya Āraṇyaka*,[178]

In one of his *Ugra* forms Śiva is said to have cut off the fifth head of Brahman, the story being found in great details in the *Skanda*,[179] *Padma*,[180] *Vāmana*,[181] *Kūrma*[182] and *Varāha Purāṇas*. The story, as found in the *Varāha Purāṇa*,[183] is like this: After creating Rudra, Brahman addressed him as Kapālin. Feeling insulted, Śiva cut off with his left thumb-nail the fifth head of Brahman. But the head stuck to his hand, of which he could only get himself rid after observing the severe Kāpālika life for

173. *ERE*, Vol. VII, p. 475.
174. Rao, T.A.G., *op. cit.*, Vol. II, pp. 156-58.
175. Chapter 96, *Pūrva-Khaṇḍa*.
176. V. 44ff.
177. Banerjea, J.N., *DHI*, p. 488, Pl. XXIV, fig. 2.
178. X. 1. 6.
179. *Brahmakhaṇḍa*, Setu-Māhātmya, 23-24ff.
180. Sṛṣṭikhaṇḍa, 14, 105ff.
181. Adh. 2; Kennedy, *Hindu Myth.*, p. 296.
182. Uttarabhāga, Adh. 31.
183. *cf.* Rao, T.A.G., *EHI*, Vol. II, p. 174.

twelve years. Brahman's tendency to tell lies is to be found in the somewhat sectarian story of the *Kūrma Purāṇa* explaining the Liṅgodbhavamūrti of Śiva whose Bhairava form is described as Brahmaśiraśchedakamūrti. In this form, he cut off, the fifth head of Brahman which talked to Śiva haughtily and disrespectfully and claimed to be the originator of the universe.

Kapāla, the most characteristic emblem of some of the fearful aspects of Śiva, is a cup made out of a human skull for drinking wine.[184]

The Kāpālas as a class of adherents of Paśupati are referred to in the *Vedānta Sūtras*.[185] Bhavabhūti in his *Mālatīmādhava* mentions Śrīśailam in the Andhra country as the most important sanctuary of the Kāpālikas. K.A. Nilakanta Sastri[186] has shown that the Kālāmukha sect was very powerful in many parts of Southern India in between the ninth and eleventh centuries A.D. The worship of Śiva as Kapāleśvara was also widely prevalent in the seventh century A.D. as proved by the Nirmand (Kangra District, Punjab) and Igātpurī (Nasik District, Maharashtra) Copper plate inscriptions[187] of *Mahārāja Mahāsāmanta* Samudrasena and Nāgavardhana respectively.

Destruction of Dakṣa's sacrifice

The description of the terrific (*ghora*) aspects of Rudra-Śiva will remain incomplete if we do not mention the story of *Dakṣa-yajña-nāśa*. That Śiva was regarded as an outsider standing apart from the other Vedic gods may appear from this episode.

184. Banerjea, J.N., *DHI*, p. 304.

We come to learn from the Chinese annals that the victorious leader of the Hiung-nu tribe drank out of such a cup made out of the skull of the Wu-Sun chief who was defeated and killed by him. The custom of using skulls as drinking cups is to be found even in Europe, among the old Germans and Livy tells the same tale of the celts.

See *ERE*, Vol. I, p. 212.

185. II. 2.36; *SBE*, Vol. 48, p. 520.

186. *The Colas*, pp. 648-49.

For a recent detailed discussion about the Kāpālikas and Kālāmukhas, see Lorenzen, David N., *The Kāpālikas* and *Kālāmukhas : Two lost Saivite Sects*, Berkeley, 1972.

187. Banerjea, J.N., *PTR*, pp. 96-97.

The kernel of the story is that Dakṣa Prajāpati invited all the gods to participate in the sacrifice performed by him, but excluded his son-in-law Rudra-Śiva due to his outlandish, unsocial and unorthodox behaviour. Satī, the daughter of Dakṣa and wife of Rudra-Śiva, went uninvited to attend the sacrifice, and gave up her life on her father insulting her and reviling Śiva in her presence. Śiva became furious at this and shot the sacrifice with an arrow so that its embodied form fled as a deer. Śiva broke Savitṛ's arms, kicked out Pūṣan's teeth, knocked out Bhaga's eyes, paralysing all the assembled gods who failed to honour him. He was assisted in this task by Vīrabhadra and other spirits born of his hair-pits.

The nucleus of this mythology is to be found in the Vedic literature. We have already seen that the Ṛgvedic tradition about the incestuous relation of a father with his daughter was elaborated in the *Śatapatha,*[188] *Tāṇḍya,*[189] and *Aitareya*[190] *Brāhmaṇas*, where Rudra pierced Prajāpati for this crime. In the *Tāṇḍya Mahābrāhmaṇa*[191] it is related that the gods were sharing among themselves the animals [sacrificed to them in the ceremonies]; but they avoided Rudra[in this sharing]. In the *Gopatha Brāhmaṇa*[192] we are told that Prajāpati, while performing a sacrifice, did not offer the requisite share of offerings to Rudra who thereupon 'seizing and piercing it (*yajña*) cut off a portion from it'. A look at it made Bhaga blind and Pūṣan toothless.

The *Rāmāyaṇa*[193] has the story in its simplest form. Śiva is simply said to wound the gods with his bows, without any reference to either Vīrabhadra or Umā, wife of Śiva. In the *Mahābhārata* the story is related thrice[194] where the wife of Śiva is only responsible for pointing out to Śiva Dakṣa's impertinence, but she is neither Dakṣa's daughter, nor did she die. In the Śānti-parvan we have Dadhīci—a staunch votary of Rudra-

188. I. 7.4.1; II. 1.2.9.
189. VIII. 2. 10.
190. III. 83. 1.
191. VII. 9. 16.
192. II. 1.
193. Bombay ed. I. 6. 8. 7ff.; *cf.* Muir, J., *OST*, IV, p. 372.
194. *Mbh.*, Sauptika-parvan, vv. 786-808, Śānti-parvan, vv. 10226-10258 and in V. 10275ff.; cf. Muir, J., *OST*, IV, pp. 373-74.

Śiva—warning Dakṣa in a rather lengthy speech about the impudence of his decision in not inviting Rudra-Śiva for the sacrifice. Dakṣa replied: "True it is that there are many Rudras numbering eleven, who wear spirally braided matted locks of hair, and who hold trident in their hands; but I do not know of Maheśvara".[195] Here is a clear attempt to distinguish between Vedic Rudra and post-Vedic Rudra-Śiva.

The *Purāṇas* reproduce the story with many embellishments. The variants of the episode told in Śivaite *Purāṇas* tend to insert references to Rudra-Śiva's almighty power as creator, preserver and destroyer; for example, in the *Vāyu Purāṇa* the gods attending Dakṣa's sacrifice took Rudra-Śiva's permission beforehand. In the *Liṅga Purāṇa*[196] Viṣṇu is beheaded. The *Bhāgavata Purāṇa*,[197] on the other hand, refers to the cause of Dakṣa's neglect of Rudra-Śiva by citing the following story: In an assembly of gods all present showed their respect to Dakṣa-Prajāpati by rising from their seats when he came in, but Brahman and Mahādeva did not. Dakṣa was willing to pay respect to Brahman; but he was offended with the insolence of his son-in-law and censured him before the other guests so that Rudra-Śiva departed in a rage. The followers of Rudra-Śiva were cursed and were declared by Bhṛgu as heretics and opponents of the true scriptures.[198]

We have the story in a slightly modified form in the *Kumārasambhava*[199] of Kālidāsa where Satī, the wife of Śiva and daughter of Dakṣa, abandoned her body owing to the insult offered by her father.

Thus we see that the two strains of the legend, as found in the Vedic literature, namely, Prajāpati insulting his daughter and disregarding Rudra-Śiva have been very 'cleverly accommodated'[200] in the later literature, and the Paurāṇic account of

195. *Santi no bahavo Rudrāḥ śūlahastāḥ kapardinaḥ* |
Ekādaśasthānagatā nāhaṁ vedmi Maheśvaram ||
Mbh., XII. 283. 26-27.

196. 100. 32.

197. IV. 2ff.

198. Muir, J., *OST*, IV, p. 382.

199. Canto I, 21.

200. Sircar, D.C., *The Śākta Pīṭhas*, p. 6. See also Kramrisch, S., *The Presence of Śiva*, pp. 322-330.

the blinding of Bhaga's eyes and the breaking of Pūṣan's teeth are pointedly mentioned in the *Brāhmaṇas.*

Associates

In the Vedic literature Rudra is surrounded by a plurality of Rudras or Maruts, called his *gaṇas* and *pramathas*. He thus appears as the leader of troops. The Maruts are often graphically depicted in the Vedic literature as young warriors, armed with spear and battle-axes, wearing helmets, decked with golden ornaments and riding on golden cars which gleam with lightning. But in the Epics and the Purāṇas, the *Pāriṣadas* or associates of Rudra-Śiva have become increasingly repugnant and obnoxious and are said to be his manifold forms. They are now dwarfish, pot-bellied, cock-faced, long-necked, big-eared, with deformed organ of sex, fiercely energetic, gigantic in size and outlandishly dressed.[201] Śiva is the lord of ghosts (*bhūtas*) and is called Bhūteśvara. The Maukhari chief Anantavarman installed in the fifth century A.D. an image of Bhūtapati in one of the caves of the Nāgārjuni hills.[202] True, we have in the *Śatapatha*[203] and *Aitareya*[204] *Brāhmaṇas* the story how the gods out of their most fearful forms fashioned a divine being called Bhūtavat (that is Rudra) to punish Prajāpati for his incestuous deeds. But the terms *bhūta*, meaning in Sanskrit 'formed' or 'created', is in the earlier sacred literature applied to the powers of Nature, and even to deities.[205] In fact, the *bhūtas* (ghosts), as associates of Rudra-Śiva is a post-Vedic development. The two notable associates of Śiva, that is, Bhṛṅgin and Mahākāla were so named as the former was as black as bee and the latter as dark coloured as pressed collyrium.[206]

201. Hopkins, E.W., *op. cit.*, p. 221.

202. Sircar, D.C., *Studies in the Rel. Life of Anc. and Med. India*, 1971, p. 52.

203. I. 7. 4. 1.

204. III. 33.

205. *ERE*, Vol. II, p. 488.

206. Mitra, H., 'Sadāśiva Worship in Early Bengal' in *JASB*, Vol. XXIX, 1933, No. 1, p. 244. For the images of Sadāśiva, see also a recent work by Sharma, B.N., *Iconography of Sadāśiva*, New Delhi, 1976. Sahai, B., in his

Rudra and the Sun

In the Vedic literature Rudra is identified with Agni and, in some passages of the *Ṛgveda*, Agni is identified with the sun.[207] The *Mahābhārata*[208] and the *Kūrma*,[209] *Padma*,[210] and *Garuḍa*[211] *Purāṇas* describe Śiva and Sūrya as identical. In the *Matsya Purāṇa*[212] both occur in the compound *Ravi-Śaṅkarau*. The composite icons combining in them features of Sūrya and Śiva—as Mārttaṇḍa-Bhairava—are not rare in Indian art.

Again, the Sun in the course of the year travels through the eight constellations of the Zodiac. Curiously enough the reflection of this idea is traced in the later literature, though in a different sense.[213] In Kālidāsa's *Abhijñānaśākuntala*[214] and *Mālavikāgnimitra*[215] Śiva is described as *aṣṭamūrti* or *aṣṭatanu* (eight-bodied), and the eight forms are: earth, water, light, wind, space, sacrificer, sun and moon.[216] In the *Matsya Purāṇa*[217] the presiding deities of these eight forms are as follows: Śarva of the earth, Paśupa of the fire, Ugra of the sacrificer, Rudra of the sun, Bhava of the water, Īśāna of the wind, Mahādeva of the moon and Bhīma of the space.

Trimūrti

Historically the most important fact is the rapproachement of two rival sects—the Śaivas and the Vaiṣṇavas. The *Mahābhārata* contemplates Viṣṇu in the form of Śiva, and Śiva in the form of Viṣṇu—Harirudra or Harihara—a dualism antecedent

---

Iconography of Minor Hindu and Buddhist Deities (Ph.D. dissertation, Patna University), New Delhi, 1975, described the iconographic features and representations of the Bhairava images. See pp. 119-131.

207. *cf.* Macdonell, A.A., *Vedic Mythology*, p. 93.
208. 'Śānti Parvan', 290. 86.
209. 'Pūrva-bhāga', Adh. 10.
210. Adh. 24, Vs. 68-69.
211. 'Ācāra kh.', Adh. 23, 6.
212. 68. 35.
213. Karmarkar, A.P., *The Religions of India*, Vol. I, 1950, p. 41.
214. I. 1.
215. I. 1.
216. Hopkins, E.W., *op. cit.*, p. 223.
217. 93, 66, 275. 38ff., 278. 17.

to trinitarianism.[218] In the *Matsya Purāṇa*[219] we have a *vrata*, suggested by Anaupamyā, the wife of Bāṇa, where Hari and Śaṅkara are recommended for being jointly worshipped. The *Mahimnaḥstotra* of Puṣpadanta is interpreted as applying to both Hari and Hara. The *Skanda*,[220] *Bhāgavata*,[221] *Śiva*,[222] *Liṅga*,[223] *Vāyu*[224] *Purāṇas* relate various stories how Śiva and Viṣṇu were combined into one. It took place possibly for the first time in Indian art in the Kuṣāṇa age, as proved, by a coin of Huviṣka, where the figure of Śiva is shown as having in the hands a *cakra*, along with *triśūla* and *vajra*.[225]

This dualism prepares the doctrine of *Trimūrti* which is often regarded as of a much later date.[226] The *Mahābhārata*[227] seeks to unite the gods of the three important theistic sects and teaches that in the form of Brahman he creates, in the form of Puruṣa (Viṣṇu) he preserves and in the form of Rudra (Śiva) he destroys. This affords the inspiration for the *Ekā mūṛtis-trayo devāḥ* of the *Matsya Purāṇa*[228] which is variously interpreted. We can trace the idea, however, to the *Maitri Upaniṣad*[229] though the part of the Upaniṣad in which it occurs is regarded as a late addition.[230] The same triad is also found in other early texts. The nucleus of the idea of *trimūrti* is also to be found in the *Ṛgveda* representing Agni as having three forms : Sun in the sky, lightning in the aerial waters, and fire on the earth.[231] Keith points out that in the Ṛgvedic prayers such as 'May Sūrya protect us from the

218. *Mbh.*, III. 39. 76f.; *cf.*, Hopkins E.W., *Epic Myth.*, p. 221.

219. 187. 49; *cf.* Kantawala, S.G., *Cultural History from the Matsya Purāṇa*, Baroda, 1964, p. 185.

220. VII. 2.17, 187ff.

221. VIII. 6-7.

222. *Sanat-kumāra-saṁhitā*, XXIII, 30.

223. Pūrvārdha, Adh. 96.

224. XXV, 20.26.

225. Benerjea, J.N., *DHI*, p. 124.

226. Hopkins, E.W., *Epic Myth.*, pp. 77, 88, 94, 170, 221, 223f.

227. III. 271. 47.

228. Farquhar, J.N., *An outline of the Religious Literature of India*, 1967 (Indian Reprint), p. 149n.

229. IV. 5-6; V. 2.

230. Radhakrishnan, *Indian Philosophy*, Vol. I, 1958, p. 715n.

231. *cf. ERE*, Vol. XII, p. 457.

sky, Vāta from the air, Agni from the earthly regions', appears a tendency to reduce all the gods to manifestations of three chief deities, each representative of one of the three divisions, sky, air and earth.[232]

Marshall[233] thinks that the three-faced proto-Śiva of the Mohenjodaro seal may be a syncretic form of three deities rolled into one. Again, the conception of the triad or trinity is a very old one not only in India but also in other parts of the world. In Mesopotamia, such triads as those of sin, Shamash and Ishtar, or of Anu, Enlil (Bel), and Ea were long antecedent to the Aryans.

Natesa Aiyar[234] describes a Gandhāra relief as a three-headed and six-armed *Trimūrti,* the head to the proper right being that of Viṣṇu and the one to the proper left being that of Brahman, and the central head is that of Śiva. Adoration to Hari-Hara-Hiraṇyagarbha or to Hara-Nārāyaṇa-Brahman are recorded in some early Kadamba inscriptions of the fifth and sixth centuries A.D. It will be of interest to note that the famous oft-reproduced *Trimūrti* image of the cave-shrine at Elephanta is taken by both Gopinatha Rao[235] and Stella Kramrisch[236] as a representation of the Maheśamūrti of Śiva.

As a healer god

We have seen that the twofold aspect of Rudra is well summarized in the Vedic literature. On the one hand, he is armed

232. *Loc. cit., RV,* X. cl. viii. 1.
233. *MIC,* Vol. I, p. 53.
234. *ASIAR,* 1913-14, pp. 276ff., pl. LXXIIa.
235. *EHI,* Vol. II, pp. 380-85, pl. cxvii.

Side by side with the masterpieces of Classical Hindu Sculpture, as at Elephanta, we have also the popular illustrations of Śiva in his different forms. Vitsaxis, Vassils G. (*Hindu Epics, Myths and Legends in Popular Illustrations,* OUP, New Delhi, 1977) introduces a form of popular religious art well known in India. Vitsaxis has given a clear and well-written account of the main myths and legends of Śiva (pp. 67-73) along with the popular illustrations. Regarding Trimūrti, Vitsaxis observes : "In popular iconography the three faces of Shiva Trimurti usually look similar to each other" (p. 71), whereas in the classical sculptures, the three faces of Śiva have different expressions corresponding to his different aspects.

236. *Ancient India,* Nl. II, 1946, pp. 4-8, Pls. I-VII.

with a 'cow-slaying' and 'man-slaying' missile; on the other hand, as the sender of diseases,[237] he is best qualified to cure it. His healing powers are mentioned in the *Ṛgveda*[238] and *Atharvaveda*[239] with great frequency and he is styled, like his later counterpart Śiva-Pañcānana, the most eminent of physicians. The *jalāṣa*, his distinctive remedy, is shown by the Atharvan ritual[240] to be cow's urine, the medicinal use of which goes back to Indo-Iranian times, as *gaomaēza* is prescribed in the *Avesta*.[241] The Maruts, as children of Rudra, have pure, salutary, and beneficent remedies, which they are asked to bring from various places.[242]

Rudra and Soma

We have reasons to believe that one of the drugs by means of which the Vedic Rudra cured the afflicted and even raised up the dead, was Soma, the elixir of immortality.[243] The Soma plant grew on the slopes of mountains, specially the Muñjavat,[244] beyond which Rudra was entreated to depart.[245] We have a hymn in the *Ṛgveda*[246] where Soma and Rudra are jointly implored. In the *Atharvaveda*[247] Rudra and Soma are requested together to drive away the hostile disease. In the *Taittirīya Saṁhitā*[248] Rudra is described as the 'lord of the Soma plant'. In fact, in later

237. *AV*, VI. 90.
238. *RV*, II. 33; *Rudraṁ jalāṣa bheṣajam* (*RV*, I. 43.4).
239. *Rudra jalāṣabheṣaja* (*AV*, II. 27. 6).
240. *AV*, II. 27. 6. For the early iconographic representation of Śiva as *Jalāṣa*, see also, Joshi, N.P., 'A Unique Figure of Śiva from Musanagar' in the *Bulletin of Museums and Archaeology in Uttar Pradesh*, Vol. 3, Lucknow, 1969, pp. 25ff. For a sculpture of Śiva with a small vessel of circa 50B.C.-50 A.D., Harle, J C., *Gupta Sculpture:Indian Sculpture of the Fourth to the Sixth Centuries A.D.*, Oxford, 1974, pls. 53, 54, 128.
241. *cf.* Bloomfield, M., *Am. Journ. Phil.*, Vol. XII, pp. 425-29.
242. *RV*, II. 33. 13; VIII. 20. 23ff.; *cf.* also V. 53. 14.
243. Venkataramanayya, N., *Rudra-Śiva*, Madras, 1941, p. 8.
244. *RV*, X. 34. 1.
245. *Taitt. Saṁ.*, I. 8. 6. 2; *Kāṭhaka Saṁ.*, IX. 7; XXXVI. 14; *Mait. Saṁ.*, I. 4. 10. 20; *Vāj. Saṁ.*, III. 61; XVI. 2.4.; *Śat. Brāh.*, II. 6. 2. 17.
246. VI. 74.
247. VII. 42. 1-2.
248. IV. 5.10; I. 8. 22. 5.

literature Soma and Rudra came to be identified. The *Kātyāyana Śrauta Sūtra*[249] states that the *caru* for Soma-Rudra is a cure for leprosy. There is an attempt now to show that Soma is mushroom.

In some of the latest hymns of the *Ṛgveda*[250] Soma begins to be somewhat obscurely identified with the moon.[251] In the *Atharvaveda*[252] and the *Yajurveda* this identification is explicit and in the later Vedic literature a commonplace occurrence. In several places of the *Ṛgveda*[253] Soma is addressed as *Indu*, which means 'moon' in later literature. In one passage of the *Ṛgveda*[254] at least the waning of the moon is caused by the gods drinking up nectar (*amṛta*). This somewhat remarkable coalescence of Soma with the moon must have started from the exaggerated terms in which the Ṛgvedic bards describe the celestial nature and brilliance of Soma.[255] In the *Chāndogya Upaniṣad,*[256] the Maruts have Soma at their head. However, when Rudra rose into prominence and became the great Rudra-Śiva, the Moon, that is the deified Soma, was placed upon his head; and stories—suitable to his new exalted position as Somanātha, Candraśekhara, Candramauli, Candracūḍa—were invented to account for it. It recalls the sovereignty which was assigned to him when the moon was recovered from the depths of the ocean. The Purāṇas[257] record how *Candra*, due to the curse of Dakṣa approached Śiva who gave him an abode on his forehead. In Śūdraka's *Mṛcchakaṭika*[258] Śiva had to place the moon on his head to allay the burning effect of poison which he had drunk during the churning of the Ocean.

Rudra and the Gaṅgā

Through the matted locks of Rudra-Śiva flows the heavenly

249. XV. 3. 39.
250. X. 85. 1-2.
251. Hillebrandt's main thesis that 'everywhere in the *Ṛgveda* Soma means the moon' is itself an exaggeration. *cf.* Hopkins, E.W., 'Soma' in *ERE*, Vol. XI, p. 686,.
252. XI. 6. 7.
253. *RV*, IX. 86, 24, 26, 37; VIII. 48. 2, 4, 5, 12, 13.
254. X. 85. 8.
255. Macdonell, A.A., 'Vedic Religion' in *ERE*, Vol. XII, p. 606.
256. III. 7. and 9.
257. *Padma P.*, 'Sṛṣṭikhaṇḍa', Adh. 34, 108f.; *Varāha P.*, Adh. 35; *Brahmavaivarta P.*, 'Brahmakhaṇḍa', 9, 58.
258. IV. 23.

Ganges (also known as Jāhnavī, Bhāgīrathī and Haraśekharā). Though mentioned twice in the *Ṛgveda*[259] the *Gaṅgā* does not appear to be a well-known or important stream in the Ṛgvedic period. In the *Yajurveda* and *Atharvaveda* we find no references to the Gaṅgā at all.[260] The name *Gaṅgā* is in all likelihood of Austric origin and the original meaning of the word is still preserved in its modern Bengali equivalent *gāṅg*, *gāṅ* which means 'any river or water-channel'.[261] In the *Rāmāyaṇa*[262] we have that famous mythology of the origin of Gaṅgā and how the royal saint Bhagīratha, descendant of Sagara, induced the celestial Gaṅgā to come down from heaven and how Śiva caught the river and compelled her to circle for ages in the labyrinth of his matted locks to check the impetus of her fall and ultimately allowed her to flow to the sea and purify the ashes of the sons of Sagara. We have another account of her descent in the *Mārkaṇḍeya*, *Vāyu* and *Matsya Purāṇas*,[263] and in the *Mahābhārata*[264] the great heroes Bhīṣma and Śāntanu were associated with her. However, the Gaṅgādhara aspect of Śiva is well exemplified in the sculptures hailing from the Gangaikondacolapuram temple.

Some scholars[265] suggest that Śiva's connection with Gaṅgā was partly due perhaps to Iranian influence on Indian religion because the close companionship which existed between Anāhita and Mithra bears a striking resemblance. But the hypothesis is not very convincing.

Weapons

The Epico-Paurāṇic Rudra-Śiva finds, rather, a closer parallel in Teshub—a god worshipped by the ancient Hittites in Western

259. VI. 45. 31 and X. 75. 5.

260. Raychaudhuri, H.C., *Studies in Indian Antiquities*, 1958, p. 56n.

261. Chatterji, S.K., *Indo-Aryan and Hindi*, Calcutta, 1960, pp. 38-39.

262. *Rāmāyaṇa*, I. 38-44, Griffith, R.T.H., *Rāmāyaṇa*, Banaras, 1895, pp. 51ff.

263. *Mārkaṇḍeya*, Chap. 55.

264. I. 98ff.

265. Venkataramayya, H., *op. cit.*, pp. 24-25; Cumount, 'Anāhita' in *ERE*, Vol. I, pp. 414-15.

Asia in the second millennium B.C.[266] Among other important common features of the two deities, we may note here the martial equipments of the two. The distinctive weapon of this storm god Teshub is the three-pronged thunderbolt;[267] and Śiva is also armed with the *triśūla* or trident, which is just a tribal insignia and found as a type on the coins of the Śibis, Vemakis, Audumbaras and others. In the Vedic literature Rudra is invariably represented as an archer with drawn bow and sharp pointed arrows,[268] spear,[269] thunderbolt[270] and club.[271] But *daṇḍa, aṅkuśa, śūla, paraśu, Khaṭvāṅga* and other curved weapons, in opposition to straight Aryan swords,[272] are found in the hands of Epico-Purāṇic Śiva to represent his terrible aspects. In the representation of Teshub at Malatia, he stands on a bull and bears bow and thunderbolt as weapons.[273] In the procession in the sacred gallery at Boghaz Koui his weapons are the trident and mace and in the Zinjerli sculpture Teshub is a bearded god armed with trident and dagger.[274]

Marshall[275] thinks that the horned-headdress of proto-Śiva at Mohenjodaro took the form of *triśūla* or trident in later days and in that guise continued to be a special attribute of Śiva signifying the three aspects of the god as Creator, Destroyer and Regenerator. The Rudras, a sect of the Śaivites had the trident branded on their forehead; the Jangamas, another sect, bore it on the head.[276]

266. Raychaudhuri, H.C., *Studies in Indian Antiquities*, pp. 200-04.
267. Charles, B.B., 'Hittites' in *ERE*, Vol VI, p. 724.
268. *RV*, II. 33. 10-11; V. 42. 11; X. 125. 6; VII. 46. 1; *TS*, IV. 5.3 and IV. 5.10.
269. *TS*, IV. 5. 10.
270. *RV*, II. 33. 3.
271. *AV*, I. 28. 5; *SB*, IX. 1. 1. 6.
272. Mitra, H., 'Sadāśiva Worship in Early Bengal' in *JASB*, Vol. XXIV, 1933, No. 1, pp. 196ff.
273. *ERE*, Vol. VI, p. 724.
274. *Loc. cit.*
275. *MIC*, Vol. I, p. 55. Regarding the Trident-signs on Indus-Seals and the head-wear of proto-Śiva as the plausible forerunner of trident, Dhaky, M.A., 'The Morphology of the Trident Emblem' in the *Journal of the Asiatic Society*, Vol. XIX, Nos. 1-2, 1977, p. 30.
276. *Loc. cit.*; Wilson, H.H., *Religious Sects of the Hindus*, pp. 122-130.

Kṣetrapāla

In the *Ṛgveda*, *Kṣetrasyapati*, 'lord of the field', is besought to grant cattle and horses and to confer prosperity.[277] In the *Vājasaneyī Saṁhitā*[278] Rudra is the lord of the fields and he exists in the soil and in the threshing floor.[279] In the *Atharvaveda*[280] we have a hymn which is redolent of fields, plants and ploughing and calls upon the 'lord of the field'. The *Hiraṇyakeśin*[281] and *Āpastambīya Gṛhyasūtras*[282] prescribe sacrifices to Kṣetrapati. In Aufrecht's *Catalogus Catalogorum*,[283] we have references to two works relating to the manner of worshipping Kṣetrapāla.[284] The Dravidian god Bhūmiyā—another form of Śiva—is also known as Kṣetrapāla.[285] According to the *Liṅga Purāṇa*, Kṣetrapāla is an incarnation of Śiva who, for the welfare of the world, assumed the form of a child, suckled the breast of Kālī and drank off in that manner her wrath and indignation. The energy thereby infused into the system made him the protector of the field and he had eight forms.[286] In the *Skanda Purāṇa*[287] we have another account, that is, how Śiva in his child-form created sixty-four Kṣetrapālas from his mouth with the aim of removing fear of the gods from Kālī. In fact, the cult of Kṣetrapāla who is always nude, is highly popular amongst the common folk of India who are connected with agriculture.

Musician and Dancer

The Epico-Paurāṇic Rudra-Śiva is a great musician (*gīta-śīla* and *gīta-vādya-rata*) and a Naṭarāja. The ancestor of Naṭarāja is

277. Macdonell, A.A., 'Vedic Religion' in *ERE*, Vol. XII, p. 608.
278. XVI. 18.
279. *VS*, XVI. 33.
280. II. 8. 5.
281. II. 3. 9. 8-12.
282. VII. 19. 13; VII. 20. 12-18.
283. Vol. I, p. 134; Vol. III, p. 29.
284. Chakravarti, Chintaharan, 'The Śaivite deity Kṣetrapāla' in *IHQ*, Vol. IX, 1938, p. 237.
285. Crooke, W., 'Dravidians (North India)' in *ERE*, Vol. V, p. 9.
286. *IHQ*, Vol. IX, 1933, p. 238. For a philosophical exposition of the symbolism of Śiva and also for the eight *Mūrtis* of Śiva in the *Purāṇas* or the eight handfuls of flowers prescribed in the religious cult of Śiva, see Agrawala, V.S., *Śiva Mahādeva : The Great God*, Varanasi, 1966.
287. *Kumārika Khaṇḍa*, 62. 16.

to be found in the Harappa civilization.[288] Although in the *Ṛgveda*[289] we have a faint allusion of the dance and music of Rudra, yet it was only in the post-Vedic Śiva that the above two features are prominent. The *Tumba-Vīṇā*, is now his favourite instrument.[290] He is often pictured as holding a *ḍiṇḍima* (a small drum) and *tamburā*, the instrument the drone of which is identified with the mystic syllable *Oṁ*.[291] It is believed that in Indian music there are six *rāgas*, each *rāga* had six *rāginīs*. Of the six *rāgas* five are said to have come from Śiva's mouth, and one from his spouse Pārvatī. In the *Bṛhaddharma Purāṇa*,[292] Śiva sings a song in praise of Viṣṇu, which ultimately gave rise to the Ganges. As a great teacher of *yoga*, *vīṇā* (music) and *jñāna* and an exponent of *śāstras* (*vyākhyānamūrti*) Śiva is known by the name of Dakṣiṇāmūrti in Indian art which is mostly south Indian in character.[293] The dance of Śiva, according to the Purāṇas, took

288. Marshall, J., *MIC*, Vol. I, p. 46.

289. *RV*, I. 43. 4.

Śiva is a cosmic dancer, and in the words of Kosambi, D.D., (*Myth and Reality*, Bombay, 1962, p. 4) "a dance by the tribal medicine-man or witch-doctor is essential in most primitive fertility rites". Upadhyaya, P. (*Female Images in the Museums of U.P. and their Social Background*, Varanasi, 1978, p. 165) thinks that the life of divinities is nothing but a reflexion of the life of man and as such dancing is natural equally with them. Upadhyaya wonders, 'Why the Indian treatises on music take pains to ascribe the invention and origin of dance to Śiva....'

290. *Vāyu Purāṇa*, 24. 142-43.

Sivaramamurti, C. (*Nataraja in Art, Thought, and Literature*, New Delhi, 1976, p. 169, fig. 4) points out an early terracotta image of Śiva as *Vīṇādhara*, belonging to the Suṅga period, Second Century B.C.

Sivaramamurti, in his other recent monumental work, *The Art of India*, New York, 1977, also exposes the *Vīṇādhara* with Devī from Lakhamandal, 'a very-early and exquisite figure, far outshines several others, though the expression of the same theme in the Vijayalayacholisva temple at Nartamalai is very charming.' (p. 80).

291. Clements, E., 'Music (Indian)' in *ERE*, Vol. IX, p. 46.

292. *Śivagānam*, II. 44.

293. For the *Vyākhyānamūrti* of Śiva, see Long J.G., 'Śiva as Promulgator of Traditional Learning and Patron Deity of the Fine Arts' in *ABORI*, 52 (1972), pp. 67-80.

To quote Sivaramamurti, C. (*The Art of India*, New York, 1977, p. 78): "Shiva as the Lord of Wisdom has two forms—Lakulisa and Dakshinamurti. Lakulisa is found in northern temples (fig. 268), while Dakshinamurti

its origin from the manner in which he sought to curb the pride of the sages of the Tāraka forest.

The Nṛtyamūrtis of Śiva[294] are found in all parts of India, but it had many well-marked varieties in southern India. The 108 kinds of dance carved on either side of a *gopura* in the Chidambaram temple of Naṭarāja correspond to a great extent with the 108 dance-modes as described by Bharata in his *Nāṭyaśāstra.*

Such was the great and composite god Śiva of the Epic and Paurāṇic times round whom the cult developed. The pre-Aryan Father-god, and a large number of local or village deities, amalgamated with Vedic Rudra, gradually came to be, as Rudra-Śiva, a great force in the composite religious life of Ancient India.

---

appears in the Southern shrines. In the South Lakulisa is represented in a long carving at Tiruvottiyur, which was commissioned in a spirit of connoisseurship by the appreciative Rajendra after his conquest of Kalinga. While Lakulisa is represented in the west at Modhera in Gujarat, in the north at Payar in Kashmir, and in the east at Bhuvaneshwar in Orissa, Dakshinamurti in several forms occurs throughout the South."

294. For the *Nṛtyamūrti* of Śiva, see Sivaramamurti, C., *Nataraja in Art, Thought, and Literature*, New Delhi, 1976. For the images of Naṭarāja as a visual embodiment of *Aṣṭamūrti*, or the eight realities, see pp. 25ff. In the words of Sivaramamurti, 'Śiva's dance is only the dance rendering of himself' (p. 4).

For Śiva's Dance, see also:

Ghosh, Oroon, *The Dance of Shiva and other Tales from India*, New York, 1965.

Leeuw, G. van der, *Sacred and Profane Beauty: The Holy in Art*, Weidenfeld and Nicolson, 1963, Part I, 'Beautiful Motion'.

Coomaraswamy, A.K., *The Dance of Shiva*, New York, 1953.

Moore, Albert C., *Iconography of Religions: An Introduction*. London, 1977, points out that the fusion of both destructive and creative aspects found characteristic expressions in the Naṭarāja images. In the words of Moore, "A classic synthesis was reached with the type of 'dancing Shiva' developed in the bronze images of South India from the tenth century. It may well be that this, along with other features of Shiva, derives from the ancient pre-Aryan cultic and sculptural forms which re-emerged in the Dravidian south. The dance itself is the most elemental form of religious expression, requiring only the movement of the human body, and represents the primal unity of religion and the arts." (p. 117).

Dehejia, V., (*Early Stone Temples of Orissa*, New Delhi, 1979) cbserves that all the early Naṭarāja images in Orissa have the peaceful form (p. 60).

Zimmer, H., *Myths and Symbols in Indian Art and Civilization*, New York, 1962, pp. 151-57.

(iii) Śiva's Admission to the Brāhmaṇical Pantheon

The story of the admission of Śiva to the Brāhmaṇical pantheon is part of the bigger story of the absorption of non-Aryans, after conflict and compromise, into the Aryan society. The Indian people is a 'Mixed people, in Blood, in Speech and in Culture'[1] of the four 'races', namely, Austro-Asiatics, Mongoloids, Dravidians and Aryans. Similarly, the cult of Śiva accommodated multifarious Aryan and pre-Aryan faiths and beliefs ranging from the Austric notions of Phallus and Zoomorphic deities (particulary the Bull and Serpent cults), the Dravidian conceptions of a great Father God and a Mother Goddess, the institutions of *Yoga*, *Pūjā* and *Bhakti* and both Austric and Dravidian myths and legends relating to petty godlings and hero-worship. Thus the concept of Rudra-Śiva is an amalgam of the proto-Śiva of the Harappa civilization, Rudra of the Vedic literature and several other gods conceived during the post-Vedic period.

That Rudra did not comply with the ideal of a Brāhmaṇic god even in the Vedic literature can be proved by a number of concurrent testimonies.

In the *Śatarudriya* section of the *Yajurveda*,[2] Rudra is closely connected with the artisan and craftsman classes and the Niṣādas belonging to the Austric race. In the *Atharvaveda*[3] he is *Eka-vrātya*, and the intimate relation of the non-sacrificing vrātyas with the people of the Harappa civilization is tempting assumption.[4] In the *Yajurveda Saṁhitās*[5] and *Śatapatha Brāhmaṇa*,[6] Rudra is repeatedly entreated to depart beyond the Muñjavat and according to the *Atharvaveda*,[7] Muñjavat is the name of a people dwelling far away, perhaps beyond the pale of Aryandom[8],

1. Chatterji, S.K., *Indianism and Indian Synthesis*, Calcutta, 1962, p. 125.
2. *Vājasaneyī Saṁhitā*, XVI. 27.
3. Book XV.
4. Mukherjea, Radhakamal, *A History of Indian Civilization*, 1956, p. 123.
5. *Taittirīya Saṁhitā*, I. 8. 6. 2; *Vāj. Saṁ.*, III. 61.
6. II. 6, 2, 17.
7. V. 22. 5. 7. 8. 14.
8. Venkataramanayya, N., *Rudra-Śiva*, Madras, 1941, p. 22.

to whom fever and other diseases are banished. In the *Atharva-veda*[9] and *Aitareya Brāhmaṇa*,[10] Rudra appears in black raiment and in some *Brāhmaṇas*[11] the name of this 'terrrible' god is not sometimes directly mentioned out of fear. The dreadful, fearful, un-Aryan characteristics of Rudra are in fact so prominent in the *Brāhmaṇas* that even the gods are afraid of him[12] lest he should destroy them.[13] The place and time of the *Śūlagava* sacrifice to Rudra, that is, at the outskirts of a village and preferably at midnight, as outlined in the *Gṛhya-sūtras*,[14] are particularly notable. The *Śatapatha Brāhmaṇa*,[15] *Kātyāyana-Śrauta-Śūtra*[16] and *Śāṅkhāyana Gṛhyasūtra*[17] enjoin the worshipper of Rudra to touch purifying water after performing ceremonies relating to him. Due to his formidable character, Rudra is isolated from the other gods and the *Pañcaviṁśa*[18] and *Śatapatha*[19] *Brāhmaṇas* represent him as crying for exclusion from sacrifice.

That the god was not originally within the orthodox Brāhmaṇical pantheon perhaps due to his association with the non-Aryan tribes is again proved by the fact that in the *Śatapatha Brāhmaṇa*[20] offerings are deposited to him at a cross-road which is known to be his favourite haunt. Cross-roads are universally believed to be the common resort of evil spirits and the Greek foreign goddess Hekate or the gods Hermes and Theoi Apopompaioi[21] and the Japanese phallic deity Saruta-hiko or Dosojin[22] are similarly worshipped at a place where four roads meet. In the *Mṛcchakaṭika* we have a reference of the worship of Śiva and

9. II. 27. 6; XI. 2. 18.
10. V. 14.
11. *Aitareya*, III. 33 and 34. 7; *Śatapatha*, I. 7. 4. 3.
12. *Śatapatha Brāhmaṇa*, IX. 1. 1. 1-6.
13. Macdonell, A.A., *Vedic Mythology*, Strassburg, 1897, p. 76.
14. *Āśvalāyana*, IV. 8; *Śāṅkhāyana*, III. 11; *Pāraskara*, III. 8; *Hiraṇyakeśi*, III. 3. 8.
15. II. 6. 2. 18.
16. I. 10.14.
17. V. 6. 1-2.
18. VII. 9. 16.
19. I. 7. 3. 1.
20. II. 6. 2. 7.
21. Harrison, J.E., *Prolegomena to the Study of Greek Religion*, second ed., pp. 8ff.
22. Aston, W.G., *Shinto*, London, 1905, pp. 187-91, 306.

Kārttikeya at such a crossing. Even now in the villages of West Bengal, the worship of Dharmarāja, who is sometimes identified with Yama, and sometimes as an incarnation of Śiva, usually takes place near a cross-road.

The *Skanda Purāṇa*[23] says that leaves, flowers, fruits etc. become unfit for consumption when offered of Śiva. Apologists have offered several ingenious explanations for this prohibition, such as a curse of his spouse Durgā whom he did not give a share of the food offered to him;[24] or the fear[25] that the food offerings would come in contact with the poison in his throat, which he had swallowed during the churning of the ocean. However, these cannot remove the suspicion that Śiva was not originally a god of the Brāhmaṇical pantheon. The Epics and the Purāṇas record a large number of legends which express the hostility between the old-fashioned Brāhmaṇas and the worshippers of Śiva.[26] The weak position of Śiva in the company of orthodox divinities is best exemplified in the south Indian Bhikṣāṭanamūrti of Śiva, mythologically associated with the Kaṅkālamūrti, in which a bell is tied to one of his legs and this reminds us of the fact that the Pariah untouchables of South India had to sound the bell before entering into a village of the Brāhmins.[27]

The cult of Śiva expanded because of its catholic spirit and its power to assimilate or amalgamate the innumerable petty godlings of the ruder faiths who seem to have lent much of the coarser elements of their characters to Śiva and the process of this adoption is very often masked by a large number of legends or myths. The pre-Aryan Bull and Serpent cults were absorbed by Śaivism by placing the Bull as Śiva's mount and putting the snake about his neck, and the process necessarily led to the votaries of those cults becoming ultimately Śiva's followers. We have reserved a separate chapter to describe how the pre-Aryan phallus worshippers were associated with the cult of Śiva.

23. See *Viśvakoṣa*, 1st ed., Vol. XVII, p. 258.

24. *Brahmavaivarta Purāṇa*, *Kṛṣṇa-janmakhaṇḍa*, Ch. XXXVII.

25. *Liṅgārcana Tantra*, 13th and 14th Paṭalas.

26. Eliot, C., *Hinduism and Buddhism*, London, 1954, Vol. I., p. XXXVI; Rao, T.A.G., *EHI*, Madras, 1916, Vol. II, Part I, pp. 49-50.

27. Dubois, J.A., *Hindu Manners, Customs and Ceremonies*, Oxford, 1906, pp. 49-51.

It is instructive to note the gradual progression of the peasant godling Bhairava (Bhairon) who, from an attendant and representative of Śiva, ultimately metamorphosed into a form of Śiva, although the epithet Śvāśva ("whose Horse is a Dog") perhaps indicates his real origin,[28] because carrion-eating animals were despicable in Aryan eyes. In his malignant aspects, Śiva closely corresponds with Aiyanar ('honourable father'), a primitive tutelary deity of the fields, who is recognized by the incoming Aryans and later on came to be known as the son of Śiva from Mohinī form of Viṣṇu.[29] Khaṇḍoba or Kānhoba ('sword father'), probably a deified non-Aryan hero who had close connection with the forest tribes of western India[30] was later on promoted to be an incarnation of Śiva. Murukaṉ, the primitive Dravidian God of Youth, became ultimately Kumāra or Kārttikeya, the son of Śiva.[31] Even the names *Śiva* and *Śambhu* come respectively from the old Tamil *Śivaṉ* (*Chivaṉ*) meaning 'red', and *Chempu* or *Śembu* meaning 'red metal'[32] as already referred to.

Signor Gorresio[33] expresses the opinion that Śiva is a deity of the Cushite or Hamitic tribes who preceded the Aryans on the soil of India. The close connection of Śiva with the non-Aryan Koch girls, like that of Kṛṣṇa with the Ābhīra women, even in comparatively late period, as we find in medieval Bengali literature, no doubt resulted from his prior identification with a

28. Rislay, H.H., *Tribes and Castes of Bengal*, Calcutta, 1891, Vol I, pp. 79ff.; Crooke, W., *Popular Religion and Folklore of Northern India*, London, 1896, Vol. I, p. 108.

29. Oppert, G., *Original Inhabitants of India*, London, 1st ed., p. 105.

30. *Bombay Gazetteer*, Vol. XVIII, pt. I, pp. 290, 413f.

31. Srinivasa Aiyangar, P.T., *Pre-Aryan Tamil Culture*, Madras, 1930, pp. 126ff.

Gaṇeśa, another son of Śiva, seems to have been originally a pre-Aryan sun-god. Not only the elephant-head shows his pre-Aryan origin, but the rat on which Gaṇeśa rides is a totem of at least the Oraons. See Crooke, W., *Popular Religion and Folklore of Northern India*, Vol. I, pp. 8, 287; Risley, H.H., *op. cit.* Vol. II, p. 113.

32. Barnett, L.D., 'Munda and Dravidian Languages' in *Linguistic Survey of India*, Vol. IV, pp. 279ff.

33. *Rāmāyaṇa*, Vol. X, p. 291, note 35; *vide* Muir, J., *OST*, Vol. IV, p. 411.

deity of the Hinduized Koch Tribes.[34] In the *Skanda Purāṇa*[35] the other name of the spouse of Śiva is *Śavarī*. The gradual approximation of the aboriginal Śavaras[36] to Hinduism is shown by their belief that by worshipping Śiva they will be united with the god in future life.[37] As the Śavaras were Hinduized, their deity Buḍhā Deo or Baḍ Rāul became Bhairava, a form of Śiva.[38] Śiva's close association with the Indo-Mongoloid Kirāta tribes is evident in the well known Kirātārjuna episode. In the *Brahmāṇḍa Purāṇa*,[39] Śiva appeared to Paraśurāma in the guise of a hunter and Paraśurāma made an image of this deity of the hunting folks and continued his austerities when the lord blessed him with his wish.

Demonolatry appears in the Vedas as an opposite force hostile to the orthodox gods.[40] But ultimately Brāhmaṇism was forced to come to terms with it and the fusion of the two opposite faiths manifested itself in the acceptance by the priests of the devils, demons and goblins as the followers or assistants of the already recognised gods.[41] Thus Śiva, due to his great power of absorbing kindred spirits and godlings of the popular creed, became ultimately 'lord of goblins' or Bhūteśvara or Bhūtapati. Vīrabhadra whom Śiva commissioned during Dakṣa's sacrifice and who is particularly noted for his un-Aryan ghastly appearance, is perhaps a Dravidian deity merged into Śaiva pantheon. The ghost companions of Śiva resemble the characteristics of the primitive Vetāla of south India who haunted cemeteries and animated dead bodies attended by troops of imps.[42] It is interest-

34. Sircar, D.C., *Studies in the Religious Life of Ancient and Medieval India*, 1971, p. 29.
35. *Māheśvara*, 35.
36. Muir, J., *OST*, Vol. II, 1860, p. 381.
37. Fawcett, F., in *JRAS*, Bombay branch, Vol. I, 1886, p. 242.
38. Crooke, W., *op. cit.*, Vol. I, pp. 119ff.
39. III. 23. 7-62.

The horned archer on the copper tablets of Mohenjodaro is none but Śiva himself.—See Marshall, J., *MIC*, Vol. III, pl. CXVII, 16.

40. Macdonell, A.A., *Vedic Mythology*, 1897, pp. 156ff.
41. Max Müller (*Contributions to the Science of Mythology*, 1897, Vol. I, p. 212) and J. Muir (*OST*, Vol. II, pp. 380ff.) however, deny that the Vedic Aryans borrowed the idea of evil spirits from the aborigines of India.
42. See the *Vetāla-pañcaviṁśatikā* in Somadeva's *Kathā-Saritsāgara*.

ing to note that, as the guardian of a village, the Vetāla is represented in a stone smeared with red paint in the top of which a human face is depicted, and in the pre-historic stone circles the centre stone represented Vetāla and the surrounding pillars his attendants.[43] In fact, Śiva's power of absorption is so great that any male tribal deity is easily identifiable with him.

Śiva might be a deified human being, the hero or lord of the Śivas, and this conception of deification is of non-Aryan origin. But we have not enough material to sketch a complete biography of this hero-god. In the Epics and the *Purāṇas,* he leads a very ordinary life in human fashion. In the *Vāmana Purāṇa*[44] he is homeless and a constant wanderer with his wife from forests to hills. In the *Brahmāṇḍa Purāṇa*[45] he is not ashamed to live a pretty long time in his father-in-law's house whereby Meru insulted him as poor and useless. The love-quarrel on trivial matters between Śiva and Pārvatī is to be found in the *Rāmāyaṇa* and *Mahābhārata*[46], the *Matsya,*[47] *Skanda*[48] and *Śiva*[49] *Purāṇas* and in a big mass of literature of later days. A great many of the Epic and Purāṇic myths and legends associated with his life are of pre-Aryan antiquity. With the gradual Aryanisation of the vast pre-Aryan people through blood, speech and culture there came "the inevitable commingling of the legends and traditions of two races united by one language, a commingling which has now become well-nigh inextricable."[50]

The attempt to admit Śiva is to be found even from the early Vedic period. The immigrant Aryans who first tried force had ultimately to adjust with the original inhabitants[51] and the

43. *Bombay Gazetteer*, Vol. XVIII, pt. I, pp. 291, 553; Vol. XXIV, p.415.

44. VIII. 48-61; see Kennedy, J., *Ancient and Hindu Mythology*, London, 1831, p. 293.

45. III. 31. 35ff.; see *Purāṇa Index*, Vol. II, p. 672.

46. Ward, W., *A View of the History, Religion and Literature of the Hindus*, Serampore, 1818, Vol. II, p. 179.

47. 155. 1-2.

48. *Māheśvara*, 34th chapter.

49. *Pūrva*, 12th chapter.

50. Chatterji, S.K., *Indo-Aryan and Hindi*, 1960, p. 56.

51. "When a country is successfully invaded by a new religion, the old ods are not immediately dismissed from being. Their existence is still recog-

Vedic period witnessed this process of absorption of pre-Aryans and their deity and the onward march of Rudra-Śiva from a minor to a major position. His identification with a host of Vedic deities—namely, Agni, Indra, Prajāpati, Vāyu and others—facilitated this process. Although in Indian religion epithets of one god are freely transferred to the other, still, in the eight names ascribed to him in the *Śatapatha,*[52] *Kauṣītaki*[53] and *Śāṅkhāyana*[54] *Brāhmaṇas,* in the *Śatarudriya* (enumeration of the hundred names) hymns of the *Yajurveda*[55], in the *Śivasahasranāmastotra* (enumeration of the thousand names) of the later literature we easily discern the process of Śiva's gradual admission and supremacy. In the *Pañcaviṁśa Brāhmaṇa*[56] we have allusion to the admission of the followers of Śiva in the Brāhmaṇical fold by allowing them to recite some Vedic verses. We have here the Vrātya-stomas by means of which the Vrātyas became eligible for social intercourse with the Brāhmaṇical order.[57] The *Atharvaveda* perhaps speaks of a period when the admixture of the Aryans and non-Aryans through blood and culture had already started and the mystic glorification of the Ekavrātya[58] is a great pointer in this respect.

Śaivism, like Hinduism in its present form, involves a double framework—the *Nigama* and *Āgama,* the *smṛti,* that is, 'tradition' and *śruti,* that is, direct revelations from Śiva to Pārvatī. The *Nigama* stands for the Veda and Vedānta. The Śaivas advocate not only Vedic *Karmakāṇḍa* but the Aryan world of ideas. Although the Āgamas stand for pre-Aryan tradition of *Yoga* and *Bhakti,* they are not always positively hostile to the Vedas. In

nised by the new religion but their position is altered. For those of them who are rooted too deeply in the affection of the people to be dethroned entirely, some position in the new religion is found by accommodation.".—Jevons, F.B., *Comparative Religion,* Cambridge, 1913, p. 92.

52. VI. 1. 3.

53. VI. 1. 9.

54. VI. 1ff.

55. Section XVI of the *Vāj. Saṁ.* and section IV. 5 of the *Taitt. Saṁ.*

56. XVII. 1. 1.

57. Winternitz, M., *A History of Indian Literature,* Vol. I, Part I, Calcutta, 1959, p. 167; Macdonell, A.A., *A History of Sanskrit Literature,* Delhi, 1965, pp. 177-78.

58. *AV.,* Book XV.

the *Kūrma Purāṇa*[59] the sage Śvetāśvatara is said to have founded the Pāśupata order and Śiva is even made to say: "Oh Brāhmaṇas, my form is the Vedas".[60] But there are twenty-eight branches of the Āgama, each of which has got a number of the *Upāgama*, the total number of texts reaching about two hundred. The genesis of the declaration of the non-Vedic pseudo-scriptures of the heterodox school by Śiva himself is to be found in the *Kūrma*[61] and *Varāha*[62] *Purāṇas* where the story of Gautama is told. The story runs thus:—

Once upon a time the sage Gautama entertained in his hermitage at Dāruvana a number of ascetics badly affected by a severe draught and famine and requested them to stay for some years even when the famine was over. But the ungrateful guests, being very much eager to go home, created a magic cow and by their trick ultimately made the host responsible for the death of the cow which was a great sin and left the hermitage on this pretext. Finally, Gautama saw through the plan and cursed the sage to be *Veda-bāhya*. The condemned and fallen sages praised Śaṁkara through *laukika stotras* for immunity from sin and Śiva finally compiled for their deliverance the delusive scriptures out of which sprang up the extreme offshoots of the Pāśupatas, namely, the Kāpālikas, the Kālāmukhas and 'thousands of others'.[63]

However, all the branches of the old tree of Pāśupata Śaivism have been fully Brāhmaṇised, by being based partly on the authority of the Upaniṣads and partly on the doctrine of Śaiva philosophy, into the cohesive components of a comprehensive synthesis. A host of great *Ṛgvedic* deities such as Indra, Agni, Varuṇa, Soma and others receded into the background; but a minor *Ṛgvedic* deity like Rudra, due to his fusion with the pre-Aryan proto-Śiva and a large number of post-Vedic godlings, arose in majestic splendour as a supreme god in the Brāhmaṇical pantheon.

59. I. 14. 22ff.
60. *Kūrma Purāṇa*, II. 37. 148.
61. I. 16, 95ff.
62. 70 and 71.
63. Hazra, R.C., *Studies in the Upapurāṇas*, Vol. II, Calcutta, 1963, p. 161n. See also Lorenzen, David N., *The Kapalikas and Kalamukhas: Two lost Saivite Sects*, 1972.

The great reluctance to acknowledge Śiva's legitimate divine status finally produced a great commotion typified in the magnificent and pompous sacrifice of Dakṣa, where he was excluded. The Epic and Purāṇic account of the story of Dakṣa points out the mode of transition from a period of religion based on the Vedic and upper-class supremacy to a period when it became necessary to recognise the phallic deity and deified heroes worshipped by the outlying non-Aryan Niṣādas, the Dāsa-Dasyus, and the Kirātas, who were not allowed to enter into the Vedic world of learning and religion. The pre-Aryan divinity was ultimately recognised and dressed up to suit Brāhmaṇical tastes. Frazer[64] has found that in some well-known Śiva temples of south India, the primitive "blood rites and drunken orgies are permitted to be revived yearly as a compromise with the aboriginal worshippers, whose primitive shrines were annexed" by the upper class of the society. Dubois[65] has cited some examples where the untouchable Pariahs of south India have the prior right to enter into some Hindu temples and act as priests, and the Brāhmaṇas follow them. In fact, the history of the socio-religious life in early India suggests that many of the doctrines and rites that distinguish Śaivism are manifestly accretions of later Hinduism and the result of the Aryan touch of sophistication, but the basic elements are just as certainly non-Aryan as seventy-five per cent of Indian culture is of non-Aryan origin.[66]

How the non-Aryan tribes were admitted into the fold of the Hindu society, or how kṣatriyahood was extended to the non-Aryan ruling houses and even to foreign potentates is a fascinating story on which little modern work is done. However, with the admission of Śiva into the Brāhmaṇical pantheon a large number of non-Aryans were also Brāhmaṇised to meet the requirement of the reformed Indo-Aryan religion and taste.[67] The spirit of reconciliation and compromise is expressed in a superb manner by the classic emergence of the concept of Harihara[68]

64. 'Saivism' in *ERE*, Vol. XI, p. 92.

65. *Hindu Manners and Customs*, Oxford, 1906, p. 583.

66. *The History and Culture of the Indian People*, Vol. I, 1957, p. 164. See also Slater, G., *Dravidian Element in Indian Culture*, New Delhi, 1976.

67. Thurston, E., *Castes and Tribes of S. India*, Madras, 1909, Vol. I. p. 54.

68. For the iconographic features and representations of Harihara, cf. Sahai, B., *Iconography of Minor Hindu and Buddhist Deities*, New Delhi, 1975, pp. 133-140.

and Trimūrti where Śiva is raised as one of the supreme triads—a concretisation of the historical process—although the germ of this concept of triad is probably traceable to the Harappa Civilization.

CHAPTER II

ŚIVA AND THE BULL

(i) *Representation of Śiva as Bull on Ancient Indian Coins*

Since the Harappa civilization the bull is represented as if being worshipped. In the *Ṛgveda*[1] Rudra himself is called a bull and we have definite numismatic data in support of the theriomorphic representation of Śiva as a bull in ancient India. The custom of issuing coins with the representation of Śiva in his three forms—theriomorphic, anthropomorphic and phallic—by kings and chiefs and mint masters was very common in ancient India.

It is interesting to note that not a single figure of the cow is seen on the punch-marked coins,[2] though the Kāmadhenu was known from very early days. The general absence of the buffalo on the ancient Indian coins is also remarkable.[3] The figure of the bull is found either with hump or without hump, standing or recumbent and is used as a type in ancient Indian coins.[4]

On the coins of the Indo-Greek rulers like Apollodotus in Gandhāra and the Punjab, the figure of a humped bull is frequently used to represent Śiva in his theriomorphic forms. Two classical writers, Hesychius and Stobaeus, prove that Śiva was an object of worship among the people of North-Western India. When Hesychius wrote that bull was worshipped by the Indians in Gandhāra (*Gandaros O Taurokrates par Indois*), he evidently

1. II. 33, 8.
2. *JASB*, XXX, 1934, 34N; Numismatic Supplement, No. XLV.
3. Theobald, W., *Copper Coins of Ancient India*, 1st ed., p. 73.
4. Chakraborti, S.K., 'The Tribal Coins of Northern India' in *JRASB*, 1936, Vol. II, 64N.; Numismatic Supplement No. XLVI—Article 335.

referred to the worship of Śiva in this form.[5] In fact, the bull design device on the coins of the early foreign rulers of North-Western India may represent Śiva.

It is most likely that the city of Puṣkalāvatī, the old capital of Gandhāra (modern Peshawar region of Pakistan), had the bull form of Śiva as one of its tutelary deities. This is indicated by a unique gold coin of an unidentified Indo-Scythian king containing the figure of a bull on one side with the legends *tauros* and *uṣabha* in the Greek and Kharoṣṭhī scripts above and below the device, both meaning 'bull', and on the other side a standing female figure holding a lotus with the kharoṣṭhī legend *Pakhalavatidevata* (the deity of Puṣkalāvatī) on its two sides.[6] Coomaraswamy idedtified the latter as Lakṣmī, but Banerjea rightly suggests that the goddess might stand for Ambikā (Pārvatī), the consort of Śiva, because the figure is presented in association with the theriomorphic form of Śiva.[7] Here we are indebted to Hiuen Tsang, who in his description of Puṣkalāvatī, says : "Outside the west gate of the city was a Deva Temple and a marvel-working image of the Deva",[8] the word *Deva* here undoubtedly is referring to Śiva.[9] The 'Bull' can be shown to have been the distinctive badge of Puṣkalāvatī, and here the Greek artist, as Rapson[10] observes, has represented in accordance with Greek ideas an Indian deity who was supposed to bear the form of a bull. In fact, Gandhāra was the region where Śiva was being worshipped in his bull form at the time of the Bactrian Greeks and afterwards.[11] The theriomorphic form of Śiva was not altogether forgotten during the rule of the Indo-Parthians and

5. Banerjea, J.N., *Religion in Art and Archaeology*, Lucknow, 1968, p. 45.

6. Banerjea, J.N., *The Development of Hindu Iconography*, Calcutta, 1956, p. 257, Pl. IX, fig. 7 (Discovered by Cunningham and now in the British Museum).

7. *Loc. cit.*

8. Watters, *On Yuan Chwang*, I, p. 214.

9. Banerjea, J.N., *Paurāṇic and Tāntric Religion*, 1966, p. 77.

10. Rapson, E.J., ed. *The Cambridge History of India*, Vol. I, 1962, p. 502.

11. Banerjea, J.N., *DHI*, p. 236. cf. O'Flaherty, W.D., 'The Hindu Symbolism of Cows, Bulls, Stallions and Mares' in *Art and Archaeology Research Papers*, no. 8, 1975, pp. 1-7.

the Kuṣāṇas, though the god began to be anthropomorphically represented. Even as late as the eleventh century A.D., the bull continued to appear on the coins of Gandhāra as is proved by the 'Bull and Horseman' Coins of the Shāhis.[12]

The magnificent humped bull on the coins of Azes I, Agileses I and Kadphises I unearthed at Taxila[13], evidently supports the identification of Śiva in his animal form. Even in seals, with which we are not concerned here, Śiva is represented as bull. Thus the humped bull appears on Rudrakṣita's seals from Spooner's find at Basarh[14] with a globular object placed between the horns of the animal, and some scholars traced Sassanian influence on it. The Bhiṭā seal No. 44, also depicting the standing bull with a round object between the horns, is no doubt interesting because in it the main device is flanked by a wheel in side elevation[15] and 'an uncertain symbol' as Marshall points out.

Tradition associates the city of Ujjayinī with the worship of Śiva and some coins found at that place contain the theriomorphic, anthropomorphic and phallic forms of the deity as their devices.[16] The wide range of the circulation of bull-marked device coins in the extreme-northern, northern and north-western regions of the Indian subcontinent not only testify to the favourite theriomorphic representation of the divinity, but also the wide prevalence of the Śaiva cult among the foreign potentates of the localities.[17]

Though Kaṇiṣka and Huviṣka were somewhat eclectic in their religious belief, still the emblem of Śiva is found on their coins; but the notable point is that the deity is nowhere accompanied by the bull on this group of Kuṣāṇa coins. On the other hand, on Vāsudeva's coins[18] the bull is almost always placed behind the deity.

12. Rapson, E.J., *op. cit.*, p. 503.

13. Marshall, J., 'Excavations at Taxila' in *ARASI*, 1912-13, pp. 45, 48, 52, Nos. 2, 19, 20, 22, 51.

14. Banerjea, J.N., *DHI*, p. 180.

15. *Ibid.*, p. 184.

16. Banerjea, J.N., *Religion in Art and Archaeology*, p. 45.

17. Banerjea, J.N., *Paurāṇic and Tāntric Religion*, p. 76.

18. Whitehead, R.B., *op. cit.*, pp. 187, 189-93, 197, 199, 200, 203, 208 and corresponding plates and figures.

Kujula Kadphises issued a number of 'Bull and Bactrion Camel' type coins[19] on the obverse of which the humped bull standing to right is found, bearing the issuer's name with full-fledged imperial titles. Marshall[20] ascribes the 'Bull and Camel' type of coins to Wema Kadphises and not to Kujula Kadphises. Again, the bull represented on the coins is associated with the Nandipada symbol; probably it is also a theriomorphic representation of Śiva.[21]

That Vāsudeva II, the Kuṣāṇa monarch, was overthrown by the Sassanians is clear from the Kuṣāṇo-Sassanian coins[22] which bear on the reverse 'Śiva and Bull', the only type issued by the former. The successors of Vāsudeva II also used on their coins the images of Śiva and bull.

Let us now have a look on the tribal coinage. Sircar[23], observes that the word Bhagavata, sometimes used in the legend of certain tribal coins in relation to a deity, has often been wrongly taken to be *Bhāgavata* and as an epithet of the people who circulated the monetary issues, but that the Audumbara coins bearing the Prākṛta legend, in both Brāhmī and Kharoṣṭhī, indicating *bhagavato mahādevasya rājarājasya*[24] were issued in

19. Gardner, P., *British Museum Catalogue of Coins of the Greek and Scythic Kings of Bactria and India,* 1886, pl. XXIII, fig. 7; Whitehead, R.B., *op. cit.*, Vol. I, 1914, Kuṣāṇa coin No. 18.

20. *Guide to Taxila*, Vol. I, p. 68.

21. Chattopadhyay, B., *The Age of the Kuṣāṇas*, 1967, p. 29.

22. Majumdar, R.C., and Altekar, A.S:, *The Vākāṭaka-Gupta Age*, 1946, p. 18. New researches by Soviet Archaeologists on Kuṣāṇa coins brought to light close relations between Central Asia and India during the Kuṣāṇa period. In the words of Bongard Levin, G.M., (*Studies in Ancient India and Central Asia*, Calcutta, 1971, p. 206) "The Kushan pantheon, amply represented on Kushan coins, attests to the spread of Zoroastrianism (current at that time in Central Asia) and its coexistence with the Indian religions of Buddhism and Saivism."

23. *Studies in the Religious Life of Ancient and Medieval India*, 1971, p. 86.

24. Sircar, D.C. 'Northern India After the Kushāṇas' in *The Age of Imperial Unity*, Bombay, 1960, p. 161n.

Scholars differ on the attribution of the Mahādeva coins which invariably bear the humped bull either on the obverse or on the reverse. According to one group (*The Journal of the Numismatic Society of India*, Vol. XXX, pp. 61-67), the coins belong to the Vaimakis struck in the name of their favourite god Mahādeva or Śiva in a critical period of their history. But Sircar treats

the name of the god Mahādeva. That the Audumbara coins were not issued by a *Bhāgavata* or 'a devotee of the god Viṣṇu', is quite evident from the representations among other Śaiva symbols of the humped bull[25], the theriomorphic form of Śiva. The bull on the Mahādeva coins is boldly conceived and well-executed and recalls its counterparts on the Indus seals and on the pillar at Rāmpurvā.[26]

The Audumbara bull is a humped one and so is that of the Ārjunāyanas, Vemakis, Uddehikas, Yaudheyas, and the Rājanyas. The bull before a particular curved object on the earliest coins of the Ārjunāyanas and Yaudheyas is identified by Allan[27] with a *liṅga*. But the object has been taken to be a sacrificial altar.[28] A comparison of this object with a similar one on the reverse of a Kanauj coin,[29] perhaps of Viṣṇumitra, may lead us to conclude that in both cases the curved object is nothing but a *yūpa*[30] or sacrificial post. Regarding the reverse of the Kanauj coin, Allan[31] remarks that it has "a horse apparently before a sacrificial post (*yūpa*) and may commemorate an *aśvamedha* sacrifice". The bull before the *yūpa* device represents the *śūlagava* sacrifice.[32]

---

these coins as belonging to the Audumbaras issued in the name of the god Mahādeva. The coins of the Audumbara chiefs Dharaghoṣa, Śivadāsa and Rudradāsa were also issued in the name of the same deity. To K.K. Dasgupta (*The Audumbaras*, 1st ed., p. 12) this Mahādeva was no other than the Audumbara king or leader who struck a number of coins, both in copper and silver. Allan (*Catalogue of Coins of Ancient India in the British Museum*, London, 1936, p. lxxxiii) observes that the word Mahādeva is used either as a regal title or it may have been the name of a ruler when we have also a silver coin bearing it.

25. Sircar, D.C., *Studies in the Religious Life of Ancient and Medieval India*, 1971, p. 87.

26. Dasgupta, K.K., *A Tribal History of Ancient India—A Numismatic Approach*, 1974, p. 61.

27. *Op. cit.*, p. 307.

28. Banerjea, J.N., *DHI*, p. 109.

29. Allan, J., *op cit.*, p. 147, pl. XIX, 13.

30. *Vide RV*, V. 2. 7; *Śat. Br.*, III. 6.4 to III. 7.1 for an extensive treatment of everything regarding the *yūpa*, and also *Ait. Br.*, VI. 1-3.

31. *Op. cit.*, p. xciv.

32. Dasgupta, K.K., *A Tribal History of Ancient India—A Numismatic Approach*, 1974, p. 24.

The humped bull couchant before a Taurine symbol on the punch-marked coins raised controversy among scholars. This is an interesting example of the interchangeable characters of the symbols of Mithraism of Persia and Śaivism of India.[33] In the Mithraic religion, the bull represents the sun[34] so that the present symbol is capable of appearing to the worshipper of either Mithra or Śiva.

In another instance, the bull is couchant before an object which may be intended for a fish, whilst a similar symbol is seen over the bull's rump. The small size of the symbol renders it difficult to determine what is really meant. It represents in reality, to quote Theobald,[35] "the ears of the bull, though the die-engraver himself may not have correctly understood the true meaning of the symbol, and failed accordingly to give it an intelligible character".

Some of the figures of bull, have either a Brāhmī *ma* or a fish placed on the back or in front of it, reminding us of the symbols seen on the Mohenjodaro figures of bulls with some appendage in front.[36] The figure of a bull is also a conspicuous symbol seen on some silver punch-marked coins.[37]

In the 'Elephant and Bull' type coins of Vaimaki Rudravarman, the humped bull is found with a symbol which cannot be a flower as suggested by Cunningham.[38] It has a similarity with the symbol on the Vṛṣṇi coins so that we may take it to be a *cakra* or discus.[39] On the coins of the Uddehika[40] prince we find the tree within railing in a horizontal line above the humped bull. Among the three groups of the Yaudheya coins, the 'Bull

33. Theobold, W., 'Notes on some symbols found on the punch-marked coins' in *JASB*, 1890, Nos. III and IV, p. 219.

34. *Loc. cit.*

35. *Op. cit.*, p. 242, Fig. 17.

36. *JASB*, XXX, 1934, Numismatic Supplement No. XLV, 42N, Fig. 32, pl. IX.

37. *Ibid.*, Figs. 32, 32a-32d, pls. IX, XII-XVI, XIX and XX.

38. Cunningham, A., *Coins of Ancient India*, London, 1891, p.168, pl. IV fig. 15.

39. Chakraborti, S.K., "The Tribal Coins of Northern India' in *JRASB* II, 1936, p. 86.

40. *Ibid.*, p. 88.

and the Elephant' type[41] is important for our purpose. As these are of rough workmanship and have some resemblance with the earlier coins of Kuṇindas and others, Smith[42] assigns them to a date slightly before or after the Christian era.

On the Rājanya coins the hump of the bull is not always distinct on all specimens due to the corroded condition.[43] The placing of the bull in a rayed circle in both the Rājanya and Agra coins[44] is interesting; it shows not only the sanctity enjoyed by the animal, but also a divine character attributed to it and the veneration of the tribes for the great god.[45] The Mālavas had all the three types, that is, with hump, without hump and recumbent. The Nāga bull is usually recumbent.[46] The circular legend on the obverse of a Nāga coin from the Gwalior Museum, which has on the reverse a bull standing in front within dotted border, showing a globular mark between its horns, is read by some[47] as *Mahārājā Śrī Vṛṣanā[ga]*: but should be *Vṛṣabha* as suggested by other numismatics.[48] Vṛṣabha might have been 'the first ruler to strike the bull type coins amongst the Nāga kings', and his successors followed him, although the bull is almost invariably shown in profile on their coins.[49]

Marshall[50] points out that bull worship was at first perhaps an independent cult and only absorbed by Śaivism at some later period. Even in the neolithic age in Southern India the bull is supposed to have been worshipped without any human or divine

41. Smith, V.A., *Catalogue of Coins in the Indian Museum*, Vol. I, pl. XXI, 13, 14, pp. 180-81; Cunningham, A., *Coins of Ancient India*, pl. VI, figs. 2-4.

42. *CCIM*, p. 165.

43. Dasgupta, K.K., *op, cit.*, p. 144.

44. Rapson, E.J., *Catalogue of Coins in the British Museum*, London, 1908, pl. XLV, 21.

45. Dasgupta, K.K., *op. cit.*, p. 18.

46. *JRASB*, 1936, Vol. II., Numismatic Supplement No. XLVI—Art. 335, 64N.

47. *cf. The Journal of the Numismatic Society of India*, Vol. XV, pp. 121-22.

48. Lahiri, Bela, 'The Coins of Vrishabha' in *JNSI*, Vol. XVI, 1954, p. 279.

49. *Loc. cit.*

50. *Mohenjodaro and the Indus Civilisation*, Vol. I, London, 1931, p. 72.

master to ride him.[51] Still, there cannot be much doubt in identifying the bull appearing on many coins as representing Śiva; the best example of which is to be found on the coins of the Śaiva Hūṇa ruler Mihirakula who adopted the symbol of bull with the legend *jayatu vṛṣaḥ* on the reverse of his copper coins.[52]

Under the Guptas Śaivism became a very vigorous integrating movement although the Gupta emperors were devoted to Viṣṇu. Mahārāja Vainyagupta Dvādaśāditya, whose association with the earlier members of the dynasty is not clear to us,[53] was described as 'meditating on the feet of the Lord Mahādeva' (*Bhagavan-Mahādeva-pādānudhyāta*) in his copper-plate inscription[54] found at Gunaighar (Comilla District, Bangladesh) and the device of his coin and seal was the *Vṛṣabha*,[55] i.e. Śiva himself in his theriomorphic form. Devagupta and his son Viṣṇugupta,[56] two of the later Gupta kings of Magadha, were *Paramamāheśvaras*,[57] and the seal device (bull) of the Maukhari chiefs of Kanauj as well as the names of a good many of them such as Īśvara, Īśāna, etc., probably indicate their cult affiliation.

The coins and inscriptions of some other Indian chiefs of the Gupta and early post-Gupta periods prove that the creed continued to be patronised by many of them. Śaśāṅka, king of Bengal, some members of the Puṣyabhūti family, the Maitraka dynasty of Valabhī and most of the rulers of the Deccan, namely, the Bṛhatphalāyanas, Ānandas, Viṣṇukuṇḍins, Vākāṭakas, Śālaṅkāyanas, Kadambas and Eastern and Western Gaṅgas were great devotees of Śiva and some of them issued bull type coins. As Śaivism was the 'dominant religion in different parts of the country in all ages of history',[58] the representation of the bull,

51. Kosambi, D.D., *The Culture and Civilisation of Ancient India*, 1st ed., p. 170.

52. Smith, V.A., *CCIM*, Vol. I, p. 236, pl. XXV, 5; Gardner, P., *op. cit.*, p. 162, pl. XXIX, 15.

53. For the suggestion that he was the son of Puru-gupta, *cf. IHQ*, XXIV, p. 67.

54. *IHQ*, VI, p. 40.

55. *Ibid.*, XIX, p. 27.

56. *CII*, III, p. 215.

57. *EI*, XXVI, p. 241.

58. Sircar, D.C., *Indian Epigraphy*, 1965, p. 151.

either as the theriomorphic form of Śiva or as his mount, is necessarily found on the coins and seals of these royal personages.

A large number of coins have been discovered in different parts of Northern India, namely, at Bhiṭā,[59] Taxila,[60] Pāṭaliputra,[61] Basarh,[62] Besnagar,[63] Lauriya-Nandangarh,[64] Vaiśālī, not to mention innumerable minor hoards. The symbol is nothing but Śiva in his theriomorphic form.

In a copper coin unearthed in the Konkan,[65] a humped bull walking to the left, his horns forming a crescent on the top of the head, is found. Beneath the bull there is a soild square mound and below it an oblong object representing perhaps a tank. In two other coins[66] from the same place a small triskeles is found revolving to the left, over the bull's rump, and an upright staff in front of the bull. The humped bull with the crescent on his head is found on the coins of Mahārāja[67] or Rājanya Janapada,[68] which is nothing but Śiva bearing the crescent moon (*Śaśāṅkaśekhara*).[69] The same device also occurs in one class of Yaudheya[70] and Ārjunāyana[71] coins.

On the Ayodhya coins,[72] the humped bull has a dominant position and is found on all the die-struck coins of Satyamitra,

59. *ARASI*, 1911-12, pp. 47, 48, 51-55.
60. *Ibid.*, 1912-13, pp. 45, 48, 52.
61. *Ibid.*, p. 82.
62. *Ibid.*, 1903-04, p. 109.
63. *Ibid.*, 1914-15, p. 81.
64. *Ibid.*, 1912-13, cf. *JBRS*, Vol. XLV, 1959, p. 492.
65. Theobald, W., 'Karshapana Coinage' in *JASB*, LXX, 1901, p. 62, No. 31.
66. *Ibid.*, No. 32-33.
67. Mahārāja is the name of a state and is referred to by Pāṇini in a rule which contemplates a man owing loyalty to it.—Jayaswal, K.P., *Hindu Polity*, Vol. I, 1st ed., p. 159.
68. Rapson, E.J., *CHI*, I, p. 485, pl. V, 13.
69. *JRASB*, 1936, II, p. 62.
70. Smith, V.A., *CCIM*, Vol. I, p. 182, No. 19.
71. Cunningham, A., *CAI*, pp. 89-90, pl. VIII, figs, 19, 20.

Dharmadeva, the king of Nepal, is said to have dedicated a large statue of Bull to the Paśupati temple and on many coins found from Nepal we have on the obverse the recumbent humped bull.

72. Cunningham, A., *CAI*, p. 93.

Sūryamitra, Saṁghamitra and Vijayamitra.[73] The bull is a common symbol on the coins of Kauśāmbī,[74] the capital of the Vatsas, and a good specimen of bull moving to left towards a standing symbol, is given by James Prinsep.[75]

Turning towards the Deccan, the Śātavāhana coins tell the same story. On the above coins a pyramid of balls or dots is found along with the bull which has frequently been called a 'caitya' by earlier numismatists, but it is now usually regarded as the representation of a hill.[76] On certain Śātavāhana coins, the bull has a disc between its horns.

The great Vākāṭaka king Rudrasena I and his successors were devout worshippers of Śiva and the former became a Śaiva through the influence of his maternal relatives, the Bhāraśiva Nāgas, who were noted for their devotion to the deity. The Kalacuri kings were great patrons of Śaivism and the silver coins bearing the legend *paramamāheśvara Kṛṣṇarāja* and the figure of bull, have been discovered not only in Nasik District but also in the islands of Bombay and Salsette.[77]

73. *Ibid.*, Figs. 12, 14, 16, 17, 18.

74. *Ibid.*, pp. 56, 73, fig. 7.

75. Thomas, E., *Essays on Indian Antiquities of James Prinsep*, II, London, 1858, pl. XLIV, Fig. 6.

76. *ARASI*, 1911-12, p. 47, Nos. 14-16, 25-28, 86.

77. Majumdar, R.C., ed., *The Classical Age*, p. 178.

The seal of Bālārjuna, the Pāṇḍuvaṁśī king of South Kosala, who was a *Parama-māheśvara* has the couchant bull as its emblem. The seal attached to the Kesarkella grant [*EI*, Vol. XXII, p. 138] of the later Somavaṁśī king Uddyotakeśarin Mahābhavagupta IV bears the Śaivite emblem of a horned bull surmounted by a crescent.

On the seals of the Pallavas the bull is found. The bull-banner (*Vṛṣabha-lāñchana*) of the Pallavas is not only referred to in Tamil literature but even in one of the Vaikuṇṭha Perumāl temple inscriptions (Sircar, D.C., *Indian Epigraphy*, 1965, p. 152n.). There are numerous other instances of the Śaiva kings styling themselves *Parama-māheśvara* with the emblem of bull on their seals and coins [*EI*, Vol. II, p. 353, *Ind. Ant.*, Vol. XVII, p. 226].

It is said that through the god's favour, Kāmārṇava of the Eastern Gaṅga dynasty obtained the *Vṛṣabha-lāñchana* or bull crest and the insignia of sovereignty. The Nanda or Nandodbhava kings of Orissa had the bull crest on their seals. The kings of the Bhañja or Mayūra dynasty of Orissa had the bull as their *lāñchana* and the Bamanghati plate [*JASB*, 1871, p. 165] of Raṇabhañja displays in a circle with rim of lotus petals, bull, crescent and trident.

The Eastern and Western Cālukyas were of Śaiva persuasion; so were the Pallavas, Colas, Pāṇḍyas, Kākatiyas, Candellas, Paramāras, Gāhaḍavālas, some kings of Assam and Kashmir and of Bengal and many of them either issued bull-type coins or had as their insignia or emblem the bull-banner (*vṛṣabha-lāñchana*).

From the Panchobh copper-plate[78] we learn that the Minor Gupta kings of Bengal, namely, Kṛṣṇa-Gupta, Saṁgrāma-Gupta of Śaiva persuasion, had bull as their insignia or emblem and were described as *parama-māheśvara-vṛṣabhadhvaja*.

Thus we see that the sacred bull enjoyed a prime position in ancient Indian history. The bull was a common emblem in Indian mythology and was adopted as a badge by various tribes, indigenous and foreign, and figured on the silver and copper coins as a type from the dawn of our recorded history.

(ii) The Bull and the Bull Cult

The bull, because of its strength, and great power of procreation, was perhaps the object of an independent cult among the pre-Aryans of the Harappa civilization. Leach and Fried[1] and also Neumann[2] draw our attention to some folk tales, legends and mythologies of many ancient peoples of the world where the bull is conceived as the animal paramour of the Great Mother.

78. Majumdar, R.C., ed., *The History of Bengal*, Vol. I, Dacca, 1943, p. 261.

Vṛṣadhvaja is a great devotee of Śiva. cf. Hazra, R.C., *Studies in the Upapurāṇas*, Vol. II, 1963, p. 317.

A close scrutiny of the legends and devices on the gold coins of the Nalas reveal that the Nalas, who held sway over Dakṣiṇa Kosala, probably in the later half of the 5th century A.D., were the worshippers of Śiva. Cf. Sahoo, A.C., 'Saivism as reflected on the Gold Coins of the Nalas' in *The Journal of the Numismatic Society of India*, vol. xlii, 1980, pp. 110-111.

1. Funk and Wagnalls, *Standard Dictionary of Folklore, Mythology and Legend*, New York, 1950, p. 61.
2. *The Great Mother*, London, First ed., pp. 268ff.

Outside India, Baal of the Semitic race was conceived under the form of bull. The Greeks worshipped bull under the name of Epaphus and the phallic god Bacchus sometimes took the form of bull.[3] The Egyptian bulls Apis and Mnevis were identified with the other phallic deity Osiris, the Creatan Minotaur had a close connection with Dionysius and the bull-god was one of the chief Hittite deities.[4] Artemis, Themis, Demeter, Hestia, Apollo, Poseidon and a host of other deities were also represented in the shape of bull.

In India though Zoomorphic divinities appear to be survivals from Austric, or Proto-Australoid notions and were known to the Vedic Aryans, only to a limited extent, still Rudra was himself represented as a bull in the *Ṛgveda*[5] and the husband of a cow (*Pṛśni*).[6] In the Harappa civilization the Father God and the Mother Goddess are prominent and appear to be co-equal[7] with each other; whereas regarding animal representation though we have innumerable bull figurines, the cow is conspicuous by its absence.

Whether the bull was actually worshipped as a god at Harappa or just an emblem of some gods cannot be definitely said as we cannot yet decipher the writing that accompaines the bull seals of the Indus valley. Aurel Stein[8] points out that from the way in

3. *ERE*, Vol. I, p. 508.
4. *ERE*, Vol. II, pp. 887-89.
5. II. 33, 8.

For Rudra's relations with *Pṛśni*, see also Bhattacharji, S., *The Indian Theogony*, Cambridge, 1970, p. 158.

6. *RV.* I. 23. 10; I. 85. 3; V. 52. 16.

In the *Vāyu Purāṇa* (XXX. 267-68) Śiva was represented as a bull.

A bull plays an obscure part in the legend of Mudgala and Mudgalānī which has been interpreted in the most diverse ways.

See Keith, A.B., *RPVU*, p. 191.

7. Marshall, J., *MIC*, Vol. I, p. 111.
8. *ARASI*, 1927-28, p. 171.

Sankalia, H.D., (*Pre-Historic Art in India*, New Delhi, 1978, p. 50) points out: "That the bull was held in high regard may also be seen from the bull heads, cut in shell. These are 0.9 and 1.3 ins. high respectively, and carefully carved-with sockets for the eyes, ears and horns, which were made of some rare material. The head was probably cemented by the flat surface at the back to a body. The hair is carefully indicated by means of incised lines, and a garland is shown as worn around the neck."

which large quantities of small terracotta figurines of humped bulls, all reproducing the type of the Brahmani bull of India, were found from Waziristan and North Baluchistan, it became evident that their deposition was connected with some object of worship. Dikshit[9] thinks that the humped bull, which stands alone in so many seals, was dedicated to the prototype of Śiva and the association of the bull with the god is thus likely to have continued since the earliest time.

The Indus Valley bulls fall into three groups : (i) the real or natural species, (ii) ambiguous animals, which are not completely mythical, such as unicorns, (iii) mythical and composite creatures, viz. semi-bovine, semi-human species. The real or natural bulls belong to two distinct groups :

(a) the large, long-horned, humped Brahmani bull, the Zebu of most European naturalists, to which the name *Bos indicus* was given by Linnaeus,[10] and which, according to Marshall,[11] was closely allied to, if not identical with, the magnificent white and grey breed still common in Sind, Northern Gujarat and Rajasthan; and

(b) the small, short-horned, non-humped, species not infrequently referred to as *Vṛṣabha* or *Bos taurus*,[12] which is the parent of modern European cattle and perhaps found in present India only in the Nilgiris. We may agree with Duerst[13] when he concludes that the short-horned, humpless type of the Indus valley originated from the long-horned, humped variety as a result of the decline of cattle breeding in the valley and not a new race imported from outside. But the origin and history of the *Bos indicus* or the Zebu stock, just like the history of Rudra-Śiva, is very complicated and naturalists put forward different

9. *Prehistoric Civilization of the Indus Valley*, Madras, 1973, p. 32.

10. Prashad, B., 'Animal Remains from Harappa' in *MASI*, No. 51, 1936, p. 6.

11. *MIC*, Vol. I, pp. 28-29.

12. *MASI*, No. 51, 1936, p. 39.

13. *Cf. Ibid.*, p. 8.

Hodgson (*JASB*, Vol. X, 1841, p. 469) has divided Indian bovine species into four genera, *Bos*, *Bibos*, *Bison*, and *Babulus*. It is said that there is no true taurine at the present time living anywhere in Asia, the aberrant *Bos indicus* being the only representative in India of the genus *Bos*.

theories regarding the original form, descent and exact provenance of this group.

Mackay[14] observes that the humped cattle made their way from Elam to Egypt via Anatolia and Syria and that the original habitat of the humped bull was India from where it was introduced into Elam at a very early date. The occurrence of bull both at the Indus valley and Susa implies communications between the two contemporary civilizations.[15]

Let us now note some theri-anthropic composite creatures as found on the Indus valley seals which perhaps represent either the close identity or the intermediary stages of evolution of the anthropomorphic form of Śiva from the theriormorphic one.

A horned and tailed creature, half-human and half-bull, attacking a mythical horned tiger, is depicted on a seal.[16] This hybrid Harappa figure cannot fail to recall the semi-bovine, semi-human Sumerian mythical hero Gilgamesh and his close companion Eabani or Enkidu as found on the Sargonid seals.[17] Mackay[18] suggests that as the tiger was considered to be the emblem of a goddess it is not unreasonable to infer that the tiger-goddess in those early times was looked upon as the consort of the deity already identified as the pre-historic forms of Śiva. Moreover, as the tiger appearing with the horns of a bull on many seals—a type of horn associated with the Śiva figures—it is possible, according to Mackay that, as now, the bull was regarded as the vehicle of the god. But this view is debatable.

We find in European mythology also images compounded of man and animal; sometimes the head only is human, as in the case of the Sphinx; sometimes the head only is animal, as in the case of the sebek; sometimes some minor portion is animal, namely, the Fauns had goat's feed and Dagon a fish's tail.[19]

Mackay[20] thinks that the idea of a composite animal 'origina-

14. *Early Indus Civilisation*, Vol. I, p. 288.
15. Sharma, O.P., 'The Bull in Indian Art and Literature' in *The Journal of the U.P. Historical Society*, Vol. V (N.S.), 1957, Parts 1-11, p. 23.
16. Marshall, J., *MIC*, Vol. III. pl. CXI.
17. *ARASI*, 1926-27, p. 58; Franfort, H., *Cylinder Seals*, 1939, p. 63.
18. *Early Indus Civilisation*, Vol. I, pp. 80-81.
19. *ERE*, Vol. I, p. 494.
20. *Further Excavations at Mohenjo-daro*, 1938, p. 333.
cf. Srinivasan, D., 'The so-called Proto-Śiva Seal from Mohenjo-

ted in India and spread from there gradually to the west by the land route'. But this view needs further investigation and research.

The proto-Śiva of Harappa perhaps represents the final stage of his evolution from the zoomorphic stage. The proto-Śiva is not only Yogīśvara but also Paśupati or lord of the beasts. Although we miss the bull among the animals that grouped about him, still his bovine character is reflected as he has not simply the legs of bull but also the horns of perhaps the same animal.

Let us now note some interesting points regarding the horns which also appear on various other figures of the Indus civilization which definitely have a special sacred significance.[21] Marshall[22] thinks that these horns are the forerunners of Śiva's *triśūla* (trident) denoting the three aspects of the god, as Creator, Destroyer and Regenerator. Later on, not only the Raudras had the trident mark branded on their forehead and the Jangamas bore it on their forehead, but it was subsequently usurped by other sects as well, notably the Buddhists, with whom it stood for the three Jewels '*triratna*'. As early as 1928 Longhurst[23] observed : "These trident heads were set up in the shrine cells in place of the usual *Śivaliṅgas*. The custom appears to have been peculiar to the Pallavas as such images do not seem to have been discovered elsewhere." It is interesting to note that Longhurst, when he wrote this, was not aware that a prototype of the historic Śiva with horned headdress had already been discovered at Mohenjodaro.

Hahn has put forward a theory that it was the shape of the horns which brought them into connection with the crescent moon.[24] The gradual development of the so-called headgear of Rudra-Śiva, as found on the old Mohenjodaro types, into the crescent placed over his head in the later period is best exempli-

daro: An Iconological Assessment' in *Archives of Asian Art*, No. 29, 1975-76, pp. 47-58. For the bovine legs of Proto-Śiva, see p. 55, fig. 13.

21. Marshall, J., *MIC*, Vol. I, p. 54.
22. *Ibid.*, p. 55n.
23. 'Pallava Architecture' in *MASI*, No. 33, p. 18, pl. XVI.
24. *ERE*, Vol. I, p. 509.

fied on the Kuṣāṇo-Sasanian coins.[25] The wearing of horns, a pre-Aryan emblem of divinity or regal strength and power, did not entirely die out in later days.

In the *Ṛgveda*, the sharp horns of Brahmaṇaspati are referred to in a hymn,[26] and the horns of Agni, who is sometimes characterized as a bull, are also mentioned.[27] Indra is likened to a horned bull which will repel all peoples;[28] and other divinities including Soma are also described in the same way. Not only these great deities but even Suṣṇa, a Dasyu and an enemy of Indra, is also described in the *Ṛgveda*[29] as horned. The Viṣāṇins —a tribe in the *Ṛgveda*[30]—who took part in the *Dāśarājña* or the battle of the ten kings, used to wear, as their name indicates, helmets with horns of the Mohenjodaro types.[31] It is also worth noting that there was a pre-Vedic tribe of the Mahāvṛṣas mentioned along with the Muñjavat in the *Atharvaveda*[32] who had some special connection, as suggested by their name, with bull, the emblem of Rudra who was himself spoken of as *Vṛṣabha* in the *Ṛgveda*. The tradition of wearing horns is still retained in South India in the representation of the figure of Ayanā.[33] A. Aiyappan[34] and T.C. Hodson[35] give us valuable informations about the horned head-dress of some non-Aryan tribes of modern India, such as the Nāgas, Gonds, Koyas, Śavars and others.

Hittite and Phoenician deities and the higher gods of Babylonia and Greece usually have bull horns. Cernunnos (perhaps = 'the horned', from *cerna*, 'horn')—a god of the Gauls—is represented with bull horns, and in many of these instances the horns worn by the gods are the relic of their animal forms.[36]

25. Karmarkar, A.P., *The Religions of India*, Vol. I, 1950, p. 18.
26. *RV*, I. 140.
27. *RV*, VIII. 49; X. 155.
28. *RV*, VII. 19.
29. I. 33. 12.
30. VII. 18. 7.
31. Hazra, R.C., 'Further Light on the God of the Famous Mohenjodaro Seals' in *Our Heritage*, Vol. XVIII, Part I, 1969, p. 6.
32. V. 22. 4, 5, 8.
33. Jouveau-Dubreuil, G., *Iconography of South India*, p. 113, Fig. 36.
34. *JRASB* (Letters), Vol. V, 1939, p. 405.
35. *The Nāga Tribes of Manipur*, London, 1911, p. 23.
36. *ERE*, Vol. IV, p. 792.

Though Rudra possessed *Uṣṇīṣa* or headband, still the deity has nowhere been said in the Vedic literature to have worn horns. But in the Anuśāsana-parvan of the *Mahābhārata* Rudra-Śiva has been described as *Śṛṅgin* and *Viṣāṇin*, in the Droṇa-parvan as *Vṛṣaśṛṅga* ('having horns like those of a bull') and in the *Liṅga Purāṇa* as *Śṛṅgapriya* ('fond of horns'). It is thus evident that Rudra-Śiva's emblem of horns is purely non-Vedic and consequently it had to make room in comparatively later days for the *Uṣṇīṣa*, which was looked upon by the Vedic people as a mark of their race and culture.[37]

It is true that the bull, unlike the cow, did not play any major role in the religious cult of the Vedic period. But in the cattle culture of the Vedic Aryans where to increase the number of the cows, to render them fruitful in milk and prolific in calves was the dream, the bull was undoubtedly recognised as the great fecundator, the source of all life and wealth, as a large herd depended on good bulls.[38] It is perhaps not for nothing that even in the late *Bhāgavata Purāṇa*[39] the *gopas* (cowherds) are found worshipping Śiva although they had to propitiate Vāsudeva.

The cow was on the road to acquire special sanctity in the *Ṛgveda* and it is called *aghnyā* ('not to be killed' as preferred by the *Nirukta*)[40] sixteen times,[41] as opposed to three instances of *aghnya*[42] (masculine). Although we have three references of *aghnya*, still apparently no serious restriction in regard to the

37. Hazra, R.C., *op. cit.*, pp. 5-6, 11.
38. Conrad, J.R., *The Horn and the Sword*, London, 1959, p. 51.
39. X. 34. 1.

In the *Ṛgveda* the cow is the theriomorphic form of the cloud; the rain cloud personalized under the name of Pṛśni, is a cow, the mother of the Maruts. Gubernatis (*Zoological Mythology*, Vol. I, London, 1872, pp. 3-4) expresses very beautifully the whole idea in the following way: "The dewy moon, the dewy aurora, the watery cloud, the entire vault of heaven, that giver of the quickening and benignant rain, that benefactress of mankind,—are each, with special predilection, represented as the beneficent cow of abundance. The lord of this multiform cow of heaven, he who makes it pregnant and fruitful and milk-yielding, the spring or morning sun, the rain-giving sun (or moon) is often represented as a bull."

40. XI. 43.
41. *RV*, I. 164. 27 and 40; IV. 1.6; V. 83.8; VIII. 69.21; X. 87. 16 etc.
42. Macdonell, A.A., *Vedic Mythology*, p. 151.

slaughter of bulls is found. It seems that some composers of the Ṛgvedic hymns were pre-Aryan Indians who became Aryanised like the Asuras and the Vrātyas and labelled the whole bovine species inviolable because outside India this inviolability is utterly unknown.[43]

The Śūlagava sacrifice, in which the bull, as the name implies, seems to have been pierced with a spike or lance to appease Rudra, is described in detail in the *Gṛhyasūtras*. According to Nārāyaṇa,[44] *Śūla* here means, one who has a spit (or pointed rod), i.e. Śiva who is also called Śūlin and this sacrifice is offered to Rudra Śūlin with the bull as a sacrificial animal.

In later times the sacrifice of bull was entirely discontinued or prohibited. Even some *Gṛhyasūtras* give a description of the *Śūlagava* which has nothing to do with the killing of the victim. This probably explains in part the rite of letting lose a spotless bull (*Vṛṣotsarga*) branded with the trident dedicated to Śiva, a custom still practised in sacred cities like Banaras or Gaya or the liberation of the bull in the course of the *Śrāddha* or funeral rites which is an act of the highest merit, believed to provide a deceased person with a vehicle to the next world.

In ancient Europe the celebration of *taurobolium*, that is, sacrifice of bull performed in honour of both the Great Mother and Attis, is just a survival of a primitive practice based upon the belief that the strength of the bull "can be acquired by consumption of its actual substance or by contact with its blood".[45]

The bull was one of the chief sacrificial animals in the cult of Zeus and in the ritual of Astarte.[46] The Apis bull of Egypt—as a symbol of imperishable life—was not allowed to die a natural death, but was ceremonially killed in his prime, so that his still-existent strength and virility might be transferred to a younger

43. Bhandarkar, D.R., *Some Aspects of Ancient Indian Culture*, Madras, 1940, p. 73.

44. On *Āsv. Gr.*, IV. 9.1; *cf.* Kane, P.V., *History of Dharmaśāstra*, Vol. II, Part II, 1941, pp. 831-32.

45. *ERE*, Vol. XII, p. 214.

46. *ERE*, Vol. I, p. 508.

bull installed in his place.[47] Conrad[48] advances a theory that the ritual killing of the sacred bull was derived from a much older practice of ritual regicide, or king killing.

Let us now note the wide practices of the immolation of bull as recorded in the Vedic literature.

In a hymn of the *Ṛgveda*[49] it is said "Indra will eat thy bulls". In the *Ṛgveda*[50] Agni is styled *Ukṣānna* and *Vaśānna*, i.e. 'eater of bulls and of barren cows'. Not only for the purpose of sacrifices but for food also, the bull was killed in regular slaughter houses and this is evident from another hymn.[51]

During the Brāhmaṇa period the slaughter of bulls and cows seems to have increased. Among the *Kāmya Iṣṭis* or minor sacrifices set forth in the *Taittirīya Brāhmaṇa*, different bovine species were sacrificed to different gods. In the larger ceremonies, such as the Rājasūya, Aśvamedha and Gomedha, the slaughter of cattle was an invariable accompaniment.[52] The *Taittirīya Brāhmaṇa* notes another ceremony for the gratification of Rudra's sons, the Maruts, the notable element of which was the consecration and liberation of the seventeen five-year old, humpless, dwarf bulls, and the immolation of as many dwarf haifers under three years.[53] The *Aitareya Brāhmaṇa*[54] lists the bull as one of

47. Conrad, J.R., *op. cit.*, pp. 76-77.
48. *Loc. cit.*

The rulers of men, in the words of Conrad, "have always been expected to embody all of the highest values and qualities of their subjects. To merit the continued allegiance of his people, a king had to be strong, virile and dynamic. Indeed, in the magic-filled minds of ancient men any weakness on the part of their leader was an omen of impending disaster in battle, in the harvest, or in any other activity essential to the welfare of the group. It was imperative, therefore, that a new leader be installed before the declining powers of the old king brought evil upon the land. By killing the old king and perhaps ritually partaking of his flesh and blood, the new king thereby added greatly to his own store of power. In time, however, as bulls and kings became more closely identified it appears that bull sacrifice took the place of king sacrifice."

49. X. 86. 13-14.
50. VIII. 43. 11.
51. X. 89. 14.
52. Mitra, R.L., *Indo-Aryans*, Vol. I, 1969, p. 361.
53. *Ibid.*, pp. 362-63.
54. VI. 8.

the sacrificial animals. From the *Taittirīya*[55] and the *Pañcaviṁśa*[56] *Brāhmaṇas* we learn that the sage Agastya slaughtered one hundred bulls at a sacrifice. The *Śatapatha Brāhmaṇa*[57] gives a picture of the inordinate fondness of Yājñavalkya for beef who said : 'I for one, eat it, provided it is tender (*aṁsala*)'. But, strangely enough, we are to face two exhortations in the same *Brāhmaṇas*[58] against eating beef.

The *Sūtras*, both *Kalpa* and *Gṛhya* display less reticence and distinctly suggest beef as an item of food on different occasions of life. According to *Śāṅkhāyana*[59] a bull or a sterile cow should be killed in the house of the father of the bride on the wedding day and also in the house of the bridegroom when the husband and wife arrived after marriage. Even at *Śrāddha*, or periodical oblations to the manes, the sacrifice of a bull or cow is recommended by the *Āpastamba*[60] and *Pāraskara*[61] *Gṛhyasūtras* and the *Yājñavalkya*[62] indicates how the aroma of beef was thought to be an ailment for the spirits.

Distinguished guests like one's teachers, priests, kings and bridegrooms and of the Vedic students on their return home after the completion of their studies are to be honoured with the presentation of a bull slaughter or a barren cow. Hence, a guest is denominated *goghna*.[63] This ceremony of *madhuparka*[64] or the offering of 'honied meal', as it is called, resembles the custom of fatted calves being slain by the Jews in honour of high ranking visitors.

Madhuparka has been prescribed by both the *Manu*[65] and *Yājñavalkya*[66] *Smṛtis*. The *Yājñavalkya* distinctly lays down

55. II. 7. 11. 1.
56. XXI. 14. 5.
57. III. 1. 2. 21.
58. I. 2. 3. 6-9.
59. I. 12. 10.
60. II. 7. 16. 26.
61. III. 10. 48-49.
62. I. 258-60.
63. *gāṁ hanti tasmai goghno'tithiḥ*—Pāṇini, III. 4. 73.
64. *Āsv. Gṛh.*, I. 24. 31-33; *Pāraskara*, I. 3. 26-29.
65. III. 11. 9-20.
66. I. 109-10.

that a *mah-okṣa* or 'big bull' is to be slaughtered on such occasion. *Manu* also recommends the *madhuparka* with beef for the reception of kings, *Snātaka* students, and other dignitaries.

However, due to multifarious factors we note the gradual change of attitude in the popular mind towards bull and a feeling of sanctity went on steadily gathering volume. An interesting chapter of the *Aitareya-Brāhmaṇa*[67] on the sacrifice of animals shows us how, next to man, the horse was the supreme sacrifice offered to the gods; how the bull and the cow afterwards took the place of the horse; the sheep, of the bull; the goat, of the sheep; and at last, vegetable products were substantiated for animals.

All the above details probably suggest that gods, in the earlier stages of chalcolithic civilization, were first conceived in human mind mostly in animal or composite forms, their anthropomorphic form being unquestionably a later development.

The term *Vṛṣa* was later on used metaphorically to signify any strength and power, a synonym for 'hero' and a number of kings of ancient India used the *Vṛṣabha-lāñchana* (bull-banner), the insignia of sovereignty.

(iii) THE BULL AND THE PHALLUS

The bull, because of his strength, energy and sexual virility, was universally considered to be a fitting representative of the masculine creative force, the personification of the god of fertility and of reproductivity.[1] This symbol of generative power has always been connected with the pantheon of primitive agrarian communities. The Hellenic god Dionysios—the Greek counterpart of Śiva—was represented as a bull which was an expression of his character as a deity of vegetation specially as the bull was a common embodiment of corn-spirit in Northern Europe.[2] Osiris and Isis—the Egyptian counterpart of Śiva and

67. VI. 8.

1. Scott, G.R., *Phallic Worship*, London, 1941, p. 179.
2. Frazer, J.G., *Golden Bough*, abridged ed., London, 1949, pp. 513, 611.

Śakti—were depicted as bull and cow representing the Male and Female principles of creation respectively. These two principles were, in course of time, still more emblematically represented in the male and female organs of generation.

In all lands the bull was identified with the Sun which through its 'fecundating warmth' sows life on earth. The Egyptians continued to represent the bull carrying the sun between its horns.[3] In India we have not simply the crescent moon alone on the head of the bull as found on the Yaudheya, Ārjunāyana and Janapada coins; but the globular mark between its horns as found on the obverse of a Nāga coin or the placing of the bull in a rayed circle as found on the Rājanya and Agra coins which perhaps indicate the intimate relation of the sun and the bull as found in Mithraic religion.

Dulaure[4] gives a planetary origin of the cults of the phallus and the bull and thus states; "It is about four thousand five hundred years ago that the sun, through the effect of a third movement of the earth from which the procession of the equinoxes resulted, came, at the spring equinox, within the sign of the zodiac called Taurus. The sign of the celestial constellation which carried this name, represented an artificial zodiac, was considered as the symbol of the vernal sun of the regenerating sun of nature....The sign (Taurus) counterbalanced the object signified, became a god, and representations of the celestial bull were adored...people adored not only representations of the zodiacal bull, but later a living bull obtained the divine honors. Such is the march of the human mind. Once engaged on a career of error and superstition, it advances along it and never turns back; an admitted error then calls other errors to its aid." It is from this worshipped animal, as Dulaure proceeds, from this sacred bull that the cult of the phallus is derived; and it is the image of the genital of bull; and not those of man, as it is generally believed, that became an object of worship.

Richard Payne Knight[5] cites some specimens where to the

3. Brion, M., *Animals in Art*, London, 1959, pp. 15-16.
4. *The Gods of Generations*, New York, 1934, pp. 44-45.
5. *Sexual Symbolism*, Vol. I, New York, 1957, p. 43.

head of the bull was joined the organ of generation, which represented not only the strength of creator, but the peculiar direction of it to the most beneficial purpose, the propagation of sensitive beings. The creator, the father principle, delivering the fructified seeds of things from the restraints of inert matter by his divine strength, is depicted on innumerable Greek coins by the bull, in the act of butting against the Egg of chaos, and breaking it with his horns. Among the Nāgas and their neighbours even at the present day the horned headdress is used as emblematic of fertility and prosperity.[6] Scott[7] and Dulaure[8] enlighten us with examples how the women, of the western civilization, desirous of becoming pregnant, uncovered themselves quite indecently before a sacred white bull.

Phallic symbols were universally considered sacred. The semitic custom of 'placing the hand under the thigh', before taking an oath, is just on euphemism of touching the private member.[9] The same custom to swear solemn oath by touching a bull was also practised in the ancient world. Plutarch in his life of Marius[10] states how the Cimbri took with them on their expedition into Italy a brazen bull, on which they were accustomed to swear solemn oaths.

Let us now come to our land. Regarding the actual practice of the Indus bull religion we can only speculate. We have no clear-cut definite evidence to assume any specific association of the proto-Śiva and the bull as early as Harappan times; still, it is possible that the bull cult was early associated with the phallic Śiva cult because the bull was already a symbol of masculinity and procreation. The lower limbs of the proto-Śiva as outlined by Marshall,[11] are bare and the phallus (*ūrdhvameḍhra*) seemingly exposed and crowning his head is a pair of horns meeting in a tall head-dress. That the god of generative, creative, inaugurative, victorious, vital power and impetuousness in nature and the universe, is closely associated since times

6. *JRASB* [Letters], Vol. V, 1939, p. 404.
7. *Op. cit.*, p. 181.
8. *Op. cit.*, p. 57.
9. (Anonymous), *Phallism*, London, 1889, p. 20.
10. Cap. 23, *cf. ERE*, Vol. II, p. 889.
11. *Mohenjodaro and the Indus Civilization*, Vol. I, 1st ed., p. 52.

immemorial with the energetic, vital, sexually potent and impetuous animal, the bull, is far from surprising.[12]

Again, it would be highly unusual if the great fertility of the bull was not associated with the waters of the Indus and the growth of grain since water and grain were held in high[13] esteem and the Indus religion was a fertility cult. The reference to one-horned Ṛṣyaśṛṅga in the epic mythology who forced Indra to rain[14] may pertain to the strange and ambiguous bull-shaped unicorn which perhaps played an important role in the fertility cult of the Indus valley. In Greece also, Poseidon and the river gods generally seem to have been conceived under the form of bulls, and the festival of Poseidon was not only called *Tauria* but even his priests were also termed 'b ulls'.[15]

The Indus religion is the progenitor of Hinduism. Śiva is doubly descended from the pre-Aryan bull god of the Indus valley and the bull god of the *Ṛgveda* and each of these cultures contributed to the ultimate make-up of Śiva, the creator-destroyer. The two earthly forms of Śiva, the two creative symbols, the bull and the *liṅga*, are directly related to the quickening of crops, cattle and women.[16] The likelihood that both Śiva and *liṅga* worshippings have been inherited in part from the Harappans is perhaps reinforced by the prevalence of the bull or of bull-like animals amongst the seal symbols.[17] According to Allan[18] the bull stands before a *liṅga* on the earliest coins of the Ārjunāyanas and the Yaudheyas collectively to be dated in between the 2nd and 3rd century B.C.

The bull is both a sprinkler and a preserver of energy that is with Śiva and the roaring of the bull is a sign of his robust vitality.[19] This roaring bull represents the god of love, Kāma-

12. Gonda, J., *Change and Continuity in Indian Religion*, The Hague, 1965, p. 77.
13. Conrad, J.R., *The Horn and the Sword*, London, 1959, p. 49.
14. Hopkins, E.W., *Epic Mythology*, 1968, p. 128.
15. *ERE*, Vol. I, p. 501; *cf. JHS*, xiv, pp. 126, 129.
16. Conrad, J.R., *op. cit.*, p. 58.
17. Wheeler, *The Indus Civilization*, p. 83.
18. *Catalogue of coins of Anc. India in the British Museum*, p. 307, Pl. II, fig. 2.
19. Agrawala, V.S., *Śiva-Mahādeva*, 1st ed., p. 15.

deva, who was conquered by Śiva. Marett[20] observes "that 'the prototype' of the All-Fathers 'is nothing more or less than' the bull-roarer".

From the *Vāyu*[21] and the *Matsya*[22] *Purāṇas* we have an idea of the cult of *Godharma* and the episode of Dīrghatamas which is fully relevant for our purpose. The sage Dīrghatamas once played with a bull by firmly holding his horns, so that the bull could not move. The bull informed the sage that he had come on this earth as a mount of Tryambaka and that if he was allowed his freedom he would grant him a boon. The bull then said, "We (the bulls) are sinless creatures who do not know the difference between good and bad; nor do we observe any restrictions regarding sexual behaviour. This is known as the cult of the bulls". Dīrghatamas went home profoundly impressed by this new teaching. The lamentable fate of the sage at the hands of his younger brother's wife for approaching her, who was to him like a daughter-in-law, to practice the teaching of *Godharma* or bull cult, suggests that it was not only odious but alien to the society to which Dīrghatamas belonged.[23] It also appears that Dīrghatamas had to undergo many other persecutions and was later on thrown into the Ganges. Pargiter[24] points out that this incident finds support in the *Ṛgveda*[25] where the sage speaks of having been delivered from bodily hurt and from danger in the rivers. However, the stream of the Ganges, as the story goes on, brought him ultimately to the territory of king

20. *Threshold of Religion*, 1909, pp. 17-19; *cf. ERE*, Vol II, p. 980.

T.N. Ramachandran (Presidential Address, Ancient Indian Section I, Indian History Congress, 1956, pp. 60-64) opines that the Indus seals depict Vedic cult scenes, that the Ṛgvedic poet and the Indus valley artist have fancied and fashioned alike. According to him; the Ṛgvedic idea that the bull does all the roaring to proclaim *dharma vijaya* is caught up by the Indus seals and sealings representing the bull with its characteristic dewlap and with three heads who goes on roaring that the Great God (who is *ūrdhvaretas* in the state of *penis erectus*) has actually completely entered the mortals.

21. 99, 26-34, 47-97.

22. 48, 23-9, 43-89.

23. Patil, D.R., *Cultural History from the Vāyu Purāṇa*, Poona, 1946, p. 158.

24. *Ancient Indian Historical Tradition*, 1962, p. 158.

25. i. 158. 3, 5.

Bali who rescued him from being drowned, supported the *Godharma* of the sage and offered his queen Sudeṣṇā to the now old and blind sage to beget an issue for the king. Later on Sudeṣṇā gave birth to five sons, viz. Aṅga, Vaṅga, Kaliṅga, Puṇḍra and Suhma—who are known as the Kṣetraja sons of Bali.[26] It is difficult to suggest any historical explanation[27] for this quaint practice of *Godharma*; but may we not conclude that a custom akin to this bull cult might have existed amongst the Śiśnadevas[28]—the original settlers of India—which attracted the attention of Dīrghatamas to the extent of practisting it himself?

(iv) THE BULL AS ŚIVA'S MOUNT

The favourite mount on which Śiva is usually represented as seated or standing is a *Vṛṣa* or *Vṛṣabha* or bull, from which he derived the name of *Vṛṣabhārūḍha* or *Vṛṣavāhana*. In his *Vṛṣavāhana* form Śiva does not always ride on his bull as in *Vṛṣabhārūḍha* form; rather the animal is placed by his side and one of his arms usually rests either on the hump or horn of the bull. The Vedic Rudra was not a bull-rider; rather, as we have already seen, he was himself represented as a bull. When, however, anthropomorphic representations of the divine beings became popular, the bull, once representing Śiva theriomorphically, became his vehicle, and stories were fabricated to account for the choice of the bull as his *vāhana*.

Zimmer,[1] referring to the examples appearing on the Bhārhut pillars put forward the theory that the *vāhana* theme is of Mesopotamian origin and the idea was in early times borrowed from the western peoples "for divinities of the pre-Aryan tradition".

J. Gonda is not ready to accept Zimmer's opinion as no "god on *vāhana* appears in the many remainders of the Indus

26. *Vāyu P.*, 99. 35ff.
27. Macdonell and Keith, *Vedic Index*, Vol. I, p. 366.
28. *RV*, VII. 21.5; X. 99. 3.

1. *The Art of Indian Asia*, Vol. I, New York, 1955, pp. 43ff.

civilization".[2] But it is really very interesting to note that among the Harappa seals we have a standing figure with a humpless bull in the fore-ground and the figure seems to hold a long staff in his left hand and water-vessel-like object in his right one,[3] resembling similar figures on certain punch-marked coins of later date, which Banerjea[4] identified as Śiva.

The mount of Śiva is again represented both theriom orphically and anthropomorphically. Nandin, Nandīśvara, Adhikāranandin—the various names of Śiva's mount, the bull, as found in the epic and Purāṇic texts—are really Śiva's attendants and unlike Garuḍa of Viṣṇu, they were anthropomorphised though hybridity was not unknown.[5]

The Ujjayinī coins, belonging to the 1st century B.C. or A.D., represent the bull 'slightly prancing up' and looking at Śiva.[6] In a Gandhāra relief[7] Śiva is found recumbent on his bull. Since the days of the Kuṣāṇas the bull invariably accompanied its master. Although on the coins of Kaṇiṣka and Huviṣka, Śiva is usually found without his mount, but on the coins of Wema Kadphises and Vāsudeva particularly, the deity in various poses is found with his mount who is usually placed behind him. Śiva is found in front of his bull in some other types of Kuṣāṇa coins, viz., 'Enthroned king', 'King sacrificing at an altar' and 'Elephant rider types'.[8] The deity is always seen standing, sometimes as leaning on his bull with left hand placed on it.[9]

In a unique gold coin of Vāsudeva the mount has got a bell

2. Gonda, J., *Change and Continuity in Indian Religion*, The Hague, 1965, p.93

Cf. Lannoy, Richard, *The Speaking Tree: A Study of Indian Culture and Society*, OUP, (Paperback), 1975, p. 188, where Lannoy observes that the idea of *vāhana* and animal incarnations is probably totemic, as are in the cases of tree and snake worship.

3. Banerjea, J.N., *DHI*, 1965, p. 165; Chanda, R.P. in the *Modern Review*, August, 1932; Mookerji, R.K., *Hindu Civilization*, 1936, p. 21.

4. Banerjee, J.N., *DHI*, pl. 1, fig. 4.

5. *Ibid.*, pp. 34-35.

6. *Ibid.*, p. 117.

7. *ASIAR*, 1913-14, pp. 276ff., Pl. LXXIIa.

8. Chattopadhyay, B., *The Age of the Kuṣāṇas*, 1967, p. 47.

9. *Loc. cit.*

attached to its neck.[10] The bull Nandin is a common feature in the images of Śiva in Mathura art. Even in the images of Śiva-Pārvatī in *āliṅganamudrā,* belonging to the Gupta period, Nandin is found at the back.[11] In some images found from Bihar and Banaras[12] both Śiva and Pārvatī are found leaning on the bull. On the reverse of some coins of Harṣadeva the god and the goddess are shown seated on Nandin.

The bull occupies a very important position in the mythology of all races either as an object of worship or as the associate or mount of some god. Besides the nameless god and goddess of Minean Crete and the Anatolian Cybele, the characteristics of Nergal, the benevolent Babylonian god of the fields granting fertility recalls the deity of the *Śatarudriya* litany of the *Yajurveda.*[13] Like Śiva, the Hittite deity Yeshub also stands on a bull. In an old coin of ancient Syria[14]—belonging to the Hittites—we have the figures of a goddess mounted on a lion (resembling the goddess Durgā of the Hindu pantheon) and of a god mounted on a bull—an exact replica of Śiva.

Mythologically the god's vehicle and attendant, the bull is, in the eyes of the students of history, a theriomorph duplicate manifestation or representation of the fertility and procreation aspect of Śiva's nature and energy.[15] On entering the sacred complex of a Śiva temple, one passes in the precincts his bull Nandin squatting on a raised platform facing the Śivaliṅga, in order that he may always look at his lord in the symbolic form or *deva-vīkṣaṇa-tatpara* as mentioned in the *Matsyapurāṇa.* The merit of presenting images of seated bull in the outer halls of Śiva temples is extolled in the *Mahānirvāṇa Tantra.*[16] At the entrance into many an important temple of Śiva in southern

10. Cunningham, A., *Coins of the Indo-Scythians and Kuṣāṇas,* Pt. III, p. 74, Pl. XXIV, fig. 9.

11. Agrawala, V.S., *A Catalogue of the Brāhmaṇical Images in Mathurā Art,* 1951, p. 27, No. 2495.

12. *IHQ,* Vol. XI, pt. III, 1935, pp. 584ff.

13. Raychaudhuri, H.C., in *Science and Culture,* Vol. V, October, 1939, p. 207.

14. Das, A.C., *Rigvedic India,* 1st ed., p. 296.

15. Gonda, J., *Viṣṇuism and Śivaism,* London, 1970, p. 76.

16. XIII. 32.

India one similarly meets with Adhikāranandin, a male figure, who resembles Śiva in his Candraśekharamūrti aspect; with the only difference that whereas the front hands of the former are folded on the chest in the *añjali* pose, those of the latter are in the *varada* and *abhaya* poses[17] and the figure of Adhikāranandin is sometimes mistaken by the less informed people for that of Śiva.

The most notable point of distinction between the north Indian and south Indian images of Naṭarāja Śiva is that whereas in the case of the former we have the bull beneath the feet of the god, dancing in unison in ecstatic joy; in the case of the latter the place of the bull is taken by the Apasmāra Puruṣa, a demon and the bull is usually found lurking behind the god.[18]

Śiva's *Vṛṣavāhana* forms have been referred to by Kālidāsa at several places of the *Kumārasambhava*.[19] The picturesque description of Kālidāsa inspired Śaśāṅka's mint master in setting his details,[20] even the bull's golden bells have been shown on Śaśāṅka's gold coins, and the deity is found reclining to left on couchant bull, with his right hand resting on the hump.[21] On all the coins of Śaśāṅka we have the bull as mount on the obverse with the moon and the image of Śiva.[22] Whether it was standing Śiva, as on the Kuṣāṇa coins, or seated as on Śaśāṅka's coins, the deity could be said to be supporting himself on the horn of his mount. According to Bāṇabhaṭṭa the bull hump, usually round and lustrous like the full-moon, was covered with mud in this coin, comparable to the spots on the moon.[23]

The *Mahābhārata* relates a story how the bull (Nandin) came to be associated with Śiva. In the Anuśāsana parvan it is stated that Dakṣa Prajāpati offered the bull (*Vṛṣabha*) to Śiva to appease him and the latter made the bull his vehicle.[24]

17. Gopinatha Rao, T.A., *EHI*, Vol. II, Part 2, Madras, 1916, p. 455.

18. Bhattasali, N.K., *Iconography of Buddhist and Brāhmaṇical Sculpture in the Dacca Museum*, Dacca, 1929, p. 112.

19. VII. 49.

20. Sohoni, S.V., 'Vrisha-vāhana Śiva and Kālidāsa' in *JBRS*, Vol. 42, 1956, p. 427.

21. Smith, V.A., *CCIM*, Vol. I, Pl. XVI, 12; Altekar, A.S., *The Coins of the Gupta Empire*, pp. 328-30, Pl. XIX, A. 89.

22. Smith, V.A., *CCIM*, pp. 121-22.

23. Sohoni, S.V., *op. cit.*, p. 425.

24. Hopkins, E.W., *Epic Mythology*, p. 223.

The process of anthropomorphising the *Vāhana* of Śiva began, however, in the early centuries of the Christian era.[25] That it was complete by the Gupta period can be substantiated by Kālidāsa's description of Nandin guarding the entrance of Śiva's place of meditation : "Nandin posted at the entrance of the bower, having a golden staff resting against his forearms, bade the Gaṇas to observe stillness with a gesture in which a finger of his right hand touched his mouth".[26] In the *Rāmāyaṇa*[27] we have the description of Nandin having the appearance of a monkey, but the body of a fierce dark-brown, short-armed and powerful dwarf.

In the *Mahābhārata*[28] we get the reference to the image of Nandīśvara. The little godling with a bull's head standing by the side of Śiva in the cave No. 1. at Badami is none but Nandīkeśvara.[29]

The *Skandapurāṇa*[30] narrates the story how Śiva asked Nandin to watch the doors, and how Nandin (who was represented in his anthropomorphic form) was cursed by Agni to descend to the world below. We have in the same Purāṇa another account, how on being asked for a boon, Dharma promised that he would assume the form of bull and would become the *vāhana* or vehicle of Śiva and the iconographic texts depict Dharma having four feet.[31]

For the art specimens, Sivaramamurti, C., *The Art of India*, New York, 1977, "In the version characteristic of Bengal, seen in a sculpture from Shankarbandha near Dacca, Shiva dances atop the bull (fig. 70). A parallel form from Southern India depicts Shiva dancing on the dwarf Apasmara. The bull and the dwarf symbolize ego and ignorance, which Shiva conquers through his dance. The only known metal representation of this form from Bengal was carried to the South as a war trophy by Rajendra and is now in the Melakkadambur temple (fig. 275). " p. 80.

25. Banerjea J.N., *DHI*, p. 535.
26. *Kumarāsambhava*, III. 41.
27. VIII. 16, 14.
28. XIII. 25, 21.
29. Jouveau-Dubreuil, G., *Iconography of Southern India*, p. 54n.
30. *Avantikhaṇḍa*, II. 20. 13ff.
31. *Vṛṣ hi bhagavān dharmaścatuṣpādaḥ prakīrttitaḥ.*

Gopinatha Rao[32] cites three different accounts about the origin of Nandīśvara or Adhikāranandin from the *Śivapurāṇa*, *Liṅgapurāṇa* and another unnamed text where he is primarily described as a human being having some iconographic traits of Śiva.

According to the *Śivapurāṇa*,[33] Viṣṇu became satisfied at the austerities practised under a śāla tree at a place called Śālagrāma by the ṛṣi Sālaṅkāyana who longed for a son, and granted him the boon and immediately Nandīkeśvara sprang from the right side of Viṣṇu who resembled Śiva in every way.

The *Liṅga*, *Kūrma* and other *Purāṇas* narrate how Śiva himself was born as Nandin, the son of the blind ṛṣi Śilāda. Nandīkeśvara, internally perturbed on hearing the prognostication that the duration of his life is small, began to meditate upon Śiva so intently that the latter appeared to him, took hold of him in his arms, threw round his neck his own garland and blessed the metamorphosed Nandin—who was now endowed with ten arms, three eyes etc.—to be free from old age and death and also anointed him as the head of his *gaṇas*.[34]

The third account runs as follows : Being pleased with the severe penance of Nandin, a *ṛṣi* in the Tretā-yuga, on the peak of the Muñjavat, Śiva granted him the boon as the head of his *gaṇas*.

We have in the *Bhāgavatapurāṇa*[35] a description how Nandikeśvara, during the Dakṣa-yajña, grew angry at the insult of his lord Śiva and pronounced maledictions against Dakṣa and other revilers of Śiva.

The *Viṣṇudharmottara*[36] paints Nandin as three-eyed, four-armed, wearing a tiger skin garment, holding a *triśūla* and a *bhindipāla* (a kind of javelin) in two of his hands, a third hand being placed over his head and the fourth held in *tarjjanīmudrā* as if he is commanding a host of people.

Thus Nandin, the mount of Śiva, is represented both as a

32. *EHI*, Vol. II, Part 2, pp. 455-48.
33. *Uttarā-śatarudriya saṁ.*, Adh. 3.
34. Gopinatha Rao, T.A., *EHI*, Vol. II, Part 2, pp. 457-58.
35. *Cf.* Muir, J., *OST*, Vol. IV, pp. 376ff.
36. III. 73, 15-17.

bull-faced human being or as a duplicate of Śiva. The bull as Śiva's mount is perhaps derived from the prehistoric cult of the bull that had once reached India from the Mediterranean area.[37]

37. *Encyclopaedia of World Art*, Vol. XIII, 1st. ed., p. 828.

Cf. Hiltebeitel, A., 'The Indus Valley' 'Proto-Siva' Re-examined through Reflections on the Goddess, the Buffalo and the Symbolism of Vahanas' in *Anthropos*, No. 73, 1978, pp. 767-97.

CHAPTER III

ŚIVA AND THE PHALLUS

(i) PHALLUS WORSHIP IN ANCIENT INDIA AND OUTSIDE

Phallism or Phallicism, an anthropological term, is applied to the worship of the generative or reproductive power of nature symbolized by the phallus, that is, male organ. Phallus worship in India is of pre-Aryan origin. The phallic conception is expressed by the ithyphallic representation of proto-Śiva in the Harappa Civilization; by the representation of detached organ of generation; and by the ascription of phallic significance to a host of objects. Marshall[1] has enlightened us with three classes of aniconic objects found at the Indus valley. The first phallic specimens were more or less realistically modelled, and Aurel Stein[2] has found such parallel phallus on Chalcolithic sites at Mughal Ghundai in North Baluchistan (Pakistan). The second specimens are conventionalized in shape and resemble the baetylic stones of western Asia, such as the semitic *maṣṣebhāh*, etc. To the third belong the miniature specimens which as amulets were perhaps carried by persons, as miniature *liṅgas* are commonly carried by the Liṅgāyats of the latter days.

These phallus worshippers of the Indus valley were perhaps deprecatingly alluded in the *Ṛgveda*[3] as *Śiśnadeva*. The *liṅga* and *yoni* cults, though of pre-Vedic and non-Aryan origin in India, prevailed throughout the ancient world. Like Śiva in India, we have Khem and Osiris in Egypt, Vul in Assyria, Pan and Dionysius in Greece, Fricco in Scandinavia, Hortanes in Spain, Adonis in Phoenicia and Attis in Phrygia.[4]

1. *Mohenjodaro and the Indus Civilization*, Vol. I, London, 1931, pp. 59-60.
2. *Ibid.*, Pl. XIII. 1.
3. Vol. III. 21, 5; X. 99, 3.
4. (Anonymous), *Phallism*, London, 1889, p. 27.

Two outlooks on phallus worship in the ancient West were current side by side. The first is the so-called 'Sin' or 'Fall' of man, and the phallic symbols—the tree, serpent, apple, etc.—are brought into the scene. The Zoraostrian Aryans particularly looked upon the phallus as the source of all evil.[5] On the other hand, the Semites and the Turanians looked upon it with feelings of veneration and glorified sexual ideas.[6]

True, some form of obscenity and immoral practices were associated with phallic worship in later days and that religion has broken out in Bacchanalian, Dionysian, Saturnalian, and other orgiastic revels; but it would be wrong to presume that licentiousness invented the rites and to judge primitive thought in the light of twentieth century ethical and moralistic ideals. The worship of phallus is so common and widespread that it is to be regarded as a part of the general evolution of the human mind and part of the history of religion. With the onward march of civilization, sophistication crept in and it was carried on by means of symbolism. Scholars are divided today about the interpretation of most symbols. Sometimes the symbolic language is hardly understood; sometimes the hidden or underlying meaning is grossly exaggerated. Thus, to writers whose imagination outpaces proof, whatever was upright and long rather than broad became the symbol of the Father; whatever was hollow, or oval, or rounded became the symbol of the Mother.[7] Hence, a great deal of circumspection is needed in identifying phallic symbols.

Primitive man saw birds, animals and women to bear youngs or carry them in their wombs but understood nothing of the process,[8] and wondered at the mysterious phenomenon. This wonder, coupled with ignorance, would lead to a veneration for the organs whose operation conducted the phenomenon.[9]

5. Mitra, R.L., *The Antiquities of Orissa*, Vol. I, 1961, p. 224.

6. *Loc. cit.*

7. Inman, T., *Ancient Pagan and Modern Christian Symbolism*, New York, 1874, p. xxiii.

8. Scott, G.R., *Phallic Worship*, London, 1941, p. vi.

9. Westropp, H.M., and Wake, C.S., *Phallism in Ancient Worships*, New Delhi, 1970, p. 34.

Thus perhaps arose the practices connected with the *liṅga* and the *yoni* among the primitive peoples of the world.

Faber[10] has referred to a universal primitive belief in a Great Father and found in phallic worship a degradation of this belief. The pre-Aryans, particularly the Dravidians, had a conception of a Great Father God and a Mother Goddess and when compared with the *Ṛgvedic* idea of Sky Father (*Dyaus pitṛ*) and Earth Mother (*Pṛthivī Mātā*) the Dravidian concept appears to be 'more profound, more mystic, more all-embracing'.[11] Forlong[12] thinks that it is the phallic faith which has taught us to honour our father and mother and from this has sprung the social organization of all primitive peoples. In fact, the worship of the *liṅga* of Śiva originated from the conception of the god as the Great Father or procreator and this Father-god and the Mother-goddess were worshipped in both anthropomorphic and symbolic forms by the pre-Aryan peoples of the Harappa civilization.

To the primitive man his tremendous struggle for existence in this world centred on fertility.[13] Everything in the first age of human society, that is, existence, growth, power, riches and happiness resulted from a great number of individuals.[14] Everything that made the earth fruitful or tended to increase production was eagerly seized upon and honoured[15] and necessarily everything that could injure or prevent that increase was considered bad and combatted with the same zeal. Thus theology has linked itself with man's reproductive instinct. It is not for nothing that the very first blessing in the Bible[16] mentioned in connection with the creation of man is: 'Be fruitful, and multiply, and replenish the earth'. In the post-Vedic literature, Śiva, a god of procreation, is worshipped mainly for the boon of a son.

The phallic cult is apt to become specially developed in the

10. *Cf. ibid.*, p. 33.
11. *The History and Culture of the Indian People*, Vol. I, 1957, p. 158.
12. *Rivers of Life*; cf. Marr, G.S., *Sex in Religion*, London, 1936, p. 26.
13. Cutner, H., *A Short History of Sex Worship*, London, 1940, p. 2.
14. Dulaure, J.A., *The Gods of Generation*, New York, 1934, p. 218.
15. Cutner, H., *op. cit.*, p. 3.
16. Genesis I 28; cf. *ERE*, Vol. II, p. 653.

agricultural stage of civilization,[17] as hunger and incest intermingle in the work of agriculture. Frazer in his *Golden Bough* has fully expounded and abundantly illustrated sexual acts from various mythologies of the world in relation to agricultural rites. The fecundity of earth and women are taken as one and of the same quality. The bedrock of Indian civilization is agriculture and it dates back to the Austrics or proto-Australoids who used the digging stick, resembling penis, to till the hill-side for depositing the seed.[18] There are evident analogies between copulation and the act of ploughing, between the Austric words *liṅga* (phallus) and *lāṅgala* (plough),[19] and Śiva is both a god of cultivation and procreation.

In most cases agricultural deities are phallic deities. That the proto-Śiva of the Harappa civilization is a vegetation or fertility god is suggested by the headdress on two seals which is surmounted by a plant motif with three branches in one case and a single branch on the other.[20] Like Osiris and Dionysus, Rudra personifies the reproductive power of nature in the Vedic literature. The placing of the Ganges on his head in the post-Vedic period was to emphasize his fertilising power. The moon on the forehead of the deity is also a 'source of moisture and fertility.'[21] In the *Mahābhārata*,[22] Upamanyu, the propagator of the *liṅga* cult, prayed to Śiva for rice and milk in plenty. As an agriculturist, Śiva is Mahādeo to the Kiṣān tribe.[23] Buḍādeo, Kodopen or Liṅgo to the Goṇḍs, Bābā Deo to the Bhīls,[24] Bīranātha to the Āhīrs,[25] Bhairon or Bhūmiyā to the Kuṇbī

17. Hertland, E.S., 'Phallism' in *ERE*, Vol. IX, p. 828.

18. *The History and Culture of the Indian People*, Vol. I, p. 151.

19. Przyluski, J., *Pre-Aryan and Pre-Dravidian in India*, (Translated from French by Bagchi, P.C.), Calcutta, 1929, pp. 10-11; Chatterji, S.K., *Indo-Aryan and Hindi*, 1960, pp. 251-52.

20. Mackay, E.J.H., *Further Excavations at Mohenjodaro*, Delhi, 1938, Vol. I, p. 335; Vol. II, Pl. LXXXVII, figs. 222 and 235.

21. Crooke, W., *Popular Religion and Folklore of N. India*, 1st ed., Vol. I, p. 39.

22. VII. 218-26.

23. Dalton, E.T., *Descriptive Ethnology of Bengal*, p. 132.

24. Rislay, H.H., *Tribes and Castes of Bengal*, Vol. II, p. 203.

25. Crooke, W., *Tribes and Castes of N.W. Provinces and Oudh*, Vol. I, p. 63.

cultivators of the South, Muni to the Eravallers of Cochin[26] and Kṣetrapāla all over India.

The phallus is regarded as the foe of sterility. To renew the strength and fertility of the soil the annual symbolic marriages of the agricultural deities are held all over the world. The marriage of Kṣetrapāla with the earth-goddess, or Buḍhā-Buḍhī or Hara-Gaurī, is annually celebrated in Eastern Bengal[27] since ancient times. Such periodical reunions of the divine pairs of fertility, namely, Dih and Deohārin and Ningo Bāghiyā amongst the Majhwārs of Mirzapur,[28] Darhār and Ḍākin amongst the Kharvārs of Bihar,[29] Ekaliṅga and Gaurī amongst the people of Rajasthan, and Sarvarāyam and the goddess of the Kāverī river amongst the Mālayālis of southern India, are age-old practices. The other phallic deities of the world, namely, Zeus in Greece, Dionysis in Athens, and Nabu in Assyria, were also annually married.[30] The ancient Teutonic phallic deity, Frey, was drawn round the country during the annual spring festival, accompanied by his young priestess, who was called the god's wife.[31] In Rome, like Tutunus or Mutunus, the other agricultural and phallic deity Liber was similarly reunited with Libera.[32]

Phallic Flora

The cult of the phallic tree embraces certain rites in the life of many ancient peoples. We have some seals which show the existence of tree-forms: one was the worship of the sacred tree in its natural form and the other was that of its indwelling spirit.[33] On some seals we have the representation of the *triśūla-*

26. *ERE*, Vol. IV, pp. 602, 605.
27. Wise, J., *Notes on the Races, Castes and Traders of Eastern Bengal*, 1883, pp. 132ff.
28. Crooke, W., *Tribes and Castes of N.W. Provinces and Oudh*, Vol. III, pp. 435, 447.
29. *Ibid.*, pp. 247ff.
30. *ERE*, Vol. IV, p. 828.
31. *Loc. cit.*
32. *Ibid.*, p. 822.
33. Mookerji, R.K., *Hindu Civilization*, 1936, p. 21.

horned figure standing nude between two branches of a tree, showing it to be the pipal.[34]

The botanical name of pipal is *ficus religiosa*, made famous as the Bodhi tree in Buddhist literature, and is associated with the sacred fig tree in Hindu religion. In the Bible the Tree of Life in the Garden of Eden was the fig tree, symbolical of the male creative power, and the fruit represented the formula principle; and eating the forbidden fruit was a figurative method of describing the sex act.[35]

In Ancient Britain the Druids worshipped Aesus in the form of an oak tree and the ancient Teutons considered the oak tree to be of the male sex as the acron looks like a *glans penis*.[36] How important a part the pine cone played in the worship of Bacchus is described by Inman.[37] Aston[38] points out that, in China and Japan, the peach is the acknowledged representative of *Kteis*, as pestle and mushroom are of the phallus. The various customs and ceremonies connected with the May-pole in Europe indicate that it was purely a phallic symbol[39] at first. In the sacred books of the Parsis, the original human pair, Maschia and Maschiana, sprang from the tree homa or haoma in Heden.[40] In Scandinavian mythology, the ash and the elm appear as the first man (Ask) and the first women (Embla).[41]

The tree with its waving leaves and branches, apparently dying in the autumn and waking to a new life in the spring, is universally regarded as the life-index.[42] Crooke[43] has collected from North India numerous examples of the practice of marrying brides to trees before the regular marriage. Although the object of this custom is obscure; in some cases, the intention is undoubtedly to communicate the vigorous reproduc-

34. Vats, M.S., *Excavations at Harappa*, pl. XCIII, 307 and 317.
35. Scott, G.R., *op. cit.*, pp. 35-36.
36. Wall, O.A., *Sex and Sex Worship*, Kimpton, 1920, p. 129.
37. *Ancient Faiths*, Vol. II, p. 491.
38. *Shinto*, London, 1905, p. 189.
39. Payne Knight, R., *Sexual Symbolism*, Vol. II, New York, 1957, p. 91.
40. Philpot (Mrs.), *The Sacred Tree*, London, 1897, p. 130.
41. *Chambers's Encyclopaedia*, Edinburgh, 1889, *s.v.* '*Ash*'.
42. Smith, W.R., *Religion of the Semites*, Edinburgh, 1889, pp. 469ff.
43. *Popular Religion and Folklore of N. India*, Vol. II, pp. 115ff.

tive power of the tree. In the marriage ceremony of the Agaria, a Dravidian tribe of Chotanagpur, Bihar, the Śāl tree plays an important role.[44] Even today, in many parts of south India, a tiny plate of gold, shaped like the fig leaf, called the *tali,* which represents the phallus, is tied about a bride's neck at her marriage.[45] Every Mech, a Mongoloid tribe of North Bengal, looks the sij plant not only as the abode of Śiva, as the Bel (*Aegle marmelos*) is, but the emblem of conjugal fidelity.[46] Though in the *Ṛgveda* we have an entire hymn[47] devoted to the praise of plants (*oṣadhi*) and another[48] celebrating the *Araṇyānī,* the part played by the plant and tree deities is an insignificant one. However, the later Vedic texts refer to offerings and adorations paid to trees and plants passed in marriage processions.[49] In the village ritual-marriage of Śiva and Pārvatī, clay images of the divinities are attached to the ends of forked branches of trees, the prongs of which are stuck into heaps of grass and flowers.[50]

Perhaps a mythology associated with the tree spirit is to be found in a three-sided terracotta prism discovered at Mohenjodaro.[51] In later days Śivaliṅgas were associated with trees. A terracotta seal in the Dhir Singh Nahar collection has on it a Śivaliṅga described as *pādapeśvara*[52] in Gupta characters. The phallic emblem of Śiva on a pedestal placed between two different trees can be found on the obverse of Var. 'C' of Class I coins hailing from Ujjayinī.[53] Even today many of the important Śivaliṅgas are associated with particular trees among

44. Dalton, E.T., *Descriptive Ethnology of Bengal*, pp. 196, 322.
45. Thurston, E., *Castes and Tribes of S. India*, Madras, 1909, Vol. III, pp. 37ff.
46. Rislay, H.H., *Tribes and Castes of Bengal*, Vol. II, p. 89.
47. *RV* X. 97.
48. *RV* X. 146.
49. Macdonell, A.A., *A History of Sanskrit Literature*, Delhi, 1965 p. 92.
50. *Indian Antiquary*, Vol. XI , 1882, pp. 296ff.
51. Mackay, E., *Further Excavations at Mohenjodaro*, Vol. I, p. 351; Vol. II, Pl. LXXXII, Nos. 1-C and 2-C.
52. Banerjea, J.N., *DHI*, 1956, p. 114.
53. *Loc. cit.*; Allan, J., *Catalogue of Coins of Ancient India in the British Museum*, p. 85, No. 2, XI, 2; p. 233, Nos. 154 and 154a, pl. XXV, 5 and p. 243, No. 19, pl. XXXVI, 15.

which the celebrated Ap-liṅga of Jambukeśvara near Srīrangam is notable.[54]

The lotus has enjoyed an unparalleled popularity in Indian art and literature since the ancient time. A notable feature of the lotus is a large number of seeds contained in the fruit suggesting a phallic significance.[55] The self-fertilizing power of the lotus makes it peculiarly suitable as a symbol of the androgynous creative god,[56] comparable with the *liṅgodbhavamūrti* of Śiva. Again, the lotus flower is closely associated with the Sun, that is, it opens when the Sun rises and closes at sunset; and sun is the re-vivifier, resurrectors or regenerator of life. The lotus appears to have symbolized for the Hindus and the Buddhists the idea of superhuman and divine birth; and secondarily, of creative force and immortality. In the *Brāhmaṇas*,[57] the lotus appears to be associated with the creator Prajāpati in cosmogonic myths. In the *Śatapatha Brāhmaṇa*,[58] it is the symbol of the womb. Analysing a unique Harappa seal representing the Earth Goddess with a plant growing from her womb, Marshall[59] draws our attention to a terracotta relief of the early Gupta period found from Bhiṭā on which the goddess is shown in much the same posture, but with a lotus issuing from her neck instead of from her womb. As an explanation of the present shape of the *Liṅga-yoni* motif in Indian Art, F.D.K. Bosch[60] has identified the *yoni* with the lotus-root and the *liṅga* placed in the *yoni* with the stem of the lotus-plant as it rises from the lotus-root.

Some scholars[61] have found a tree-analogy behind the *Liṅgodbhava* legend wherein Viṣṇu is found digging into the ground as a boar to find the root of the liṅga and Brahman as a swan flying upwards to discover its top. Those who have tried to

54. Banerjea, J.N., *DHI*, p. 114.
55. Scott, G.R., *op. cit.*, p. 38.
56. *Loc. cit.*
57. *Taittirīya Brāhmaṇa*, I. 1. 3, 5ff.
58. VII. 4. 1. 11.
59. *MIC*, Vol. I, p. 52.
60. *The Golden Germ—An introduction to Indian Symbolism*, 1960, Holland, pp. 164ff.
61. Bhattacharyya, H., *The Foundations of Living Faiths*, Vol. I, 1938, p. 228.

prove, though not successfully, that the *liṅga* had originally a sylvan origin, sometimes trace its evolution from the *yūpastambha*[62] or sacrificial post, resembling it. The cultus-post was so closely associated with the Egyptian phallic god Osiris that it became the hieroglyphic symbol for his name in Egyptian writing.[63]

Phallic Fauna

The creative and generative power in nature is very often represented by and also worshipped in the form of an animal famed for its virility and fecundity.

The bull, because of his strength, energy and virility is universally considered to be a fitting representative of the masculine creative force, the personification of the god of fertility and reproductivity, since the prehistoric period. We have already devoted a chapter on the bull. Dulaure[64] believes that the signs of the two animals, Bull and Goat, in the zodiac, which marked the spring equinox and which in Egypt bore the same name, the celestial Bull and Goat, first worshipped in representation and then in real form, were primarily responsible for the origin of the cult of the phallus; and their genital members became the models for phalli and placed in all places where fecundity was desired and sterility was feared.

Apart from the bull and the goat, the serpent ranked as a popular representative of generative or reproductive deities. The serpent having the power of casting its skin periodically and apparently renewing its youth has become the symbol of rejuvenescence, life and vigour.[65] The serpent symbolizes 'lust', 'carnal mind', 'sex-desire', 'sex-degeneracy' and so on and the power of erection possessed by certain snakes is emblematic of male activity and suggests the phallus.[66] Forlong[67] thinks that

62. Allan, Grant, *Evolution of the Idea of God*, 1st ed., Chap. VI (Sacred stakes), Chap. VII (Sacred Trees); *The Proceedings of the Convention of Religions in India*, p. 124, f.n. 6.

63. *ERE*, Vol. X, p. 94.

64. *The Gods of Generation*, New York, 1934, p. 222.

65. Payne Knight, R., *Sexual Symbolism*, Vol. I, New York, 1957, p. 36.

66. Scott, G.R., *op. cit.*, pp. 87-88; Cutner, H., *op. cit.*, p. 176.

67. *Rivers of Life*, Vol. I, London, 1883, p. 223.

the idea of the rod of life originated from the fact that the sexual act in serpents was practised in erect formation. However, in every corner of the world tree and serpent worships are closely intertwined with phallus worship,[68] and no one can deny the universality of the serpent symbol as the principle of ever-renewing life since the prehistoric days. Though in the *Ṛgveda* we have reference to *Ahi budhnya*, the 'serpent of the Deep', representing the beneficent aspect of the serpent Vṛtra, and in the *Yajur-* and *Atharva-Vedas*, especially in the latter, the serpents are mentioned as a class of semi-divine beings along with the Gandharvas and others and in the *Sūtras* offerings to them are prescribed; still zoomorphic divinities in general were known to the Vedic Aryans only to a limited extent. The worship of serpentine deities in India would appear to have come from the Austric world.

Of the two seals found at Mohenjodaro, the Yogīśvara, proto-Śiva is surrounded on both sides by kneeling *nāgas*.[69] In the *Mahābhārata*,[70] *nāgas* figure very frequently in association with Śiva. We have a large number of numismatic and glyptic specimens of Ancient India wherein the serpent is found enclosing the *liṅga* or five-headed snakes forming canopy over it.[71] Śiva as Rikheśvara or Nāgeśvara is himself the snake god.[72] The Nāga, the emblem of Śiva, is also the name of a serpent-worshipping non-Aryan ruling tribe of North India who came after the Kuṣāṇas.[73] Some medieval dynasties of different parts of India claimed to be Nāgavaṁśis.

The serpent always accompanied the images of Osiris in Egypt. The Greek god Hermes was very often represented as holding in his

68. Cox, G.W., *The Mythology of the Aryan Nations*, Vol. II, London, 1870, p. 127.

69. Marshall, J., *MIC*, Vol. I, pp. 54, 68, Vol. III, pl. CXVI, 29 and CXVIII, 11.

70. *Udyogaparvan*, 103, 9-16; *Anuśāsanaparvan*, 150. 41.

71. Rivett-Carnac, J.R., 'The Snake Symbol in India, especially in connection with the worship of Śiva' in *JASB*, 1879, Vol. I, pp. 17ff.

72. Sherring, M.A., *The Sacred City of the Hindus*, London, 1868, pp. 75, 87ff.; Atkinson, E.T., *Himalayan Gazetteer*, Vol. II, 1884, p. 851.

73. *History and Culture of the Indian People*, Vol. II, 1960, p. 168.

hand the caduceus, or serpents in sexual congress.[74] The Phoenicians entwine the folds of a serpent around the cosmic egg to express the incubation of vital spirit as the serpent was thought to possess the power of calling the egg into action.[75] We may draw attention to the fact that the serpent worship of Rome continued in a flourishing state until the time of Constantine and that the virgins had to approach the sacred serpent in the grove of the Dodona Jove, with its food, in a state of absolute nudity.[76] In the folk-tales, myths and arts of the ancient world such instances of union of serpent and woman and the representations of half woman, half-serpent composite beings are found.

The tortoise, like the serpent, is a symbol of androgynity and immortality because of its tremendous power of retaining life in its limbs even after mutilation and decapitation. It is looked upon as a phallic symbol due to its protruding head and neck resembling the *glans penis* from a shell which was shaped like a sheath.[77] The tortoise is placed at the feet of Apollo, Mercury and Venus. In the *Śatapatha Brāhmaṇa*,[78] Prajāpati, when producing creatures, is said to have changed himself into a tortoise. Gopinatha Rao[79] points out how the fanciful rendering of the names of certain important places has sometimes given rise to a new god and his image. For instance, Kāñcīpuram (Conjeevaram) is known in ancient Tamil literature as Kacci and the phonetic similarity between this Tamil word and Sanskrit *Kacchapa* (meaning 'tortoise') has given rise to a new god and his image in Kāñcīpuram, namely, Kacchapeśvara where Viṣṇu in his tortoise incarnation is seen bathing a *Śivaliṅga*.[80]

The fish as a phallic symbol was common to many races of antiquity. Freud finds in fish a symbol of the male organ; but it—especially its head and mouth—has also been recognized as a female symbol.[81] Statues of the goddess Isis often show her with

74. Forlong, *Rivers of Life*, Vol. I, London, 1883, p. 223.
75. Scott, G.R., *op. cit.*, p. 85.
76. Cutner, H., *op. cit.*, pp. 176ff.; Scott, G.R., *op. cit.*, pp. 31ff.; Wake, C.S., *Serpent Worship*.
77. Marr, G.S., *Sex in Religion*, London, 1936, p. 32.
78. VII 5. 1. 5; *SBE*, Vol. 41, p. 390.
79. *EHI*, Vol. I, p. 42.
80. *Ibid.*, Pl. D.
81. *Encyclopaedia of World Art*, Vol. XII, 1st ed., p. 895; Cutner, H., *op. cit.*, pp. 185-86.

a fish on her head.[82] Dagon, the god of the Philistines mentioned in the *Old Testament*, was half-man and half-fish[83] resembling somewhat the *matsyakanyā* of Indian folklore. In the processions of the Bacchus-festival, the women carried the symbol of fish alongside the phallus.[84] In the marriage rites of many Indian sects and tribes, the fish is caught by the bride as an emblem of fertility.[85] The close association of the fish with Śiva is to be found in the *Kālikā Purāṇa*[86] where Kāma, after being restored to life installed the image of the fish-form of Śiva on the Maṇikūṭa mountain in Assam. In the topmost tableau of the Kailāsa temple at Ellora,[87] we have two fishes combining in arch-like fashion, amidst a lotus and three successive *liṅgas,* quite in keeping with the details of the sculpture to represent the creator-god.

Other Phallic Symbols

Mountains are symbolic of strength, vigour, vitality and everlasting quality and peaks of hills or mountains, roughly resembling a human phallus, were revered as the *Svayambhū-liṅga* or self-wrought phallus of Śiva since ancient times. We have already seen that due to his close association with hills and mountains, some Greek writers identified Śiva with the phallic god Dionysus.[88] In the mythology of the churning of the ocean for ambrosia, we have a suggestive image of Mount Mandara which formed the stick.[89] Although in the *Ṛgveda*[90] we have a direct appeal to the mountains, still the cult of mountains has been regarded as purely non-Aryan. The Muṇḍās, Santāls, Mohilīs, Hos and other agricultural Kol tribes of Eastern

82. *Loc. cit.*
83. Scott, G.R., *op. cit.*, p. 31.
84. *Ibid.*, p. 32.
85. Dikshit, S.K., *The Mother Goddess*, Poona, 1st ed., pp. 32-33; Thurston, E., *Castes and Tribes of S. India*, Vol. II, 1909, p. 306.
86. *Adh.*, 82, 50-52.
87. Mysore Gazetteer, Vol. II, pt. 1, pp. 156-57; Karmarkar, A.P., *The Religions of India*, Vol. I, 1957, p. 151.
88. McCrindle, J.W., *Ancient India as described in Classical Literature*, 1901, p. 64n.
89. Hopkins, E.W., *The Religions of India*, London, 1902, pp. 358ff.; Monier-Williams, M., *Brāhmaṇism and Hinduism*, London, 1891, p. 349.
90. VII. 35. 8.

India worship a mountain-god known as Morang Burū or Baḍ Pāhāḍ. Nearly all the deities of the Todas are hill-deities.[91] The Kandhs reserve their veneration for such mountain-gods like Sāru Pennū,[92] the Kurkūs for Dūngar Deo and so on.

The cult of stones and the origin of the belief that all sepulchral or upright stones consisting of menhirs, monoliths, dolmens, cairns and cromlechs, are not merely a memento of the dead and an abode of the indwelling spirit, but also a representative of the male and generative principle, are to be found in all parts of the globe from remote times.[93] Gilbert Murray[94] holds that the phallic monoliths on graves symbolise the renewal of life and the Greek god Hermes who is usually represented as a square post with a human head (like the *mukhaliṅga* of Śiva) apparently developed out of such upright stones. In India, the custom of erecting columns of standing stones to commemorate one's ancestors—which was undoubtedly a contribution of the Austrics and Dravidians—had something to do with the growth and development of the phallic cult.[95] The veneration entertained for the father of the family as the 'generator', led to the ancient custom of adoring the ancestor who founded or continued the family in the belief that he would exercise that power to grant an increase to his seed, if properly approached.[96] Thus, ancestor worship influenced phallic worship. H. Spencer[97] concludes that the cult of ancestors is the basis of all human religion or that "Gods are but ghosts of dead men, raised to a higher and finally to the highest power" and that the hero-cult is developed to its highest form into the cult of god. The upholders of the Spencerian hypothesis necessarily

91. *ERE*, Vol. XII, pp. 354-55.

92. *Ibid.*, Vol. II, p. 482.

93. Elliot Smith, G., (*The Ancient Egyptians and their Influence upon the Civilization of Europe*, London, 1911, p. 176) has made an attempt to prove that the impulse for the erection of the standing monoliths in Asia, Europe and Africa came from a single race starting from Egypt.

94. *Four Stages of Greek Religion*, 1st ed., p. 74.

95. Allan, G., *Evolution of the Idea of God*, pp. 73-74.

96. Westropp and Wake, *Phallism in Ancient Worship*, New Delhi, 1970, p. 36.

97. *Principles of Sociology*, Vol. I, 1877, pp.410ff.

may easily conclude that Śiva was originally a great human being raised to the status of god only in later times.

Ancestor worship was unknown to the Vedic Aryans, and the idea of transmigration was an Austric notion.[98] The non-Aryan tribes of Bihar, namely, the Kiṣāṇs and Bhūiyāns adore their ancestors under the name of Bīr or Vīra, 'hero';[99] the Kurubārus of Mysore revere their ancestors as Vīrika.[100] In western India, the Dhor Kāthkaris and Vaitis of Thāna, the Kunbis of the Konkan and others adore their ancestors in the shape of an unhusked coconut,[101] and coconut as a fertility symbol is very popular in many parts of India.[102] The custom of worshipping ancestor is very developed among the Khoṇḍs,[103] the Goṇḍs,[104] the Bhīls of Khāndesh,[105] and the Kharrias and Korwas of Eastern India.[106] In fact, the masses of Austric speakers of present India (that is, the Kol, Muṇḍā peoples), though somehow transformed outwardly, still retain a good deal of their original notions and set up on the ground the *Sasan-diris* or family burial stones.[107] The most typical cases of erecting such a mysterious upright conical stones on the memorial platform is found among the Khāsis,[108] Lushāis,[109] Kukis,[110] Mikirs,[111] and Nāgas[112] of North-Eastern India. Some scholars even venture to suggest that from the island of Java to Scandinavia everywhere these monoliths, and cairus testify the pre-

98. Chatterji, S.K., *Indianism and the Indian Synthesis*, 1962, pp. 202-04.
99. Dalton, E.T., *DEB*, pp. 132ff.
100. Buchanon, F.H., *A Journey from Madras*, Vol. I, Madras, 1870, p. 397.
101. *Bombay Gazetteer*, Vol. XIII, pp. 165, 182.
102. Frazer, J.G., *The Golden Bough*, Vol. I, p. 156.
103. Macpherson, *Memorials of Services*, p. 95.
104. Hislop, S., *Aboriginal Tribes of the Central Provinces*, p. 125.
105. Malcolm, J., *Memoirs of Central India*, Vol. I, 1824, pp. 516, 550.
106. Dalton, E.T., *op. cit.*, pp. 160, 229.
107. Chatterji, S.K., *Indo-Aryan and Hindi*, 1960, p. 39; *The History and Culture of the Indian People*, Vol. I, 1957, p. 163.
108. Dalton, E.T., *op. cit.*, pp. 55ff.
109. Shakespear J., *The Lushei Kuki Clans*, London, 1912, p. 85.
110. *Ibid.*, p. 165.
111. Stack, E., *The Mikirs*, London, 1908, p. 42.
112. Hodson, T.C., *The Nāga Tribes of Manipur*, London, 1911, p. 138.

valence of Śiva's worship.[113] It has also been supposed that Karaeng Lowe in South Celebes, who is usually figured under the form of *liṅga* and *yoni*, is no other than Śiva, imported via Java.[114]

Like the above, we have some other specimens of stones which have a phallic significance. The idea of fertility is the probable explanation of the use of the household grindstone at Hindu birth and marriage rites;[115] and among the Agamuḍiyan, a grindstone and a roller, representing Śiva and Śakti, is usually placed in the north-east corner at the wedding. Kosambi[116] believes that the *liṅga* might have originated out of the pestle-stone rolled about in the 'cup'. The potter's wheel similarly is looked as symbolic of the creative power because the clay is formed into a revolving lump, like a *liṅga* on the wheel, on it.[117]

The priapic form of boundary stones in India and elsewhere is probably due to a belief in its prophylactic value as protective talismans and symbols of the gods of generation.[118] The best examples of this are found in south India, and B.L. Rice[119] calls our attention how in Mysore these boundary stones are often adopted into the Śaiva cult by carving on them the symbols of Śiva.

Many theories have been advanced on perforated stones which are specially valued everywhere both as protective and fertility symbols.[120] In this context the ring-stones, found from both Harappa and Mohenjodaro, ranging from half an inch to nearly four feet in diameter, are notable. The mouth of a cave, a fissure in the rocks, a promontory of land projecting from a continent, and even the human tongue protruded from the mouth, are universally regarded as figures of the male or female organs, or both in union'.[121]

113. Mitra, R.L., *The Antiquities of Orissa*, Vol. I, 1961, pp. 224-25.
115. *ERE*, Vol. IX, p. 818.
116. *Myths and Reality*, Bombay, 1962, p. 139.
117. Thurston, E., *op. cit.*, Vol. IV, p. 191.
118. Dulaure, J.A., *op. cit.*, p. 220.
119. *Mysore*, Vol. I, London, 1879, p. 508.
120. Inman, *Ancient Faiths*, Vol. I, p. 46.
121. (Anonymous), *Phallism*, London, 1889, p. 16.

Pillars have been endowed with phallic significance by scholars since the days of Herodotus.[122] In the Bible, the pillar and pole, called respectively *maṣṣēbhāh* and *āsḥērāh*, are phalli.[123] The tops of the pillars standing before Phoenician and Punic shrines were often carved into a pyramidal shape, suggesting the top of a phallus.[124] It is alleged that many figured monuments of Buddhism have now become Hindu fetishes,[125] and that the Aśokan pillars are conversed into *liṅgas*.[126] In fact, Aśokan pillars at Araraj and Lauriya Nandangarh in the Champaran District, Bihar, are today worshipped as phallic emblems.[127] But the theory of the phallic cult from pillars has attracted so much attention that the high stump-shaped *liṅga* with a broken top in the Bhāskareśvara temple at Bhubaneswar, Orissa, was suspected by some as part of an Aśokan pillar.[128] But this has been proved to be wrong as a result of excavation.

How the cross originated is still an open question and the phallic significance of cross, like that of the *Śiva-liṅga*, has always been hotly contested by many writers who pour scorn on such attempts. But it is interesting to note that the cross was used as a symbol long before Christianity and how a straight line represented by the number I penetrating a circle, or a stick pushed through a ring and looked at Sideways, gives a perfect impression of cross.[129] Incidentally, we should note that in the *Śiva Purāṇa*[130] the unification of *bindu* (that is, dot over a letter representing the *anusvāra*, symbolic of the goddess) and *nāda* (that is the nasal sound represented by a semicircle, symbolic of Śiva) is outlined, and the fusion of *bindu* and *nāda*

122. Smith, W.R., *The Religion of the Semites*, London, 1894, pp. 456ff.
123. *ERE*, Vol. IX, p. 819.
124. *ERE*, Vol. XI, p. 877.
125. Barth, A., *The Religions of India*, p. 271.
126. *Corpus Ins. Ind.*, Vol. I, pp. 40-41.
127. Banerjea, J.N., 'Phallic Emblem in Ancient and Medieval India' in *JISOA*, Vol. III, 1935, p. 37.
128. Mitra, R.L., *The Antiquities of Orissa*, Vol. II, Calcutta, 1880, p.89. Devala Mitra (*JAS*, Vol. I, No. 1, 1959, 1-2) does not find any trace of Aśokan Brāhmī letters on a vertical portion of the *liṅga* as found by K.C. Panigrahi (*JAS*, Vol. XVII, 1951, p. 98).
129. Cutner, H., *op. cit.*, pp. 158, 160, 189.
130. Chap. XVI, 86-90.

is the phallic emblem of Śiva.[131] Sha Rocco[132] concludes that "the cross bespeaks evolution in religion. It is the product of time and the relic of the revered past. It begins with one thing and ends with another." In fact, the fundamental basis of Christianity was "more purely phallic than that of any other religious faith now existing".[133]

Fire-drills have received phallic interpretation. The mode of producing fire by wooden apparatus in the ancient world by rapidly rotating a piece of upright hard wood upon a softer wood lying on the ground is so suggestive that the upper and lower sticks, resembling male and female, have received sexual interpretation.[134] Thus wooden apparatus is called *araṇi* in India. It is interesting to note that even in the *Ṛgveda*[135] the rubbing of the two fire-sticks is represented as an act of generation because it resembles the phallus in the *yoni*. The upper wood made of aśvattha and the lower made of śamī are distinguished in the *Atharvaveda*,[136] *Śatapatha Brāhmaṇa*,[137] *Taittirīya Brāhmaṇa*[138] and *Kātyāyana Śrauta Sūtra*.[139] In the *Śatapatha Brāhmaṇa*,[140] the two sticks have been compared with Purūravas and Urvaśī. In the *Bṛhadāraṇyaka Upaniṣad*,[141] a great similarity is drawn between *araṇi* and human procreation. All the above details prove that the idea of procreation also affected or contaminated the thought of the Vedic Aryans, though they hated phallus-worship. Definitely it does not prove that the origin of the *liṅga* is to be found in the *araṇi*, for the phallus-worship was already very popular with the people of the Harappan civilization, which antedates the Vedic.

131. *Ancient Indian Tradition and Mythology*, Vol. I (*Śiva Purāṇa*), 1970, p. 103.
132. *The Masculine Cross and Ancient Sex Worship*, London, 1898, p. 6.
133. Marr, G.S., *op. cit.*, p. 27.
134. *ERE*, Vol. IX, p. 819.
135. III. 29. 1-6. See *SBE*, Vol. XLVI, p. 302.
136. VI. 11. 1.
137. III. 4.1. 22; XI. 5.1. 15.
138. I. 1, 3, 11.
139. IV. 7. 22; V. 1, 30.
140. III. 4. 1. 22.
141. VI. 4. 22.

The hand was euphemistic symbol of the phallus. The ancients had two forms of what antiquarians have named the phallic hand, one in which the middle finger (*digitus impudicus* or *infamis* to the Romans) was expanded at length signifying the *membrum virile* and the thumb and other fingers doubled up representing the testicles; while in the other the whole hand was closed, but the thumb, resembling the phallic symbol of the libido, protrudes between the first and the second fingers.[142] In the *Śiva Purāṇa*,[143] we have the recommendation of the worship of the phallic emblem on the thumb. In the *Jātaka*, Sakka rendered Śīlavatī, the favourite wife of Okkāka, pregnant of the future Bodhisattva with a touch of his thumb.[144]

And in this way the story of the phallic cult goes all over the world. The phallic significance of the symbol was not always understood because religions in the ancient world were packed with esoteric practices, allowed to and understood by only genuine initiates.[145] An inquiry into antiquity, as represented by the beliefs and customs of the Anglo-Saxons, Assyrians, Babylonians, Chinese, Egyptians, Gauls, Greeks, Hebrews, Indians, Japanese, Phoenicians, Romans and others and into modern faiths still current among them, shows that the religion of the later days has tried not only to suppress or regulate or even to eliminate every type of phallism, but has painted gods as produced full-formed, independently of sex. It is the same story everywhere because men, considered collectively, are at all times the same animals. The story of phallus worship in India and the representation of Śiva in his phallic form is thus not an isolated and unique feature of the history of India, but a part of the overall story of mankind.

142. Payne Knight, R., *op. cit.*, Vol. II, pp. 65-66.

143. Chap. XI. 34; *Ancient Indian Tradition and Mythology*, (*Śiva-Purāṇa*), Vol. I, 1970, p. 70.

144. Cowell, E.B., ed., *Jātaka*, Vol. V, 1907, p. 141.

145. Cutner, H., *op. cit.*, p. 196.

(ii) Phallicism and Śaivism

In the Śaiva temples and sanctuaries, the most sacred object of worship is the *Śiva-liṅga* which is enshrined in the *garbhagṛha* and the anthropomorphic figures of the deity are usually carved in different parts of the temples more or less as accessory figures. Little is known about the antiquity of the custom of worshipping only *liṅga* in exclusion of the image; but this is traceable to the early Gupta period as indicated by the Mathura stone inscription[1] of the Gupta year 61 (381 A.D.). A hazy beginning of the association of phallicism and Śaivism is to be found in the Harappa civilization where the proto-Śiva was perhaps worshipped both in his anthropomorphic and phallic forms. That the cults of Śiva and the *Liṅga* have been inherited from the Harappans is further reinforced by the prevalence of the bull cult in the Indus valley.

That phallus worship is quite repugnant to the Vedic religion becomes quite clear from the references in a curt and deprecatory manner to a class of people called *Śiśnadevas* in the *Ṛgveda*.[2] The interpretation of the epithet as 'persons addicted to sexual pleasures' etc. by Yāṣka,[3] Sāyaṇa and others,[4] is today rightly called in question by most scholars who interpret it as phallus-worshippers. In fact, the opprobrious terms *mūradeva*, *avrata*,

1. *Ep. Ind.* Vol. XXI, pp. 1ff.

cf. Joshi, N.P., *Catalogue of the Brahmanical Sculptures in the State Museum, Lucknow*, Part I, Lucknow, 1972, figs. 24-27.

2. VII. 21. 5; X. 99. 3.

3. *Nirukta*, IV. 19.

4. Muir, J., *OST*, Vol. IV, p. 409; Macdonell and Keith, *Vedic Index*, Vol. II, p. 382.

Siddhantashastree, R.K., (*Śaivism Through The Ages*, Delhi, 1975) opines, "The popular idea among the modern educationists that Śiva, originally was a non-Aryan deity, and that the term *Śivaliṅga* stands for the phallus of the God, are belied by innumerable evidences found even in the earliest portions of the Vedic texts...". p. vii.

Jash, P., (*History of Śaivism*, Calcutta, 1974) points out that "the *liṅga* has nothing to do with the Phallus in its realistic sense. " p. 5.

Kramrisch, S., (*The Presence of Śiva*, Princeton Univ. Press, 1981) observes, "The *liṅga* is the phallus of Śiva. Śiva is in the phallus. God resides in whatever is part of God. The erect *liṅga* is full of seed. Śiva is the carrier of the seed. At will, he may release or restrain it." p. 170.

adeva, anāsa, mṛdhavāk, yātu, yātudhāna, etc., were extravagantly used in the *Ṛgveda* most probably to denote the *Śiśnadevas*, the pre-Aryan phallus-worshippers of the Indus valley culture. However, even when phallicism came to be intimately associated with Śaivism, the orthodox section of the society who upheld the original Vedic tradition were at first tardy in its recognition, for no clear reference to the phallic emblem for a part of their ritualism is found in the later Vedic and *Sūtra* literatures. It is noteworthy that although Upamanyu in the *Mahābhārata*[5] inculcates the *liṅga* cult, still Śiva did not appear to him either in his ithyphallic or *liṅga* form—a fact which perhaps indicates that phallism was as yet loosely associated with Śaivism.

Although phallus worship was deprecated in the *Ṛgveda*, still in one verse[6] we find an allusion to phallism as it refers to the joy expressed by Āsaṅga's wife Śāśvatī describing her husband's organ in seeing her husband restored to full sexual powers as a result of the austerities practised by her. To Hopkins this verse seems to have crept in by mistake.[7] But this opinion is open to criticism. We have already seen when we discussed *araṇi* (see the Section on *Phallus Worship in Ancient India and Outside*, p. 122) how phallic symbols sometimes influenced the ideas of the Vedic Aryans.

The *liṅga* worship does not appear to have been popular at the time of Patañjali (second century B.C.), for, in his commentary on the Sūtra of Pāṇini[8] (fifth century B.C.), the word used in respect of Śiva is *pratikṛti* or likeness and there is no reference to the symbolic representation of that god. R.G. Bhandarkar[9] believes that the worship of *liṅga* was introduced in India after the time of Wema Kadphises, because, on the reverse of his coins, there is both theriomorphic and anthropomorphic figure of Śiva but not the phallic emblem. However, in view of the discoveries of the Harappa civilization and

5. XII. 14. 231-33.
See De, S.K., 'Sects and Sectarian Worship in the Mbh.' in *Our Heritage*, Vol. I, 1953, pp. 9-10.
6. *RV*, VIII. 1, 34.
7. Hopkins, E.W., *Religions of India*, London, 1902, p. 251.
8. V. 3. 99.
9. *VSMRS*, p. 115.

numismatic evidences of the pre- and post-Christian period Bhandarkar's opinion is no longer acceptable.

Marshall[10] is at a loss to explain how, having once worshipped Śiva and the *liṅga* as in the Harappa civilization, the people ceased to do so in the Vedic period, but returned to the worship later. It should be noted that the dark and suggestive realism of the phallus did not find favour with the Vedic Aryans. But a commingling of blood and culture of the Aryans and non-Aryans led ultimately to its recognition although the realism of the *liṅga* was suppressed under the gradual conventionalization of its outward form.[11] The process started in the early Gupta period as the shape of the inscribed *Śiva-liṅga* of the Gupta year 117, corresponding to 436 A.D., found at Karamdāṇḍā[12] (Faizabad District, U.P.) is a pointer in this respect. Although the realistic representation of the *liṅga* was not altogether forgotten even in the Gupta Age, still, with the passage of time, the process of conventionalization was carried out to such a perfection that its original phallic character was forgotten and some scholars like Havell[13] wrongly thought that the Buddhist worship of the votive *stūpa* is absorbed in Hinduism in the form of the worship of *liṅga* by the Śaivites.

In the Foote collection of the Madras Museum, we have a phallus of highly realistic shape made of pale gneiss stone, which, according to R.B. Foote,[14] is of neolithic origin. Some other specimens of neolithic times, made of clay, are also to be found from various parts of Gujarat.[15] But these surface collections cannot be specifically dated. In one of the early punch-marked coins, Theobald[16] has found the phallic emblem of Śiva But this does not seem to be accurate. Cunningham has interpreted one of the three symbols on the coins of the so-called Mitra dynasty of Pañcāla, as a *liṅga* guarded by two

10. *MIC*, Vol. I, pp. 111-12.
11. Banerjea, J.N., *Religion in Art and Archaeology*, 1st ed., p. 66.
12. *Ep. Ind.*, Vol. X, pp. 71-72; *JRASB*, Vol. V, p. 458, pl. XIX.
13. *The Ideals of Indian Art*, London, 1911, p. 87.
14. *Indian Prehistoric and Protohistoric Antiquities*, 1916, p. 61.
15. *Ibid.*, p. 139.
16. *JASB*, 1890, pt. I, pp. 193, 200; Pl. X, 186; XI, 263-64.

snakes.[17] But this is also doubtful. A somewhat realistic representation of *liṅga*, in close association with tree, appears on an uninscribed cast coin (provenance unknown) which, according to Allan,[18] is definitely a 'liṅgam on square pedestal'. The central device on a very fine large temple seal, discovered by Spooner at Basarh,[19] represents, though in a schematic way, the somewhat realistic *liṅga* on a wide base and the outline of a stouter tree with spreading base.

A black polished small stone *liṅga* wrapped in fragments of cloth and with two wire rings and a similar one with *Panivattam* —as is used by the Liṅgāyats—have been excavated from Peddamudiyam.[20] The excavations at Lauriyā-Nandangarh[21] have yielded a terracotta matrix representing the *Śiva-liṅga* which, stylistically, is related to the Śuṅga period. The figure of *liṅga* with a crescent on its top and flanked by female attendants on either side is found on a seal discovered at Nālandā.[22] A circular terracotta seal, found from Rājghāṭ and now in the Bhārat Kalābhavan (Varanasi),[23] with indistinct legend in Gupta characters bears a *Śiva-liṅga* flanked by a combined trident-axe on left and a double-faced thunderbolt on right. Again, we have the reference to a stucco *liṅga* figure on the circular wall of the Maniyārmaṭha at Rājgīr.[24] Bloch, who unearthed this unique conventionalized colossal *liṅga* covered with a garland of flowers, standing on circular base, moulded in the shape of a flower pot, is inclined to regard its form and details being suggested or influenced by the Buddhist stūpas in adjoining areas.[25]

17. *JASB*, 1880, pt. I, pp. 21-28.
To Rapson (*Coins of the Andhras and the Western Kṣatrapas*, p. CLXXVI, pl. VIII, fig. G. p. 1) it is a Naga symbol. To D.R. Bhandarkar (*ASIAR*, 1913-14, p. 211) it is the *Kaustubha-maṇi*.
18. *Catalogue of Coins of Ancient India in the British Museum*, p. 85.
19. *ARASI*, 1913-14, p. 142, No. 369, pl. XLVIII.
20. *Ibid.*, 1905-06, p. 130, Nos. 8 and 9.
21. *Ibid.*, 1935-36, p. 64, Pl. XXIIe.
22. *MASI*, No. 66, p. 51.
23. Banerjea, J.N., *DHI*, p. 188.
24. *MASI*, No. 58, p. 34.
25. *ARASI*, 1905-06, pp. 104-05.

A very interesting and much discussed realistic representation of the *liṅga* with the figure of Śiva standing on a crouching *yakṣa*, discovered by Gopinatha Rao[26] at Guḍimallam, near Renigunta in Andhra Pradesh, throws considerable light on the point of association of phallicism and Śaivism. The artist perhaps felt it necessary to carve the figure of Śiva on the huge *liṅga* to minimise any doubt regarding its nature which proves that the intimate connection between phallicism and Śaivism may not have yet been definitely established in the area. But scholars differ about the date of this *liṅga*.[27] The *mukhaliṅgas*, that is, the *liṅgas* which show on their *Rudra-* or *Pūjā-bhāgas* one or more human faces standing for one or more aspects of Śiva, illustrate the close and intimate association of Śaivism and phallicism. We have reserved a fuller discussion of the topic in the Section on Art.

The assimilation of phallicism with Śaivism is perhaps due to the previous association of the Father God with that of the Mother Goddess. The conception of the Mother Goddess, namely, Ambikā, Durgā, Kālī, etc., though not found in the *Ṛgveda*, is to be found in later Vedic texts. In fact, to the higher class people of the early Vedic society, who were primarily responsible for the texts, the worship of the Mother Goddess does not seem to be popular, although later on she was recognised as subordinate to Śiva. Barth[28] rightly observes that, though the personification of Śakti is not peculiar to Śaivism, it is in Śaivism that the ideas centering round Śakti have found a soil most favourable for their expansion, and that they have been distorted into the most monstrous developments. The close connection of Śiva and Śakti ultimately helped the development of the phallic cult and its ultimate absorption by Śaivism. Although we have the Father God and Mother Goddess in both iconic and aniconic forms in the Harappa civilization, still the joint symbols of *liṅga* and *yoni* are not

26. *EHI*, Vol. II, pt. 1, pp. 55-71.

27. Gopinatha Rao (*loc. cit.*) assigns it to 1st century B.C.; D.R. Bhandarkar (*Carmichael Lectures*, 1921, p. 20) to 4th century A.D.; Longhurst (*MASI*, No. 40, p. 24) to 8th or 9th century A.D.

28. *Religions of India*, London, 1921, pp. 199-200.

found in the Indus valley.[29] It is only in course of time that the *liṅga* was united with the *yoni*, representing the two great generative principles of the universe.

In the Vedic literature Rudra's association with the vegetable kingdom and the whole animal world is perhaps due to a deliberate tendency to see in him the reproductive power of nature. The Mother Goddess, worshipped by the non-Aryans, is similarly associated with the vegetation world which is well emphasized in her *Śākambharī*[30] aspect and in the *Navapatrikā* ceremony in later days. The nuclei of this vegetation aspect of both Śiva and the Devī can be traced back to the Harappa civilization. In fact, a great deal of the Purāṇic and Epic myth, legend, tradition and semi-history of Śiva's association with the Vegetation and necessarily with the Mother, which ultimately helped the assimilation of phallism and Śaivism, is of pre-Aryan origin, later on adopted by the Aryans with the gradual Aryanization of the people among whom these traditions grew. The story that Upamanyu's unnamed mother first revealed the phallic cult of Śiva to her son, as we find in the *Mahābhārata*, need not necessarily imply that the cult arose in a matriarchal society.[31] In fact, what we find in the epic is the result of a prolonged operation of various influences of unascertained origin.

While commenting on Pāṇini's *sūtra*,[32] Patañjali described the exclusive worshippers of Śiva as *Śiva-bhāgavata* denoting those who carried an iron lance (*āyaḥśūlika*). In this context we should note that the Mother Goddess is popularly known as *Bhagavatī*, that is, a deity possessing *bhaga* or *yoni*. Sircar[33] suggests that the epithet *Bhagavatī* "originally indicated the female deity who was thought to have given birth to all creatures, and that the epithet *Bhagavat*, applied to Śiva and other gods, is merely a masculine form afterwards coined on the basis of

29. Marshall (*MIC*, Vol. I, pp. 59ff.) observes that "the *liṅga* and *yoni* worship may have been associated then, as they were later under the aegis of Śaivism".

30. *Mārkaṇḍeya Purāṇa*, *Devīmāhātmya*, 91, 48-49.

31. De, S.K., in *Our Heritage*, Vol. I, 1953, p. 10.

32. V. 2, 76.

33. 'The Śākta Pīṭhas' in *JRASB*, Vol. XIV, No. 1, Letters, 1948, p. 8.

Bhagavatī". The suggestion of Hopkins,[34] Oppert[35] and others that Śaivite phallic worship was due rather to late Greek influence has been proved to be wrong now by the fact that Hinduism borrowed not simply the cult of the *liṅga* from the pre-Aryans, but even the name of it is of Austric origin.

Rudra's identification with Agni in the *Ṛgveda*,[36] *Atharvaveda*,[37] *Taittirīya Saṁhitā*,[38] and *Śatapatha Brāhmaṇa*[39] might have facilitated his association with the Mother Goddess, as Agni was connected with a large number of female deities, and this ultimately paved the way for the assimilation of the phallic cult with Rudra-Śiva. In the *Muṇḍaka Upaniṣad*[40] Kālī and Karālī (the well-known names of the Great Mother and consort of Śiva in later days) are mentioned as two of the seven tongues of Agni.

Whether the proto-Śiva of Mohenjodaro was associated with the mountains, we do not know. But the close association of Rudra as *Girīśa* and his spouse as *Pārvatī* with hills or mountains—the peaks of which roughly resemble *liṅga*—might have been another helping factor in the coalescence of phallicism and Śaivism. An extremely realistic phallic emblem of Śiva shown above or beside a hill on some terracotta seals from Bhiṭā[41] can be dated in between second and third centuries B.C., if not earlier. In another oval seal from the same place and of the same design we have the legend in northern Gupta characters, *Kālañjarabhaṭṭārakasya*,[42] that is, 'of the lord of Kālañjara'. Cunningham[43] points out that Kālañjara is the name of a hill in Bundelkhand, the favourite resort of the Śaiva *tapasvins* since early days and mentioned in the *Mahābhārata* and *Matsyapurāṇa*. A pointed oval temple seal, discovered by T. Bloch[44]

34. *The Religions of India*, London, 1902, p. 414.
35. *Original Inhabitants of India*, p. 381.
36. II. 1.
37. VII. 87.
38. V. 4, 3; V. 5, 7.
39. VI. 1. 3.
40. *Vide* Muir, J., *OST*, Vol. IV, p. 425.
41. *ARASI*, 1911-12, p. 49, No. 15 and 16, pl. XI, fig. 8.
42. *Loc. cit.*
43. *ASR*, Vol. XXI, pp. 20ff.
44. *ARASI*, 1903-04, p. 110, No. 30.

from Basarh, bears on it *liṅga* and *yoni* and the legend Āmrātakeśvara, that is, the lord of Āmrātaka, which is the name of a mountain. Hiuen Tsang mentioned a great mountain peak of Gandhāra (modern Peshawar District, Pakistan) as a natural image of Maheśvara's spouse Bhīmādevī.[45]

Marshall[46] has drawn our attention to the so-called 'chessmen' pillars of Dimapur which are supposed to be memorial stones erected in memory of local heroes. "That these chessmen columns", to quote Marshall, "were originally phallic monuments is suggested by the fact that, in the, non-Aryan districts of the South, the custom still obtains, or did so until recently, of erecting *liṅgas* on the graves of local heroes".[47] An inscribed sculpture found at Bhiṭā (near Allahabad in U.P.), now in the Lucknow Museum, dated on palaeographical grounds in the first century B.C., and described by R.D. Banerji[48] as one of the earliest forms of the *liṅga*, is important for more than one reasons. The top of it, according to Banerji, is shaped as the two-armed human bust and below this are four defaced human heads, one at each corner. There is a phallus mark incised in deep lines below two of the heads. It contains a two-line Brāhmī inscription :—

1. *Khajahutiputānāṃ la* [liṃ as suggested by Benerji] *go pratiṭhāpito*
2. *Vāsēṭhi-putēna Nāgasirinā piyatā* [*ṁ*] *d* [*e*] *vatā*

45. Watters, *On Yuan Chwang*, Vol. I, pp. 221-22.
46. *MIC*, Vol. p. 60.
47. *Loc. cit.*

Dhaky, M.A., ('The Ākāṣaliṅga Finial', in *Aribus Asiae*, 36 : 4 (1974), p. 307 equates the *Ākāśaliṅga* with Space *liṅga*. But Kramrisch thinks that "This *ākāśaliṅga* does not consist of space. On the contrary, it is a soild shape and functions as the finial of the tower (śikhara) on Śiva temples (*Agni purāṇa* 102 : 4 it can be found on such temples in Orissa and Andhra Pradesh of the seventh to tenth centuries. It rises high in space directly above the *liṅga* on the ground in the inermost sanctuary, the womb chamber (*garbha-gṛha*) of the temple."—*The Presence of Śiva*, p. 176.

But to Siddhantashastree, R. K., (*Śaivism Through the Ages*, Delhi, 1975, p. vii) "The fact that the term Liṅga stands for the all-pervading *Ākāśa* (ether), a representation of the all-pervading Supreme spirit is found in the Purāṇa literature, and is quoted in this book with apt interpretation."

48. *ARASI*, 1909-10, pp. 147-48, pl. LIV.

and translated as "The *liṅga* of (i.e. worshipped by) the sons of Khajahuti, was dedicated by Nāgasiri, the son of Vāseṭhi. May the deity be pleased".

But this interpretation was called in question by Bloch,[49] who maintained that the word was *lago* of uncertain meaning and not *liṅga* signifying the phallus of Śiva. D. R. Bhandarkar[50] upheld Bloch's objections and doubted whether the Bhiṭā sculpture was a Śiva-liṅga at all and even wished to date it at least two centuries later than the one adopted by Banerji. According to Bloch 'the *liṅga* of the sons of Khajahuti', as read by Banerji, would make no sense at all. But we cannot support Bloch's objection in this regard because the practice of erecting phallic stones to keep or honour the memory of one's ancestor is common not only with the peoples of ancient India but also with many other ancient peoples of the world. Grant Allan[51] says, "on many grave stones of early date, a phallus marked the male sex of the occupant, and the stone being regarded as the ancestor of the family, it is not unnatural that early men should sometimes carve it into a phallic shape".

Gopinatha Rao,[52] Coomaraswamy,[53] Saraswati[54] and a host of other scholars have identified the Bhiṭā sculpture as a *pañca-mukha Śiva-liṅga* of the pre-Christian period. Sircar thinks that it cannot be merely a memorial pillar. The sentence *prī-yatām Devatā* suggests that a deity was mentioned in the previous sentence. However, even if the Bhiṭā specimen was not '*liṅga* of the sons of Khajahuti' or originally a *Śiva-liṅga*, still, some sort of sanctity was attached to it as it was installed by Nāgasiri to please the deity who was no other than Śiva, whose *liṅga* was

49. *Loc. cit.*, R.D. Banerji took note of this opinion in the same article.
50. *Carmichael Lectures*, Vol. III, 1921, pp. 20, 40-43.
51. *The Evolution of the Idea of God*, 1st ed., p. 68.
52. *EHI*, Vol. II, Pt. 1, pp. 63-64.
53. *HIIA*, p. 32.
54. *A Survey of Indian Sculpture*, 1957, p. 129.

Banerjea ('The phallic Emblem in Ancient and Medieval India' in *JISOA*, Vol. III, 1935, pp. 40ff.) endorsed Fuhrer's explanation of the Bhiṭā sculpture as 'the capital of a column' and interpreted *lago* as a possible contraction of the word *laguḍa*. The five faces on it were explained by Banerjea as symbolising the departed 'sons of Khajahuti' to commemorate whom the 'column' was erected by Nāgasiri, the son of Vāseṭhi.

usually placed over the mounds entombing the ashes or bodies of the departed saints, teachers, kings or heroes. The Mathura stone pillar inscription of 380 A.D. records the installation of two *Śiva-liṅgas* named Kapileśvara and Upamiteśvara, by one Uditācārya to consecrate the memory of two departed ācāryas, Kapila and Upamitā.[55] It also records that *gurvāyatana* or teacher's shrine denoted the place, where the memorials in the form of *Śiva-liṅgas* for the departed *gurus* hearing their names as well as their portraits were enshrined.[56]

In many temples of Śiva in south India, human bones and ashes have been found at some depth below the floor on which the *Śiva-liṅga* is placed.[57] This may suggest that the original shrine was erected over the relics of some saints or potentates. To cite two examples of later days, Śaiva shrines were built over the burial-ground of the Cola king Āditya I and over the spot where the father of Gaṅga Rājāditya was buried.[58] In fact, the phallic cult became fused with the cult of Śiva with the gradual recognition of the concept of Śiva as the Father God.

(iii) The Liṅga Cult in Early Indian Literature

The principal idea underlying the cult of *liṅga*—the symbolical form of the generative power of Śiva—in its primitive aspect is purely phallic in character. We have already seen how this phallic symbol of Śiva appears, both in its form and name, to be of Austric or proto-Australoid origin and how there are evident analogies between *liṅga* and *lāṅgala*.[1] In the

55. *Ep. Ind.*, Vol. XXI., pp. 1ff.
The name of *Śiva-liṅgas* ending with the word *īśvara* are more or ess found from all parts of India. *Cf. Ep. Ind.*, Vol. XXVIII, p. 182, Note 4.
56. *Ep. Ind.*, Vol. XXI, pp. 1ff.
57. *Annual Report, Arch.* Dep. S. *Circle*, 1915-16, p. 29.
58. Hultzsch, E., ed., *S. Indian Inscriptions*, Vol. III, pt. 1, 1900-1903, Madras, pp. 26ff.

1. Bagchi, P.C., *Pre-Aryan and Pre-Dravidian in India*, Calcutta, 1929, pp. 10-11.

Ṛgveda[2] and other Vedic texts,[3] *lāṅgala* is the regular word for 'plough', but *liṅga* in the sense of 'phallus' is not perhaps used. Many of the *Ṛgvedic* deities, both male and female, had *liṅgas* of their own and the four entire hymns[4] dedicated to them are perhaps *Ṛgvedic* riddles. In the first Chapter of the *Kauśika Sūtra* (belonging to the Atharvaveda) the word *liṅga* is also used in relation to several deities,[5] as in Yāska's *Nirukta*[6] Viśvaliṅga is found to represent the Viśvedevas.

We noted earlier how the *Śiśnadevas*, the non-Aryan phallus-worshippers, are mentioned twice in a deprecatory manner in the *Ṛgveda*.[7] The natural and suggestive realism of the phallic emblem does not seem to be accepted first in our literature, especially among those whose thoughts were reflected in our early literature. But the beliefs and practices of a large section of people and the admission of Śiva to the Brāhmaṇical pantheon ultimately led to the *liṅga* cult being given a convenient position in our literature. In the late *Taittirīya Āraṇyaka*,[8] we have the reference to *liṅga* in the context of the worship of Śiva. Max Müller thinks that *liṅga* worship is recognised in the context of the Mahāvīra pot in the Pravargya of the *Śatapatha Brāhmaṇa*[9] though in a faint and isolated manner. R. G. Bhandarkar[10] has found 'an allusion to physical fact of the *liṅga* and *yoni* connected together' in the *Śvetāśvatara Upaniṣad*[11] when it describes in two verses the god Īśāna as presiding over every *yoni* and over all forms and *yonis*. But the above evidences are not conclusive. It is only in the *Kṛṣṇa-Upamanyu Saṁvāda* of the *Mahābhārata*,[12] adjudged as late by Indologists, that we

2. IV. 57. 4.
3. Macdonell and Keith, *Vedic Index*, Vol. II, 1958, p. 231.
4. *RV*, IV. 13; IV. 14; X. 161 and X. 184.

Chakravorty, A.K., 'The Liṅga-daivata Hymns : A Rigvedic Riddle ?' in *IHQ*, Vol. 38, 1962, pp. 226ff.

5. *Loc. cit.*
6. Chapter XII. 40.
7. VII. 21, 5; X. 99, 3.
8. X. 16.
9. *SBE*, Vol. 44, p. xlvii.
10. *VSMRS*, p. 114, note 1.
11. IV. 11. and V. 2.
12. XII. 14. 231-33.

find for the first time unmistakable evidence of the worship of Śiva in his phallic form. It is expressly mentioned by Upamanyu that Mahādeva is the only deity whose organ of generation is worshipped even by gods like Brahmā, Viṣṇu and others and "that one should know everything which is male to be Īśāna and all that is female to be Umā; for this whole world, movable and immovable, is pervaded by [these], two bodies."[13] The *Liṅga Purāṇa*[14] exalts Śiva in the *liṅga* form as above all gods and as containing everything.

However, our philosophy has denied altogether the phallic character of the *liṅga*.[15] The term '*liṅga*' is interpreted as a symbol or source of creativity that is invisible and unmanifested[16]. Śaṅkarācārya in his *Saundaryalaharī* declares that Śiva can create only when united with Śakti, otherwise he is unable even to move.[17] The Āgamic texts extol the inextricable nature of the conjoint *Puruṣa-Prakṛti* aspect. In fact, according to the general teaching of the Tantras, the human organism is a microcosm, a mini-universe, which contains a large number of minute channels (*nāḍi*) and connected with these channels are six great centres (*cakra*) of the occult force, described as so many lotuses, one above the other. Among these six centres, Brahman in the form of a *liṅga* is the lowest and the most important centre, and coiled round this *liṅga*, like a serpent, lies the Śakti called *Kuṇḍalinī*.[18] All the above interpretations were perhaps due to the impact of the Sāṅkhya doctrine on the *liṅga* cult, and phallic worship came to be clothed with a mystic and philosophical meaning.

13. *Mbh.*, XIII. 19, 78:
puṁliṅgaṁ sarvam Īśānaṁ strīliṅgaṁ viddhi cāpy umāṁ |
dvābhyāṁ tanubhyāṁ vyāptaṁ hi carācaram idaṁ jagat ||

14. II. xlvi. 13-21.

15. *Cf.* Wilson, H.H., *Works*, Vol. VI, p. lxix;
Monier-Williams, *Brāhmaṇism and Hinduism*, London, 1891, pp. 83, 90f.; Eliot, C., *Hinduism and Buddhism*, Vol. II, pp. 142ff.

16. Agrawala, V.S., *Śiva-Mahādeva*, 1st ed., p. 3.

17. See Srinivasan, T.N., *A Handbook of South Indian Images*, Tirupati, 1954, p. 66.

18. Sastri, Mahadeva, *Yoga Upaniṣads*, pp. 505ff., 518ff.; see Pūrṇānanda Svāmī, *Śrītattvacintāmaṇi* in Vidyāratna Tārānātha's *Tantrik Texts*, Vol. II, 1913.

Though a casual reference is found in the *Ṛgveda*,[19] where Rudra is prayed for the increase in offspring, still in the Vedic literature he was not merely invoked for procreative purposes as we find in the *Mahābhārata* and the *Purāṇas*. In the *Kūrma Purāṇa*[20] we see Viṣṇu worshipping the *Śiva-liṅga* as the great generative power for obtaining a son. Kṛṣṇa, as we find in the *Mahābhārata*,[21] not only obtains a son for his wife Jāmbavatī, after practising rigorous asceticism and by the grace of Śiva; but in the *Kūrma Purāṇa*[22] he recommends the *liṅga* cult and explains its origin. Drupada in the *Udyogaparvan*[23] and Somadatta in the *Droṇaparvan*[24] of the *Mahābhārata* worship the phallus of Śiva mainly for the boon of a son. However, this god of generation subdued sexual passion and reduced Kāma, the god of sexual love, to ashes.[25] Hence, some scholars[26] could venture to interpret the phallic epithets *Ūrdhvaretāḥ*, *Ūrdhvaliṅga*, *Mahāliṅga*, *Mahāśepho nagna*, *Sthāṇu* (that is, the *liṅga* which is perpetually fixed), *liṅgādhyakṣa* etc. ascribed to him in the *Mahābhārata* and the *Purāṇas* as denoting sexual restraint or symbolic of abstention from creative activity. But, as we know, Rudra-Śiva is a phallic deity and the phallic nature of the *liṅga* cult is evidenced in early Indian literature.

Regarding the origin of the *liṅga* cult we have two different traditions. First, Śiva, either voluntarily or due to the curse of the sages, discarded his organ of generation. Secondly, the *liṅga* appeard independently as a blazing pillar of cosmic fire.

The *Skanda Purāṇa*[27] relates a story how on seeing the naked Śiva, who came to Dāruvana for begging alms, the minds of the Ṛṣis's wives became disturbed and agitated with the pain of love and all started following him. Later on, the Ṛṣis cursed

19. II. 33. 1.
20. I. 2. 5.
21. XIII. 14-17.
22. I.26.
23. *Mbh.*, V. 188f.
24. *Ibid.*, VII. 144f.
25. Kālidāsa, *Kumārasaṁbhava*, IV. 42.
26. See, Bhattacharyya, H., *The Foundations of Living Faiths*, Vol. I, Calcutta, 1938, pp. 226-27; Munshi, K.M., *Somnath the Shrine Eternal*, 1951, pp. 9-10; Hazra, R.C., 'Further Light on the God of the Famous Mohenzodaro Seals' in *Our Heritage*, Vol. XVII, Part 1, Jan-June, 1969, pp. 18-19.
27. *Nāgarakhaṇḍa*, I. 22ff. VII. 1.

Śiva for enticing their women-folk and eventually his *liṅga* fell down. The same story is repeated in the *Saura Purāṇa.*[28] In the *Liṅga Purāṇa*[29] Śiva went to Dāruvana forest not for begging alms but for examining the philosophical knowledge attained by the Ṛṣis residing there, and it was afterwards that the above event took place. The *Vāmana Purāṇa*[30] related how, after the loss of Satī, Śiva, being influenced by Cupid, roamed about naked and reached Dāruvana in an amatory mood.

The *Padma Purāṇa* however, popularised a different kind of story. In one portion[31] it records the curse of Sāvitrī to Śiva, as the latter had attended the second marriage of Brahman with Gāyatrī, saying that Śiva would miss his member as a result of the curse of the sages. However, when the latter were appeased, Sāvitrī said that the *liṅga* thus fallen down would be worshipped by mankind. Another portion of the same *Purāṇa*[32] discloses the curse pronounced by Bhṛgu. To discover which one of the triad was the greatest, a number of sages headed by Bhṛgu, came to Mount Kailāsa to visit Śiva, but they were prevented from entering into the interior of the abode by the janitor Nandin on the ground that his master was then in company of his spouse and not at leisure to talk to them. Thus insulted, Bhṛgu condemned Śiva and cursed him to take on the shape of the generative organ to be worshipped only by heretics.

The *Mahābhārata*[33] and the *Vāyu Purāṇa*[34] relate that requested by Brahmadeva to create living beings, Śiva proceeded to perform austerities and remained under the primeval water for such a long time that Brahmadeva produced another creator who performed his task. At last Mahādeva rose out of the water and seeing that new beings had already been created, he became very angry, discarded his organ of generation as no more necessary and struck it into the ground. In this connection

28. 69. 53.
29. *Pūrvārdha*, Adh. 29.
30. Chap. VI.
31. *Padma Purāṇa, Sṛṣṭikhaṇḍa*, 17.
32. *Uttarakhaṇḍa*.
33. *Sauptikaparvan*, Ch. 17, 21-23.
34. Chap. X.

we should also point out that Yāgeśvara—a unique representation of the crystal phallus form of Śiva as we find in the *Daśakumāracarita*[35]—is described in the *Naiṣadha-carita* of Śriharṣa as a water-deity lying invisible in the waters.[36] Kapāṭeśvara Śiva is described in Maṅkha's *Śrīkaṇṭhacarita*[37] and in the *Jñānārṇava Tantra*[38] as the great *liṅga* residing in the waters.

It is perhaps undeniable that all the above tales, put together, form a senseless chaotic mass. However, a great link with Egyptian mythology is to be found where Osiris, as the principle of life, is often thus represented.. Isis, the wife of Osiris, could not find her husband's missing member after his murder and at last she caused a wooden surrogate to be made which is greatly venerated by people of all ages.[39]

In order to establish the second tradition that the *liṅga* cult evolved independently with no connection with phallus in its realistic sense and that Rudra-Śiva is not an ithyphallic deity, the *liṅgodbhava* legend is invented. The story has also got a sectarian touch not simply because it represents Śiva as winning a momentous victory over the other two supreme divinities of the Hindu Triad, but it paints in a 'puerile and inept manner'[40] the inferiority of the other gods as we find particularly in the *Śiva Purāṇa*.[41] In the *Liṅga Purāṇa*[42] the myth opens in the background of familiar primeval situation of cosmic ocean and the wrangling between Brahmā and Viṣṇu over their respective superiority as the real creator of the Universe. At that moment a towering effulgent *liṅga* surrounded by expanding ever-burning flames of fire and growing into infinite space appeared before them. To prove the superiority of one above the other Brahmā took the form of a Swan and winged into the air to find the top of the *liṅga*, and Viṣṇu assumed the shape of a boar and dove into the deep to trace the end. But the attempts of both

35. I. 2.
36. Handiqui, K.K., *Naiṣadhacarita of Śrīharṣa*, p. 620.
37. III. 14.
38. XX. 18.
39. *ERE*, IX, p. 820.
40. Muir, J., *OST*, Vol. IV, p. 390, f.n. 154.
41. Vth and VIth sections.
42. Chs. XVII-XX.

to discover the reality and measure the height and depth of this pillar of fire practically proved futile and both began to praise him. The same story is to be found with slight modifications in the *Vāyu*,[43] *Matsya*,[44] *Mārkaṇḍeya*,[45] *Kūrma* and *Saura Purāṇas*. Philosophically, this blazing pillar or tower of light (and light is the progenitive power) is like Axis Mundi that fills the gap between Mother Earth and Father Heaven and like an arrow 'pierces the two ends of the creative substance or the supreme reality of the universe'.[46]

In the *Vana-parvan* of the *Mahābhārata*,[47] Arjuna, after being vanquished by Kirāta (Śiva in disguise), is seen worshipping the same deity in an alter made of earth by him. In the *Sauptika-parvan*[48] Śiva appeared before Aśvatthāmān as a huge golden altar with all-spreading flames of fire on it. The germ of this concept of Śiva as a blazing pillar may be traced to *Stambha* ('pillar' or 'support') of the *Ṛgveda* and *Atharvaveda* where its function is to beget *Hiraṇyagarbha* or *Purāṇapuruṣa*, the god of reproduction,[49] we have the following passage in the *Śvetāśvatara Upaniṣad:*[50] "He, the creator and supporter of the gods, Rudra, the great seer, the lord of all, he who formerly gave birth to *Hiraṇyagarbha*, may he endow us with good thoughts". Being not content with the unimaginative myth of Śiva discarding his *liṅga* the philosophers of later days perhaps took this conception of tower of light from the Vedic literature and adapted it to Rudra-Śiva in such a way that the original phallic foundation and significance was forgotten and lost. The famous twelve *jyotirliṅgas* or pillars of Light as we find in the *Śiva*[51] and

43. Ch. LV.
44. Ch. LX.
45. Ch. LXIII.
46. Agrawala, V.S., *Śiva-Mahādeva*, p. 43; Zimmer, H., *Myths and Symbols*, p. 128.
47. Ch. 39, V. 65.
48. *Mbh.*, Ch. XVII. 13-14.
49. *RV*, X. 1-10.

Regarding *Hiraṇyagarbha*, see also Eliade, M., 'Spirit, Light, and Seed' in *History of Religions*, 11 : 1, 1971. Eliade points out the relationship of spirit, light and seed in different religions of the world (pp. 3-4).

50. III. 4; IV. 12.
51. *Uttarakhaṇḍa*, Ch. 3.

Skanda[52] *Purāṇas* are without any phallic significance. They are:—

(1) Oṁkāra (at Māndhātā on the Narmadā),
(2) Mahākāla (at Ujjain),
(3) Tryambaka (near Nasik),
(4) Dhṛṣṇeśvara (at Ellora),
(5) Nāganātha (near Ahmednagar),
(6) Bhīma Śaṅkara (near the source of the Bhīmā river in the Sahyādri),
(7) Viśveśvara (at Varanasi),
(8) Kedāranātha (Garhwal District),
(9) Somanātha (in Kathiawar),
(10) Mallikārjuna or Śrīśaila (on a mountain on the river Kṛṣṇā),
(11) Vaidyanātha (at Deogarh),
(12) Rāmeśvara (in Madura).

To the faithful, in fact, the great *liṅgas* have no sexual connotation and absolute purity and cleanliness are rigorously demanded from the priest or *pujārī*.[53]

Gopinatha Rao[54] has quoted numerous textual references to prove the phallic nature of the *liṅga* and has already given an exhaustive account of the various types of *liṅgas* found from the length and breadth of India. All the Śivaite *Purāṇas*, namely, *Śiva*, *Liṅga*, *Vāyu*, *Skanda*, *Matsya*, *Kūrma*, *Bhaviṣya*, *Brahmāṇḍa* and *Mārkaṇḍeya*, glorify Śiva and extol in the most extravagant terms the advantages of worshipping the *liṅga*. The *Vāmana Purāṇa*[55] and the Tāntric texts, namely, the *Liṅgārcana*, *Mātṛkābheda* and *Prāṇatoṣanī Tantras* of later days recommend *liṅga* worship for the members of the four castes. The *Smṛtiratna* and *Ratnāvalī* laud the merit secured by bathing the *Śiva-liṅga* with milk, curd, clarified butter etc.[56] The *Baudhāyana Gṛhyasūtra*[57] outlines the procedure of the worship of *liṅga* and pres-

52. *Avantikhaṇḍa*, 1. 1. 32.
53. *EHI*, Vol. II, Part I, p. 71.
54. *Ibid.*, pp. 58ff.
55. Chs. V and VI.
56. Kane, P.V., *History of Dharmaśāstra*, Vol. II, Part II, 1941, p. 738.
57. II. 17.

cribes neither invocation to come nor bidding of good-bye to the *acala-liṅga*. The *Matsya Purāṇa*[58] devotes a whole chapter on *Liṅga-lakṣaṇam* and expatiates on the procedure of making *liṅgas* from metals, crystals, earth, wood etc. Varāhamihira in his *Bṛhat Saṁhitā*[59] records some valuable details about the shape and proportions of *liṅga* to be worshipped. The *Agni Purāṇa*[60] deals in details the rules for consecration of *liṅgas*. The *Pāśupata Sūtra*[61] lays down that a true Pāśupata should always be a *liṅgadhārin* (that is, 'bearing a *liṅga*'). Bāṇabhaṭṭa in his *Kādambarī*[62] refers to the fourteenth day of the dark half of a month as sacred for the worship of *Śiva-liṅga* since ancient times. Side by side with this vast literature which glorifies the *liṅga*, we have also the sectarian *Purāṇas*[63] and Smṛti works of the anti-Śiva

58. Chs. 260ff.
59. LVII. 53-55.
60. Chs. 67 and 103.
61. I. 6.

In the words of Mc Cormak, W., ('On Liṅgāyat Culture' in Ramanujan, A.K., tr. *Speaking of Śiva*, 1973): A *liṅga* is tied to the body because "*liṅga* represents the wearer's soul, which is not different from the divinity of Śiva." p. 179.

See also Gupta, A.S., 'Eulogy of Paśupati Śiva', in *Purāṇa*, 17 : 2, 1975, pp. 100-105.

Some scholars, like Werner Stark (*The Sociology of Religion*, Vol. II, 'Sectarian Religion', London, 1967, p. 95) regard the philosophy of the *liṅgadhārins* as 'contraculture' to Brahmanist learning. But the Liṅgāyat scholars, like Nandimath, S.C., (*A Handbook of Virasaivism*, Dharwar, 1942), Sakhare, M.R., (*History and Philosophy of the Lingayat Religion*, Belgaum, 1942, being an introduction to Lingadharana-Chandrika of Nandikeshvara), Sadasivaiah, H.M., (*A Comparative Study of two Virasaiva monasteries, a study in Sociology of Religion*, Ph.D. dissertation, Mysore University, Mysore, 1967) bring to light the philosophy of the Liṅgāyats and the philosophical similarities with the monism preached by the great Vedāntin Śaṅkarācārya in the eighth century.

Ramanujan, A.K. translated the religious lyrics written by four major Dravidian Vīraśaiva saints of the great bhakti protest movement in the 10th century A.D. in Kannada language. A lyrical expression of love for Śiva, Ramanujan's *Speaking of Śiva*, Penguin, 1973, mirror the urge to by-pass tradition and ritual, to concentrate on the subject rather than the object of worship, and to express kinship with all living things in moving terms.

62. Para 54.
63. The *Bṛhannāradīya Purāṇa*, (ch. xiv) calls the liṅga worshippers as heretics who must be condemned to hell.

school which not only defile Śiva in an inept manner but record fierce denunciation of the *liṅga* and its worshippers.

This, in brief, is the polemic of the *liṅga* cult as we find in early Indian literature.

CHAPTER IV

ŚAIVISM IN ART

(i) Śiva in Early Indian Art

The plastic representation of the anthropormorphic forms of Śiva must have started long before the second half of the third millennium B.C., because the three-faced, ithyphallic, horned proto-Śiva of the Harappa civilization, seated on a deer throne in yogic posture and attended by animals is already highly stylized. The two outstretched hands of the figure are covered with bangles and bracelets and on his neck and breast is placed a series of torques and necklaces. It is true that this excessive display of ornaments on the images of Śiva since the Harappa days 'hindered very considerably the development of the human figure'[1] as Indian art, unlike Greek art, always retained the conventional type for the forms; still the impact of the ornaments on the images of Śiva is not always as harmful as it is sometimes feared. The multiplicity of hands, an outstanding feature of Śiva particularly in north Indian art, is also manifest on the Harappa seals and a four-armed figure is represented among the signs of the Indus script.[2] The mutilated statue of an ithyphallic male dancer at Harappa made of dark grey slate, standing on his right leg, with the left leg raised high and the body from the waist upwards turned well round to the left and both arms thrown out in the same direction in the swing of dance, resembling Greek artistry by its striking anatomical truths, is perhaps none but the ancestor of Śiva Naṭarāja.[3] In fact, we have in the Harappa art and religion the

1. Grünwedel, A., *Buddhist Art in India*, London, 1901, p. 31.
2. Chanda, R.P., in *Modern Review*, August, 1932.
3. Marshall, J., *MIC.*, Vol. I, p. 46.
   Lannoy, R., (*The Speaking Tree : A Study of Indian Culture and*

nucleus from which evolved different art traditions of representing Śiva in later days.

Although we may have some stray allusions to images in some Vedic texts, still the Vedic religion was perhaps not idolatry. Quintus Curtias records that an image of Herakles was carried in front of the army of Porus as it advanced against Alexander's forces and Coomaraswamy[4] has identified this Herakles, though not perhaps rightly, as an image of Śiva; for Herakles is usually recognized as the prototype of Kṛṣṇa. Patañjali in his *Mahābhāṣya* refers to the exhibition and sale of the images of Śiva in his comment on Pāṇini.[5] The intervening gap between the Harappa civilization and the first historic Indian sculpture that begins with the Mauryas in the fourth-third century B.C. is shrouded in mists. The advanced stage of Mauryan court art with all its dignified bearing perhaps proves that the great heritage of the Indus art, which also shows close resemblance with the art of early Sumer and Babylonia, continued down to the Mauryan period, enriched further by the contribution of multifarious ethnic elements.

The earliest representation of Śiva with Pārvatī in the historic period in which the god touches the bosom of the goddess with his left hand, is found on a concave gold plaque discovered from Patna fort (now in the collection of R.K. Jalan). Considering the absence of nimbus and the general treatment, Jayaswal[6] assigned it to the Maurya period. Although the Maurya age is noted in the history of art for the employment of stone as the medium par excellence for sculptural expression, yet unfortunately we have no such sculptural specimen of Śiva which can definitely be dated either to the Maurya or the Śuṅga period. Jayaswal[7] discovered from Bhiknapahari (near Patna) a terra-

Society, OUP, paperback, 1975) opines: "The torso of a dancer from Harappā displays a characteristic twist and movement that became well-known in the poses of classical art and is similar to the stance in which numerous Chola bronze images of the dancing Shiva Nataraj were portrayed during the late medieval period in the Dravidian South." pp. 9-10.

4. *HIIA*, p. 42, f.n. 5.

5. V. 3, 99 *jīvikārthe cāpaṇye*.

6. 'Pāṭaliputra Śiva-Pārvatī Gold Plaque' in *JISOA*, Vol. II, 1934, p. 1. pl. 1.

7. 'Terracottas dug out at Patna' in *JISOA*, Vol. III, 1935, p. 126, pl. XXXII, Fig.1.

cotta *yogīśvara ūrdhvaliṅga* Śiva with a snake hood over his head and classed it as a pre-Maurya specimen; but the perfectly refined treatment and expression of the figure suggest clearly its Maurya-character. Terracotta—the medium of expression of the poor and humble folk to whom stone proves to be rather costly—is divided by Stella Kramrisch[8] into 'ageless' or 'timeless' (usually modelled), on the one hand, and 'timed variation' (usually moulded) on the other. Although Kramrisch dismissed such thing as a Maurya level etc., so far as terracottas are concerned, because they cannot be objectively dated, yet we cannot totally brush aside the terracotta that had been usually labelled in between the Maurya and early Gupta period, as an important source of our knowledge about Śiva.

The Śuṅgas (c. 187-75 B.C.), who supplanted the Mauryas, brought in a Brāhmaṇical revival. About 40-30 B.C. both the Śuṅgas and the Kāṇvas were swept away by the Sātavāhanas, lords of Dakṣiṇāpatha. Again, taking advantage of the weakness of the country after the fall of the Mauryas, foreign intruders, namely, Greeks, Śakas, Parthians, Kuṣāṇas entered in number through the northwestern gates of the country. Many of them became adherents of Śiva. The above chronic disturbances and unsettled political condition necessarily find reflection in Indian art and religion. Several schools of sculpture with different idioms of art flourished in course of the long 500 years that intervened between the fall of the Mauryas and the rise of the Guptas. Thus we have Bharhut, Bodhgayā, Sāñci, Mathurā and Gandhāra in the north and Amarāvatī, and Nāgārjunikoṇḍa in the south. But unfortunately we have not got from all the above schools extant sculptural representations of Śiva, and it is only the numismatic and glyptic data that present us the earliest iconic figure of the deity.

Rapson[9] draws our attention to a number of Ujjayinī coins, none of which can be dated later than the second century B.C. Cunningham[10] assigns these coins to the Sātavāhanas and it

8. 'Indian Terracottas' in *JISOA*, Vol. VII, 1939, p. 89.

9. *CCAWKTB* (*Catalogue of Indian Coins in the British Museum*, Vol. IV), London, 1908, p. xcii; CHI, Vol. I, Indian Reprint, 1962, p. 479, Pl. V, 19.

10. *Coins of Ancient India*, London, 1891, pp. 97-98, Pl. X, figs. 1-6.

was possibly Sātakarṇi I who wrested Ujjayinī (western Malwa) from the Śuṅgas. In the first type we have the two-armed standing figure of Śiva taking a staff in the right hand and a vase in the left, and the next specimen is of a polycephalous type[11] where we have a three-headed standing figure of the above deity on the obverse, carrying identical attributes, although Allan[12] wrongly identified it with Kārttikeya. However, the figures on these coins essentially appear to be indigenous in character. Just like the proto-Śiva of the Indus valley, we have on certain copper coins of Ujjayinī[13] the figure of Śiva seated on a lotus seat in yogic pose, although Coomaraswamy found in it one of the earliest representations of the Buddha.

Banerjea[14] has recognised an unquestionable representation of Śiva on two copper coin devices of the Indo-Scythic ruler Maues (c. 20 B.C. to 22 A.D.), although Gardner[15] has simply described it as a 'male figure'. The deity in these foreign coins, just like his counterpart in the indigenous Ujjayinī coins, is to be found in the *ābhaṅga* pose (that is, a slight bend both in the upper and the lower halves of the figure). Whitehead[16] has brought to light some coins of the Indo-Parthian king Gondophernes (c. 21 A.D. to 50 A.D.) where Śiva with faint traces of *jaṭā* on his head stands facing, with his left leg slightly advanced and head bent a little towards the left, clasping a long trident in his right hand and a palm-branch in his left. Rapson[17] described another variety of the coins of Gondophernes where the deity is represented with his right hand extended and a trident in his left hand. Marshall[18] has found at Taxila the terracotta bust of an androgynous figure belonging to the Śaka-Parthian lavel, resembling the Ardhanārīśvara image. However, the figure of Śiva on the Indo-Scythian, Indo-Parthian, Ujjayinī

11. Coomaraswamy, A.K., *HIIA*, p. 67n.

12. *Catalogue of the coins of Ancient India in the British Museum*, London, 1936, Introduction, pp. cxliii, 245-52.

13. Cunningham A., *Coins of Ancient India*, Plate X, Fig. 10.

14. *DHI*, p. 120.

15. *BMCCGSKI*, p. 71, pl. XVII, 3.

16. *PMC*, Vol. I, *Indo-Greek Coins*, Oxford, 1914, p. 151, Pl. XV, Fig. 43 and p. 183, Pl. XVII, fig. 33.

17. *JRAS*, 1903, pp. 285-86.

18. *ARASI*, 1928-29, p. 158.

and other pre-Christian coins are not at all impressive and some of them are clumsy and crude.

With the coming of the Kuṣāṇas on the stage a new vista opens in Indian art and Śiva assumes different forms on the coins of Wema Kadphises, Kaṇiṣka, Huviṣka and Vāsudeva. These coins are 'much more elegant and refined than the Indo-Parthian ones'.[19] The multiplication of Śiva's hands and heads and the nature of varying indigenous attributes in his hands perhaps prove that the iconography of the cult deity had already developed in the Kuṣāṇa period.[20] Cunningham[21] thinks that the various deities, on the Kuṣāṇa coins represented the seven planets, and Śiva represented Saturn—hence, perhaps the terrific attributes, namely, thunderbolt, trident, spear, battle-axe, noose, human skull, etc., are to be found on these coins. The treatment of matted locks of Śiva, particularly on the coins of Wema Kadphises, is in spirial form like 'flames rising from head' and on Vāsudeva's coins the residue of the hair, often being used to form a top knot, descends down the sides of the face in such a way as not to give a genuine appearance.[22]

Some scholars[23] detect the figure of the Ardhanārīśvara on the reverse of some gold coins of Kaṇiṣka, although to Whitehead[24] it is just a two-armed standing figure of Śiva. Śiva and Umā in one quarter stater of Huviṣka[25] with the Kuṣāṇa monogram Oeso (Bhaveśa) and Nana (Umā) is of great iconographic interest. Rapson[26] noticed another similar representation on a unique coin of the same ruler where the goddess is correctly described as OMMO (Umā). Gardner[27] described a gold coin

19. Majumdar, R.C., ed., *The Age of Imperial Unity*, 1960, p. 535.
20. Banerjea, J.N., *RAA*, p. 48.
21. *Numismatic Chronicle*, Vol. XII, 3rd series, 1892, pp. 44, 98.
22. Banerjea, J.N., *DHI*, p. 127.
23. Singh, O.P., 'Ardhanārīśvara on the coin of Kaniṣka' in JNSI, Vol. XXX, 1968, p. 195.
24. *PMC*, Vol. I, Pl. XIX, 231.
25. *Ibid.*, p. 197, pl. XVIII, 135.
26. *JRAS*, 1897, p. 324.

Biswas, K., ('Śiva on Some Kushāṇa Coins of the Indian Museum Cabinet' in *The Journal of the Numismatic Society of India*, Vol. XLI, 1979, Parts I-II, Plate VI, P. 18) thinks that Smith, V.A., is not always accurate or complete in his description of the iconographic features of Śiva.

27. *op. cit.*, p. 148, Pl. XXVIII, 16.

of Huviṣka as representing a three-headed, four-armed, ithyphallic Śiva with Viṣṇu's *Cakra* in one hand, and Banerjea[28] thinks that it may offer the beginning of the syncretic Hari-Hara icon of later days or may be similar to the Gandhāra relief of a three-headed and six-armed Trimūrti.[29]

In fact, the great cosmopolitan character of Indian culture and the eclectic mental make-up of the early foreign immigrants, the Greeks, Śakas, Pahlavas, Kuṣāṇas and others helped not only their social absorption, the identification of their gods with Indian prototypes, and the fusion of Hellenic and non-Hellenic elements,[30] but also the merger of different Indian deities as these foreign potentates paid homage to more than one deity. Again, it was under the lavish patronage of the Kuṣāṇas and others that two great schools of art flourished in ancient India—one at Gandhāra and the other at Mathurā. The best Kuṣāṇa specimen of Śiva carved in Gandhāran Graeco-Indian tradition is to be found in an intaglio in the Pearse collection, now in Indian Museum, in which the god is represented as three-headed with *jaṭā* knobs all over the head encircled by a halo and with different weapons in the four-arms and seated on his mount Nandin in the *Sukhāsana* pose.[31] In the Mathurā art of the Kuṣāṇa period Śiva is always shown as *ūrdhvaliṅga* and in one specimen (No. 2085) at least the third eye on the forehead is discernible. The total number of Ardhanārīśvara figures of Śiva of this period in the Mathurā Museum is not negligible.[32] In two other reliefs[33] of the Kuṣāṇa

28. *DHI*, p. 124.

29. *ARASI*, 1913-14, pp. 276ff., pl. LXXII, a.

30. Gardner (*BMC*, Introduction, p. lviii) used the term 'barbaro-Hellenic'.

31. Banerjea, J.N., *DHI*, pp. 468-69, pl. XXXIV, fig. 1.

32. Agrawala, V.S., *Catalogue of the Brāhmaṇical Images in Mathurā Art*, Lucknow, 1951, pp. ix, 27; Nos. 800, 874, 2520.

Dehejia, V., (*Early Stone Temples of Orissa*, New Delhi, 1979, p. 75) points out that "In the earliest Orissan temples the images of Śiva in his variety of forms are invariably depicted with the *ūrdha liṅga*. ....Dancing, Ardhanārīśvara, Seated Śiva in Śiva Pārvatī panels, Naṭarāja, Ekapāda, Harihara, Lakulisa, Vīrabhadra, Bhairava are all shown with a prominently carved upright *liṅga*. On later temples this practice seems to have been abandoned."

33. *Ibid.*, pp. 25, 27; Nos. G 52, 2495.

period in the same Museum, we have the typical *dampatī*, Śiva and Pārvatī in *āliṅgana-mudrā.*

The Audumbaras, who seem to have been subjugated by the Kuṣāṇa king Kaniṣka I, issued a number of coins in the name of their favourite god Mahādeva or Śiva. It is interesting to note that on the reverse of some square copper coins of the Audumbara chiefs, Śivadāsa, Rudradāsa and others we have the invariable representation of a Śaiva temple marked by a *dhvaja*, a trident and a battle-axe.[34] On the obverse of the silver coins of the early Audumbara chief Dharaghoṣa we find the representation of Viśvāmitra as indicated by the Kharoṣṭhī legend across the figure with the right hand in *abhaya* pose and the left resting on the hip.[35] That this Viśvāmitra stands for Śiva is proved by the combined symbols trident and battle-axe on the reverse of these coins. The over-emphasis of muscles in the figure and the general treatment of these silver coins appear to be Hellenistic in character.

Incidentally, it may be pointed out that we have perhaps the same Śiva as Viśvāmitra in the inscribed bronze seal No. 12 of the second or first century B.C. unearthed from the Sirkap site of Taxila[36] and described by Marshall as 'Herakles trampling down a bull-shaped dragon' and the Kharoṣṭhī legend read by him as *Tiḍusa Vibhumitrasa.* But Sten Konow's reading of it as *Baḍusa Viśvamitrasa*[37] ('of the young Brāhmaṇa Viśvāmitra') is more acceptable and the name of the person on this seal being after the name of the god reproduced.[38] Another similar personal seal of an individual (Śivarakṣita) who used the figure of his patron deity is found from the same site of Taxila[39] in which Śiva seems to wear an elaborate turban or *śirastrāṇa* which is usually found on the images of the Śuṅga period. The treatment of this round copper seal, belonging to the first century A.D. or a little earlier, is undoubtedly Hellenistic and Śiva appears with trident in his left hand and club in the right, bearing the

34. *JNSI*, Vol. IV, pp. 55ff.
35. Allan, J., *op, cit.*, pp. 122 to 125 and plates.
36. *ARASI*, 1914-15, p. 35, pl. XXIV, 50.
37. *Corpus Inscriptionum Indicarum*, Vol. II, p. 102.
38. Banerjea, J.N., *DHI*, p. 121.
39. *Comprehensive History of India*, Vol. II, p. 401.

legend in Brāhmī and Kharoṣṭhī characters—*Śiva-rakṣitasa*[40] ('of one protected by Śiva').

On the Kuṇinda copper coins of the second or third century A.D., which resembled Kuṣāṇa module, Śiva appears in the form of Chatreśvara.[41] The *jaṭās* on the head of Śiva are arranged in such a way as to look like a convex-shaped object.[42]

With the advent of the Guptas in the first quarter of the fourth century A.D., we enter upon the classical phase of Indian sculpture and witness "a heightening of the aesthetic consciousness leading to the fulfilment and culmination of the earlier trends and tendencies".[43] In spite of most of the Gupta emperors being dedicated to Viṣṇu, the glorification of Śiva was no less popular. We have now two aspects of Śiva in Indian art, as a God of love and a God of wisdom and the 'Indianness' of the figure is felt first of all because all loose and divergent local ideas and motifs of art are now assimilated into a synthetic and harmonised order.[44]

h On the lintel of the Śiva temple of *Bhumara*[45] (Satna District, M.P.), we have a fine bust of Śiva with the characteristic quiet poise, which is the common denominator of Gupta sculptures. The relievo sculptures of Śiva in the niches of the Daśāvatāra temple[46] at Deogarh (Jhansi District, U.P.), belonging to the 6th century A.D., though they bear the stamp of certain coarseness, still reflect the Gupta tradition of dignified pose, tranquil detachment and graceful spiritual expression. In a panel on the eastern facade we have a superb representation of Śiva as *Mahāyogin* attended by other heavenly beings hovering in the air, which in spite of the inartistic excrescence of the extra pair of arms may claim, according to V.A. Smith,[47] a place among the best specimens of Indian sculpture. In one relief Śiva and Pārvatī, being seated on their respective mounts, are seen soaring

40. Sten Konow, *CII*, Vol. II, p. 102, Pl. XX, 11.

41. D.C. Sircar thinks that the word should be Catreśvara, and not Chatreśvara.

42. Allan, J., *op. cit.*, pp. 167-68 and Plates.

43. Saraswati, S.K., *A Survey of Indian Sculpture*, 1957, p. 120.

44. Kar, C., *Classical Indian Sculpture*, London, 1950, pp. 4-5.

45. Banerji, R.D., 'Śiva Temple at Bhumara' in *MASI*, No. 16.

46. Vats, M.S., 'The Gupta Temple at Deograh' in *MASI*, No. 70.

47. *A History of Fine Art in India and Ceylon*, p. 73.

through the space.[48] The two figures of Nara and Nārāyaṇa, on one of the side niches of the above temple, which breathe 'the aroma of the classicism of Sārnāth'[49] have been wrongly identified by Gopinatha Rao[50] as the Jñāna- and Yoga-Dakṣiṇāmūrtis of Śiva.

The Mathurā laboratory in the Kuṣāṇa age released massive and ponderous images, but now in the first phase of the Gupta sculpture the images are brought under a "stern and disciplined modelling, and a firm outline and a harsh geometrical composition restrain a vigorous and monumental body of full rounded limbs within a heavy and ruthless concentration".[51] We have two remarkable three-eyed oval-shaped Śivaite heads[52] belonging to this phase of Mathurā tradition which have "not yet experienced bliss, the joy and glow of weightless existence," one in the Mathurā Museum,[53] and the other, which is qualitatively of a higher level, in the Calmann galleries, London.[54]

In the inscribed standing Śiva-Pārvatī relief from Kosam[55] of the reign of Kumāragupta I, now in the collection of the Indian Museum, both the ịthyphallic god and his consort raise the right hand in *abhaya* pose, in the left hand Śiva holds *amṛtaghaṭa* and Pārvatī carries *triśūla*. In spite of the Gupta mark of quiet poise and detachment, this specimen is strikingly simple with no stamp of beauty and excellence in comparison with the suggestive posture of the divine couple in post-Gupta statues[56] particularly of East India, where Pārvatī is usually shown seated on the left thigh of her consort. However, in the Mathurā Museum we have another specimen (No. 2084) of Śiva and Pārvatī (ht.

48. *ASR*, Vol. X, pp. 105ff. and plates.

49. Saraswati, S.K., *op. cit.*, p. 139.

50. *EHI*, Vol. II, p. 273, pl. LXXI,

51. Majumdar, R.C., (ed.), *The Classical Age*, 1962, pp. 523-24.

52. *Ibid.*, p. 524, Pl. XIX, 38, 39.

53. *Cf.*, Vogel, J. Ph., *Catalogue of the Archaeological Museum at Mathura*, Allahabad, 1910.

54. *JISOA*, Vol. VI, p. 202, Pl. XLIV; Saraswati, S.K., *op. cit.*, Fig. 89.

55. *ARASI*, 1913-14, Pl. LXXb.

See Dehejia, V., *op. cit.*, pp. 84-85, for a newly discovered Bhavani-Shankar temple at Bhubanesvar.

56. Bloch, T., *Supplementary Catalogue of the Archaeological Collection of the Indian Museum*, pp. 86-87.

3′-0″, width 1′-10″) which, though retaining the essential features of the Kuṣāṇa period, is very much transformed and is considered as an image of unusual interest.[57] Here Śiva characterised *jaṭā-jūṭa* and *ūrdhvaliṅga* is perhaps represented in his post-nuptial state. The god extends his left arm around the neck of his spouse and both the standing god and goddess hold a *nīlotpala*, symbolic of their married life. Finally, the Gupta artists also depicted the standing deities in *āliṅgana-mudrā* as is noticeable in an image (No. 474) of the Mathurā Museum.

The Ardhanārīśvara form of Śiva in which Śiva and Pārvatī are blended together, though iconographically evolved in the Kuṣāṇa period, was handled by the Gupta artists with an unexcelled perfection.[58] We have two such notable busts in the Mathurā Museum (Nos. 362, 722) where the right half representing Śiva and the left representing Pārvatī are treated more carefully and delicately. In the above Museum, we have also three heads (Nos. 1333, 1336, 2510) of the syncretic Hari-Hara of the Gupta period, showing Śiva's matted locks on the right and Viṣṇu's high *mukuṭa* on the left.[59]

In addition to the above, we have numerous seals, plaques and other terracotta and metal objects of the Gupta period found from Bhiṭā, Rājghāt, Nālandā, Ahichchhatra and Basarh, which undoubtedly form a very interesting series by themselves.

The Bhiṭā (U.P.) seals, unearthed by Marshall,[60] bear the different appellations and images of Śiva. For example, the seal No. 17, which is of the fourth or fifth century A.D., represents Śiva as Bhadreśvara and the two-armed figure is found seated in *lalit-āsana* pose on a *pādapīṭha* with flames over head and shoulders.[61] We have from Rājghāt (near Varanasi) a circular terracotta sealing of a similar character bearing the legend *Śrī-Devadevasvāmi* (*naḥ*) (representing Śiva as Devadevasvāmin), where the god stands "on an elaborate pedestal, with out-stretched arms holding a wreath (or a noose?) in the right

57. Diskalkar, D.B., 'Some Brāhmaṇical Sculptures in the Mathurā Museum' in *JUPHS*, January, 1932, p. 39. Plates 16-17.

58. Agrawala, V.S., *Studies in Indian Art*, first ed., p. 188.

59. Agrawala, V.S., *CBIMA*, 1951, p. 45.

60. *ASIAR*, 1911-12, pp. 47-49.

61. Banerjea, J.N., *DHI*, p. 183.

and a flask in the left hand, a serpent being shown to his left."[62] In the unique Nālandā clay seals[63] of the late Gupta period, we have both the two-armed and four-armed Śiva under the canopy of snake hoods, flanked by a tree and a lighted lamp on a stand on either side of the figure.[64] V.S. Agrawala[65] has found among the ruins of an ancient Śiva temple at Ahichchhatra (Bareilly District, U.P.) a very interesting terracotta plaque of the late Gupta period depicting the reposeful ascetic form of Śiva as *Jñāna-Dakṣiṇāmūrti*. On the left of the four-armed god seated gracefully in the *ardha-paryaṅka* pose, there are two figures, one male and the other female, in *namaskāramudrā*. Spooner[66] unearthed from Vaiśālī (modern Basarh near Muzaffarpur, Bihar) innumerable seals of both Gupta and pre-Gupta days, bearing numerous representations of Śiva.

Even after the departure of the Imperial Guptas from the scene, the tradition of Gupta art—expressing perhaps the entire spiritual heritage of India—continued and continued long as model of Indian art. The post-Gupta period is marked by the emergence of a set of new dynasties in north India : the Maukharīs of Kanauj, the Puṣyabhūtis of Thaneswar, the Maitrakas of Valabhī and others and many of the members of these royal families were devotees of Śiva. We have from Deo-Baramark (South-West of Arrah) an image of Umā-Maheśvara belonging to the period of the Maukharīs of Kanauj in which Śiva wears, as E. Pires[67] observes, "a singularly novel and elongated sort of head-dress, very minutely engraved and artistically embellished." The standing Śiva of Mandasor and other Malwa specimens are of a type of sturdy physique, "invariably heavy, round and tough while the eastern ones are soft, slender and delicate".[68]

However, with the coming of Harṣavardhana of the Puṣyabhūti family in the first half of the seventh century A.D., our

62. *Ibid.*, p. 188.
63. S.I. 645, 811; SIa, 442.
64. Sastri, H., 'Nālandā and its Epigraphic Material' in *MASI*, No. 66, pp. 37ff.
65. *Ancient India*, No. IV, 1947-48, pp. 169-70, fig. 3.
66. *ASIAR*, 1913-14, pp. 152ff.
67. *The Maukharis*, Madras, 1934, p. 177.
68. Majumdar ,R.C., *The Classical Age*, 1962, p. 527.

period comes to an end since medieval age begins in Indian history.

Turning to the Deccan and south India, we have very few notable specimens that can be definitely dated within our period as most of the magnificent images of Śiva—now sub-divided into *saṁhāra* (destructive) and *anugraha* (gracious) classes corresponding to his *ugra* and *saumya* aspects—belong to the later age. Indeed, it is really very difficult to trace the different representations of Śiva in Indian art dynasty-wise or chronologically and to limit the discussion within our period.

It was in the Kṛṣṇā-Godāvarī delta that the Āndhra school—under the patronage of the Sātavāhanas and represented by the remarkable specimens of Jaggayyapeta, Amarāvatī and Nāgārjunikoṇḍa—blossomed forth with all its characteristic qualities. Rene Grousset[69] opines that, in the first centuries of the Christian era, Andhra, unlike northern India, has preserved inviolate both its political independence and the original tradition of Indian aesthetics. But the impact of the north on the art of the south is today undeniable. In fact, it is with the Āndhra school, which inherited a lot both from the Gandhāra and Mathurā schools of the north and ultimately evolved a style of its own, that the curtain is drawn on an art that perhaps began its career long before. We are not sure whether the sturdy and vigorous standing figure of Śiva on a crouching Yakṣa, as found on the lower section of the famous *liṅga* of Guḍīmallam, is a product of this tradition. Considering the firm and resolute tread, as shown by the forceful attitude, Kramrisch[70] relates it with an aspect of the tradition of India that has not survived.

However, the said school continued to produce its creations at least till the fourth century A.D. and the Pallava art inherited a lot from it. The earliest remarkable specimens of the Pallava school are to be found in the open-air rock-carvings of Mahābalipuram (or Māmallapuram) and the Kailāsa temple of Kāñcīpuram. The slender elongated figures of Śiva and Pārvatī with 'pointed faces and attenuated grace of proportions'[71] are

69. *Civilisations of the East*, Vol. II (*India*), pp. 230ff.
70. *Indian Sculpture*, p. 35.
71. Rowland, Benjamin, *The Art and Architecture of India*, 1953, p. 186.

the notable marks of this school of the south. "The communication of emotional tension", to quote Benjamin Rowland,[72] "through pose and gesture, rather than through facial expression" was a common feature of both the Āndhra and Pallava reliefs. In the magnificent open-air bas-relief of Mahābalipuram 'Arjuna's Penance'[73]—the central theme of the famous Kirātārjuna episode, wherein Śiva attended by his *gaṇas* stands to the right of Arjuna in an intense naturalistic gesture—is depicted in such a way that it has become a wonderful 'fresco in stone'.[74]

In the art of south India, Śiva is not usually depicted multi-armed excluding in some aspects to emphasize his martial glory. The vast collection of different forms of Śiva in his Gajāsura-saṁhāra, Tripurāntaka, Somāskanda and Dakṣiṇāmūrti in the Kailāsanātha temple at Kāñcīpuram which is a 'veritable mine of information'[75] falls beyond the scope of our study. However, we should note that in the representations of Śiva in the above Pallava temple there is a 'thinning down of the plastic context'.[76] In south Indian art a popular mode of representing Śiva was in his Dakṣiṇāmūrti form. In this aspect Śiva is very often confused with Buddha because the former seated on a deer-throne and surrounded by sages has got incontestable resemblance with the latter preaching his first sermon before the first five disciples.

Coming to the Deccan, we have again very few records of great art belonging to our period and have the masterpieces of the rock-cut carvings of the Cālukyas of Bādāmi illustrating Śivāyana mythology at Aihole, Bādāmi, Paṭṭadakal and Ellora. The characteristic marks of the Aihole representations of Śiva are suppleness and elongation and in this respect they supply a link between the earlier Āndhra school on the one hand and the subsequent Pallava school on the other,[77] which gave emphasis on physiognomical form. In the stone panels of Bādāmi, Śiva appears as Mukteśvara, Ardhanārīśvara and Hari-Hara. In the bas-reliefs of the temples of Saṅgameśvara, Virūpākṣa and

72. *Loc. cit.*
73. Ramachandran, T.N., in *JISOA*, Vol. XVIII, pp. 58ff.
74. Munshi, K.M., *Saga of Indian Sculpture*, 1956, p. 29.
75. Banerjea, J.N., *RAA*, p. 102.
76. Saraswati, S.K., *op. cit.*, p. 170.
77. *Ibid.*, p. 149.

Mallikārjuna at Paṭṭadakal, Śiva is represented in his numerous aspects which register the impress of the Pallava tradition.[78] We notice a remarkable resemblance in details existing between the Kailāsa temple of the Pallavas at Kāñcī and of the Cālukyas at Ellora.

In the Kailāsa temple at Ellora Śiva "carved in pure lines, is smooth, chaste and soft in his nudity"[79] and here we have a perfect fusion of the southern element with the tradition of the Deccan. "The slender type of the body", in the words of Kramrisch,[80] "with its easier and quickened gestures, is assimilated by the heavier form of the Dekkan with its sustained power". In fact, the magnificent rock-cut Kailāsa temple at Ellora, clothed by Śaivite legends from the *Rāmāyaṇa*, is a 'gigantic theatrical tableau'[81] rightly considered as 'a woderful drama in stone'[82] containing in the words of Rene Grousset[83] "one of the most powerful works in the art of the whole world".

(ii) The Phallus in Early Indian Art

Right from the beginning of the Harappa civilization, we have a large number of plastic and glyptic data to prove that the anthropomorphic and phallic representation of Śiva were current side by side. Over and above the ithyphallic representation of the proto-Śiva, we have a large number of *liṅgas* of extremely realistic character, both large and small. The smaller Harappa specimens—usually less than two inches in height, made of lapis-lazuli, jasper, chalcedony and other stones and also of faience, bone, shell and ivory—most probably carried

78. Majumdar, R.C., *The Classical Age*, p. 534.
79. Munshi, K.M., *Saga of Indian Sculpture*, p. 33.
80. *Indian Sculpture*, p. 86.
81. Rowland, B., *op. cit.*, pp. 186-87.
82. Munshi, K.M., *op. cit.*, p. 34.
83. *Civilisations of the East*, Vol. II (*India*), p. 239.

See also, Chatham, Doris, C., *Stylistic Sources and Relationships of the Kailāsa Temple in Ellora*, (Ph.D. dissertation, University of California), Berkeley, 1977.

For the iconographic representations of Śiva in his different forms, see also Sivaramamurti, C., *The Art of India*, New York, 1977, pp. 77-78.

by persons as amulets like the miniature *liṅga* carried by the Liṅgāyats in later days, are very beautifully cut and finished.[1]

The two notable *liṅgas* of ancient India, namely, those from Guḍimallam and Bhiṭā, although they have anthropomorphic figures on them, resemble the somewhat naturalistic phallus of the Harappa type. A good number of phallic emblems of a highly suggestive nature without the figure of Śiva on them, belonging to the first few centuries of the Christian era, are found from various parts of north India, particularly from the Mathurā region. For example, exhibit No. H1 in the collection of the Lucknow Museum, hailing from the Mathurā region and belonging to the Kuṣāṇa period, is such a realistic '*liṅga* with a broadened top'. The nut of this red sandstone phallus is clearly demarcated from the shaft, and there is a slanting grove cut round the junction of the nut and the shaft and it is also encircled in the middle by a band of a decorative character, thus enhancing the realism of the emblem.[2] We have a bas-relief in the Mathurā Museum (No. 2661) showing scenes of worshipping, with garlands and flowers, a *liṅga* installed on a pedestal by two Kuṣāṇa noblemen wearing coats and trousers.[3] The suggestiveness is to some extent subdued in another huge specimen of the above Museum,[4] which is somewhat later in date. Here the nut is distinctly marked on one side of its lower end by a dentate groove suggesting the *Brahmasūtra* motif which is nothing but a device to show the distinction between the nut and the shaft. In fact, in this mark of *Brahmasūtra* on the *Rudra-* or *Pūjā-bhāga* of the *liṅgas* of the later days, faint traces of the original phallic character of the emblem are to be sought.[5]

Most of the phallic specimens from the Gupta period onwards show how the emphasis on their naturalistic character is subdued. A conventionalized colossal *liṅga*, perhaps of the 5th century A.D., has been excavated from Maniyār Maṭh at Rājgīr,

1. Mackay, E.J.H., *The Indus Civilization*, London, 1935, p. 78.
2. *JISOA*, Vol. III, 1935, Pl. VII, fig. 1.
3. *Annual Report of Mathura Museum*, 1936-37, Pl. II, fig. 1.
4. Banerjea, J.N., *DHI*, p. 457.
5. Banerjea, J.N., *Religion in Art and Archaeology*, 1st ed., p. 67.

and Bloch[6] compared it, as a parallel to such a colossal *liṅga* at Fatehgarh near Baramula in Kashmir and the Tirupara-kunrum rock near Madras. Another notable point is that the *liṅgas* of the pre-Gupta and early Gupta periods do not show any real base in the shape of *arghya* as the '*liṅgam in Arghya*' motif—symbolizing the antagonistic yet cooperating forces of the two sexes—is perhaps a comparatively late phase in course of its conventionalization. In the later representations the spout-like projection, from which the *pūjā-bhāga* of the *Śiva-liṅga* rises upward and which is generally taken as symbolizing *yoni*, also serves the utilitarian purpose of draining off the water profusely poured on the top of the *liṅga*.[7] As an explanation of this enigmatic shape of the motif, Bosch[8] used his theory of Lotus-stem because here the direction in which the stem, corresponding with the *liṅga*, grows, turns away from the root, the equivalent of the *yoni*. To the faithfuls, the *Śiva-liṅga* is totally devoid of any idea of lewdness and transcends iconolatry; but to the critics it was "by persisting in such abstraction that India...drove her religious art to its own annihilation".[9]

Gopinatha Rao,[10] on the basis of various Āgamas and other texts, has already outlined an exhaustive account of the various types of *liṅgas* and their merits. Broadly speaking, we have two types, *cala* (movable) and *acala* (immovable). The *cala-liṅgas* are divided into *mṛṇmaya* (made of earth), *lohaja* (made of metal), *ratnaja* (made of precious stones), *dāruja* (made of wood), *śailaja* (made of stone) and *kṣaṇika* (for temporary use). The *acala*, *sthira* or *sthāvara liṅgas* are classified under four heads according to the *Makuṭāgama*, six according to the *Kāmikāgama* and nine according to the *Suprabhedāgama*.. The nine classes are: (i) *Svāyambhuva*, (that is, the natural or self-thought *linga*,

6. *ARASI*, 1905-06, p. 105.
7. Banerjea, J.N., *RAA*, p. 68.
8. *The Golden Germ*, Holland, 1960, p. 166.
9. *Ency. of World Art*, Vol. VII, p. 427.
10. *EHI*, Vol. II, pt. I., pp. 75-99.

For a descriptive account of the varieties of *liṅga* cf. Singh, S. B., *Brāhmaṇical Icons in Northern India*, New Delhi, 1977, Chapter I.

See also, Kramrisch, S., *The Presence of Śiva*, 1981, pp. 153-196.

there being 68 places dedicated to such forms according to *Jīrṇoddhāradaśaka*), (ii) *Daivika* (associated with the Devas, the *Makuṭāgama* prescribing the shape of a flame or resembling a pair of hands in the *añjali* pose though the *brahmasūtra* design is not to be shown), (iii) *Ārṣaka* (associated with the divine ṛṣis and spheroidal in shape resembling an unhusked coconut), (iv) *Gāṇapa* (set up by *gaṇas* and resembling the cucumber, citron, wood-apple or palm), (v) *Asura* (worshipped by the *asuras*), (iv) *Sura* (worshipped by the gods), (vii) *Rākṣasya* (worshipped by demons), (viii) *Bāṇa* (natural objects or pieces of stone resembling the teat of a cow or an egg in shape, mostly picked up from the Revā or Narmadā, the *Siddhānta-sārāvalī* mentioning sizes as ranging from $\frac{1}{8}$ *aṅgula* to one cubit and having different colour), (ix) *Mānuṣa* (man-made *liṅgas* which form the largest number of *acala* or *sthira-liṅgas*, and are made of three parts known as *Brahma-bhāga* (the square lowest section), *Viṣṇu-bhāga* (the octagonal middle part), and *Rudra-* or *Pūjā-bhāga* (the cylindrical topmost portion), these *lingas* being grouped under ten classes on the basis of different criteria.

If the *Pūjā-bhāga* or cylindrical shaft of the *Mānuṣa-liṅgas* has a number of vertical fluted facets ranging from 5 to 64, such *liṅgas* are the *Dhārā-liṅga*. Sometimes, multiple miniature *liṅgas* are carved on the *Rudra-bhāga* of the main *liṅga* in parallel horizontal and vertical lines, and by chaffing the edges of the resultant criss-cross sections. Thus we have a number of *Aṣṭottaraśata* (108) smaller *liṅgas* attached on the back of the main *liṅga* and *Sahasra* (1000) *liṅgas* in many ancient south Indian temples, namely, at Tiruvaṟṟiyūr near Madras, the Ekāmbaranāthan temple at Kāñcīpuram and the Aruṇācaleśvara temple at Tiruvannamalai.[11]

The *Mukha-liṅgas*, one of the most important varieties of *Mānuṣa-liṅgas*, show on their *Pūjā-bhāga* one to five human faces, standing for one or more aspects of Śiva and the number of faces should correspond to the number of doorways of the central shirne. The *Kāraṇāgama*[12] lays down that *Mukhaliṅgas*

11. Srinivasan, T.N., *A Handbook of South Indian Images*, Tirupati, 1954, p. 68.

12. See Banerjea, J.N., *DHI*, p. 460.

with four faces should have them facing the four quarters, a three-faced one should not have a face on its back, and a one-faced one should have the face placed a little high up." According to the *Rūpamaṇḍana*[13] also, "in a one-faced type the face should be shown in front; and in a three-faced one, the back face is absent. In a four-faced variety, the western face is white, the northern red, the southern black and terrific, while the eastern face is of the colour of a well-kindled fire". The earliest extant specimens of *mukha-liṅgas* usually with one, three and four faces, are found more or less from all parts of India.

Of the *Ekamukha* type, we should first mention exhibit No. 1287 in the collection of the Mathurā Museum, whose nut is much broader than the shaft and which bears on its top portion one *jaṭāmukuṭa*-bearing Śiva-head.[14] Exhibit Nos. 770 and 899 of the above museum are unfinished or fragmentary *Ekamukha* specimens of the Kuṣāṇa period[15] and No. 2528[16] is a colossal (ht. 4′-8″) Kuṣāṇa specimen of irregular shape looking like the Bhiṭā specimen and with one face against the upper portion of the shaft. In the Lucknow Museum,[17] we have a specimen (Exhibit No. 42) of the Gupta period where the nut and the shaft are not clearly demarcated and the realism has not completely disappeared. The lower part of the Khoh[18] (Nagod, M.P.) specimen is roughly chiselled and the upper cylindrical

13. *Loc. cit.*

14. *JISOA*, Vol. III, 1935, p. 44.

Sharma, B.N., (*Iconography of Sadāśiva*, New Delhi, 1976, pl. I) thinks that the *Mukhaliṅgas*, with one to five face, date back to the Second Century B.C.

In the words of Sivaramamurti, C., "The Shivalinga from Bhita has five heads corresponding to Tatpurusha, Aghora, Sadyojata, Isana, and Vamadeva and composing Sadashiva. The complex iconography of this piece, which dates from about the second century B.C., is testimony to a deep rooted and ancient craving for iconographic forms. The representation of Shiva at Gudiamallam goes back to the early phase of the Satavahanas. Here is Shiva as Kālāgnirudra, a pillar of fire, symbolic of Agni and Rudra in unison."—*The Art of India*, New York, 1977, p. 77.

15. Agrawala, V.S., *A Catalogue of the Brāhmaṇical Images in Mathurā Art*, Lucknow, 1951, p. 27.

16. *Loc. cit.*

17. *JISOA*, Vol. III, 1935, Pl. VII, fig. 2.

18. *ARASI*, 1904-05, Pl. XXVI, figs. a-d.

section contains on one side the bust of Śiva. The Śiva temple at Bhumara[19] (Nagod, M.P.), which is all but a ruin, enshrined an *Ekamukha-linga* in the sanctum. Among the Udayagiri cave shrines, there is at least one which houses an *Ekamukna-linga.*[20]

We are not acquainted with any text which describes a *Dvimukha-linga*, although an example of it is to be found in Exhibit No. 462 of the Mathurā Museum.[21] The carving is undobtedly crude and the two heads with *jaṭāmukuṭa* on the shaft, one at the back and the other facing front, have the third eye and curiously enough, also moustaches. It is perhaps a specimen of the post-Gupta period. Incidentally, we should point out that it is particularly from the Mathurā region that we have different specimens of *mukha-liṅgas* of the Kuṣāṇa and Gupta ages.[22]

The Mahādeva temple of Nachna Kuthara in the Baghelkhand region (c. 7th-8th century A.D.), enshrined a colossal *caturmukha-linga* (4′-8″).[23] On the pedestal in the sanctum of the so-called temple of the god Brahman on the bank of the Khajur Sāgara, the *caturmukha* (an appellation usually applied to Brahman), *Śiva-liṅga* is enshrined.[24] Another specimen is to be found from Sirpur (Raipur District, M.P.).[25]

Among the Pāhārpur terracottas of Bengal, we have one *caturmukha-linga*, with signs of *brahmasūtra*, of which three faces are only discernible on account of its being a relievo representation.[26] One unique variety in red sandstone, though fragmentary, now in the collection of the Mathurā Museum,[27] shows four faces with different hair styles on four shafts joined together, and although there is a slight demarcation between the nut and the shaft the result has not

19. Banerji, R.D., 'Śiva Temple at Bhumara' in *MASI*, No. 16.
20. Banerjea, J.N., *RAA*, p. 100.
21. *JISOA* Vol. III, 1935, Pl. VII, Fig. 3.
22. Agrawala, V.S., *Studies in Indian Art*, 1st ed., p. 187; *Handbook to the Sculpture of the Curzon Museum of Archaeology*, p. 42; *JUPHS*, July, 1935, pp. 83-85.
23. Banerjea, J.N., *RAA*, p. 99.
24. *ASR*, Vol. II, p. 430.
25. *JIH*, XI, 1962, p. 163.
26. *History of Bengal*, Vol. I, 1943, p. 440.
27. *JISOA*, Vol. III, 1935, Pl. VII, Fig. 4.

been suggestively realistic. Diskalkar[28] dates it in the first century A.D. and describes it as a *Pañcamukha-liṅga.* But, on stylistic and other grounds, it can be assigned to the late Kuṣāṇa period[29] and there is no certainty that there was another head on the top of the sculpture. According to the *Rūpamaṇḍana,* the fifth face on the top usually remains invisible and though the *Kāraṇāgama* mentions *Pañcamukha-liṅga* as *Śarānanam* (the number of cupid's *śara* or arrows being five) still it does not mention the position of the fifth face. We have already seen how the Bhiṭā *liṅga* of the Kuṣāṇa period has raised a controversy among scholars. The top of it, according to R.D. Banerji,[30] is shaped as the bust of a male holding a vase in his left hand, while the right is raised in *abhaya-mudrā* and below this bust are four defaced human heads. Whether the Bhiṭā *liṅga* is a specimen of the *Pañcamukha* type is still a debatable question. However, Pañcānana images, representing the five aspects of Śiva, were a favourite theme of the Gupta and post-Gupta iconography.

The exact implication of the rarified white granite colossal Śivaite image[31] (13′-6″) from Parel, Bombay, of the Gupta period is still uncertain. To Stella Kramrisch[32] here we have a unique representation of Śiva in his three-fold presence, vertically one above the other. But the central theme is likened to a *liṅga* and from it emanate multiple representations of two-armed Śiva, two on each side, while the uppermost figure is many-handed, and all of them are depicted with a severe attitude of *yogic* concentration.[33] However, this combined mode of depicting both the anthropomorphic and phallic form of the deity in a single piece of sculpture became highly conventional in subsequent periods and it perhaps formed the next step to the rise of the conception of the *Liṅgodbhavamūrti* in which Śiva upto his knees is usually represented as rising out of the flaming *liṅga.*

28. *JUPHS,* Vol. V, pt. 1, p. 37.
29. *JISOA,* Vol. III, 1935, p. 44.
30. *ARASI,* 1909-10, pp. 147-48, Pl. LIV.
31. Saraswati, S.K., *A Survey of Indian Sculpture,* 1957, pl. XXV, fig. 115.
32. *Indian Sculpture,* Calcutta, 1933, p. 70.
33. Saraswati, S.K., *op. cit.,* p. 146.

The *Liṅgodbhavamūrti* is very popular in south India, and according to the *Āgamas*, it should be placed in the niche in the western wall of the *garbhagṛha* of the temple.[34] The iconographic texts give us a detailed description of this form of Śiva. For example, according to the *Aṁśumadbhedāgama*, Śiva in the form of Candraśekhara should be carved on the front of a *liṅga*; as per the *Kāraṇāgama*, at least one-fifth part of the *liṅga* on the top and bottom should be left out without sculpture, the flying swan soaring upwards should be on the top right section and the burrowing boar delving deep into the earth on the left bottom section and the figures of Brahman and Viṣṇu in the *añjali* pose should also be sculptured on the right and left of the *liṅga*, and among the four hands of Śiva, one should be in the *abhaya*, another in the *varada* pose, the third should carry the *paraśu* and the fourth *Kṛṣṇa-mṛga* (black buck).

Gopinatha Rao[35] has illustrated three reliefs which are more or less in accordance with the above description, one from the Kailāsanātha temple at Kāñcīpuram, the second from Ambar Mangalam and the third from the Daśāvatāra cave at Ellora. Among the late varieties, the great Cola specimen from the Bṛhadīśvara Temple of Tanjore contains the four-armed Candraśekharamūrti of Śiva which is 'beautifully carved inside an elliptical cavity on the surface of the column which is decorated with a festoon design on its top'.[36] Another notable specimen (date unknown) in the Rajaputana Museum,[37] Ajmer, wherein the long slender column on which the figure of Śiva is depicted has both the theriomorphic and worshipping anthropomorphic figures of Brahman and Viṣṇu. The *Liṅgodbhavamūrti* in art represents in a beautiful way the Indian method of depicting a continuous narrative by the repetition of figures in the same panel.[38] While referring to a grand specimen in the Musee

34. Gopinatha Rao, T.A.G., *EHI*, Vol. II, pt. 1, p. 105.
35. *Ibid.*, pp. 109-01.
36. Banerjea, J.N., *DHI*, p. 463, Pl. XXXI, fig. 4.
37. *JISOA*, Vol. IX, Pl. X.
38. *The History and Culture of the Indian People*, Vol. III, 1962, p. 439.
For the *Liṅgodbhavamūrti*, see also Sivaramamurti, C., *The Art of India*, p. 78; Kramrisch, S., *The Presence of Śiva*, pp. 158-60.

Guimet in Paris, Zimmer[39] described it 'the phenomenon of the growing, or expanding, form' because in accordance with the suggestion of the tale as something growing and the representation of Brahman and Viṣṇu speeding in opposite directions, the substance of the stone correspondingly expands, outmeasuring their movement and thus the static solid stone is converted into a dynamorphic, multiple event.

The Devadāruvana legend, where Śiva is painted in the ithyphallic form, has found expression in art in the relief in the Mallikārjuna temple[40] (Śrīśailam, Karnool District), and in the several pillar figures in the entrance hall of the Mīnākṣī temple[41] at Madura.

The proto-Śiva of the Indus valley is a priapic deity. Although Marshall[42] is not quite certain whether the phallus (*ūrdhvameḍhra*) of the deity is in reality the end of the waistband, still there is no doubt today that the *ūrdhvaliṅga* of the figure is exposed and prominent. Lakulīśa, though an incarnation of Śiva, is usually represented like the seated *yogin* of Harappa with the *ūrdhvameḍhra* emphasized.[43]

The Śaiva sannyāsins of later days, namely the Kaṛā Liṅgīs and Nāgās, go naked and the former, to quote Wilson,[44] 'to mark their triumph over sensual desires, affix an iron ring and chain on the male organ'. That the prime inspiration of representing Śiva in ithyphallic form came from the non-Aryan world is once again proved by the fact that the face of Śiva in the much-discussed and realistic specimen of Guḍimallam[45] is distinctly Mongoloid, and there is no Brāhmaṇical sacred thread or *yajñopavīta* which is insisted in all the *Āgamas*. But the organ of Śiva in the above specimen, as discernible through the diaphanous drapery, is shown not upwards (*ūrdhvaliṅga*) but hanging downwards like that of the

39. *Myths and Symbols in Indian Art and Civilization*, New York, 1962, pp. 130-31, fig. 30.

40. Longhurst, A.H., in *ASIAR*, Southern circle, 1917-18, p. 32, Pl. XIV, b.

41. Coomaraswamy, A.K., *Yakṣas*, Part II, New Delhi, 1971, p. 44n.

42. *MIC.*, p. 52.

43. *ARASI*, 1906-07, p. 186, figs. 2 and 5; *ibid.*, 1930-34, Pl. CXX(c).

44. *Religious Sects of the Hindus*, Calcutta, 1958, p. 133.

45. Gopinatha Rao, T.A.G., *EHI*, Vol. II, Pt. 1, pp. 66ff.

Tīrthaṅkaras of the Digambara Jain sect. We have seen earlier how the *vrātyas* were closely connected with Śiva and were usually divided into two main classes:[46] (i) *Jyeṣṭha* who were noted for their *śama* or restraint of passion, and worshipped their nude god with the organ hanging downwards (*nīcameḍhra*) and (ii) *Kaniṣṭha* or *Hīna* whose deity was portrayed with his organ upraised (*ūrdhvameḍhra*). The Guḍimallam specimen perhaps represents the first type; the proto-Śiva of Harappa and Lakulīśa of later days represent the second.

After the Harappa example we are to encounter the *Ūrdhvaliṅga* characteristic in a number of Śiva images in Mathurā art, belonging to the Kuṣāṇa and the Gupta periods. On the reverse of Huviṣka's gold coin we have, as pointed out by Gardner,[47] a three-headed, four armed, nimbate, ithyphallic figure of Śiva, and this *Ūrdhvaliṅga* mark is not noticed in any other early numismatic representations of Śiva. In art of Mathurā, Śiva is always shown as *Ūrdhvaliṅga*. Perhaps the main inspiration of emphasizing this feature came from the Lakulīśa sect of the Pāśupata Śaivas who made Mathurā their centre in the Kuṣāṇa and Gupta periods as is evident from the Mathurā stone inscription of the time of Candragupta II.[48] Coomaraswamy[49] has illustrated a unique specimen of 'Śiva as liṅgin' of the late Kuṣāṇa period from Mathurā, analogous to the Guḍimallam specimen, which has the image of a four-armed, standing, *Ūrdhvameḍhra* Śiva on one side of a long pillar-like emblem. In two typical *dampatī* relief slabs of the Mathurā Museum (Nos. G. 52 and 2495), belonging to the Kuṣāṇa period, the *Ūrdhvareta* Śiva is seen standing with his spouse in āliṅganamudrā.[50] In another *dampatī*

46. Bhandarkar, D.R., *Some Aspects of Ancient Indian Culture*, Madras, 1940, p. 44.

To Bhandarkar, the explanation of *śama-nīchā-meḍhrā* by *Lāṭyāyana-sūtra* (VIII. 6. 4) as 'those who through old age have lost the power of procreation' is totally unacceptable as it is impossible to single out those people and insulting to bring such people under one class.

47. *British Museum Catalogue of Coins of the Greek and Scythic Kings of India*, p. 148, Pl. XXVIII, 16.

48. *Ep. Ind.*, Vol. XXI, p. 8.

49. *HIIA*, p. 67, Pl. XVIII, fig. 68.

50. Agrawala, V.S., *A Catalogue of Brāhmaṇical Images in Mathurā Art*, 1951, pp. 25, 27.

image (No. 474) of the Gupta period the same characteristic is discernible.[51] In an inscribed Śiva-Pārvatī image from Kosam,[52] belonging to the Gupta period, the *ūrdhvaliṅga* of Śiva is shown. Even in the *Ardhanārīśvara* statuettes of the Kuṣāṇa period,[53] now in the Mathurā Museum (Nos. 800 and 874), Śiva is depicted in his *ūrdhvareta* aspect. We have in the same Museum (No. 2084) a three feet high Gupta sculpture of unusual interest wherein Śiva is represented in his post-nuptial state enjoying the company of his consort, his left arm is thrown around Pārvatī's neck but his *membrum virile* is shown aloft.[54]

The *ūrdhvaliṅga* is common and prominent in almost all types of anthropomorphic figures of Śiva found in Bengal[55] upto the thirteenth century A.D., namely, in the varieties such as Candraśekhara, Nṛtyamūrti, Sadāśiva, Umā-Maheśvara, Ardhanārīśvara, Kalyāṇasundara and Aghora Rudra. This may be perhaps due to the impact of the Tāntric or Vāmācārī cult[56] as the eastern part of India was practically its nerve-centre. In a sculptural specimen of Umā-Maheśvara, found at Chauduar[57] in Orissa, Śiva is depicted with *Ūrdhvareta.* Even in the scenes of offering *halāhala* or deadly poison to Śiva, as revealed by the Pāhārpur sculpture,[58] the god is represented with *Ūrdhva-liṅga.*

Another trend of representing the phallus in Indian art is by placing it on the head or shoulder of the worshipper or the deity himself is depicted as carrying the load. In the *Rāmāyaṇa*,[59] we have the reference of Rāvaṇa carrying a golden *liṅga* wherever he went. According to epigraphical records,[60] the antiquity of the practice of carrying the *liṅga* on the person is to be traced

51. *Ibid.*, p. 29.
52. Fleet, J.F., *Gupta Inscriptions*, p. 266.
53. Agrawala, V.S., *A Catalogue of Brāhmaṇical Images in Mathurā Art*, p. 27.
54. Diskalkar, D.B., 'Some Brāhmaṇical Sculptures in the Mathurā Museum' in *JUPHS*, Jan., 1932, p. 39, Plates 16 and 17.
55. *History of Bengal*, Vol. I, 1943, pp. 441ff.
56. Ghosh, A., in *IC*, Vol. II, p. 766.
57. *MASI*, No. 44, Pl. VII (2).
58. *ARASI*, 1926-27, Pl. XXXIII, b.
59. *Uttarakāṇḍa*, Section 31, V. 42f.
60. Fleet, J.F., *Gupta Inscriptions*, pp. 236, 245.

to the Bhāraśivas, the matrimonial relatives of the Vākāṭakas, to whom Śiva was the guardian and symbol of national resurgence and we find 'Śiva everywhere in this period'.[61] We have in the Bhārat Kalā Bhavan (Banaras),the fragment of a sculpture (provenance unknown) which depicts the *liṅga* placed on a *padmapīṭha* being carried on the head by one[62] whose broken hands on the sides of the *padmapīṭha* are still extant.

R. Sengupta[63] has brought to light some interesting panels from different parts of the Kailāsa temple at Ellora, attributed to the Rāṣṭrakūṭas. In this first example,[64] we have Umā sitting on the left lap of Śiva and the *liṅga* is apparently being carried by Śiva on the right shoulder and touched by his back right hand. In another sculpture[65] of the same nature, we find the *liṅga* on the left shoulder of Śiva and touched by his back left hand. In the next specimen[66] both Śiva and Pārvatī hold the *liṅga*. Sitting by the side of Pārvatī, Śiva here carries the *liṅga* in the left hand, raises the right hand in *abhaya* pose and Pārvatī touches it with her right hand. In the last panel of the same type from the same temple,[67] the treatment of which is better, Śiva carries the *liṅga* on a pedestal with the left hand, while Pārvatī embraces it with her right hand.

In the Cālukya temples of Saṅgameśvara, Mallikārjuna and Virūpākṣa at Paṭṭadakul (Bijapur District, Karnataka) we have many sculptures of the above types, among which the Vīṇādhara in the first temple and Maheśvara playing dice with Umā in the second, are particularly notable. In the Vīṇādhara image,[68] Śiva in *lalitāsana* holds the *vīṇā* with the proper hands, the *liṅga* supported on the right shoulder is comfortably touched by his back right hand and the back left hand is turned to left. In the

61. Jayaswal, K.P., *An Imperial History of India*, Lahore, 1934, p. 49.

62. Nilakanta Sastri, K.A., *A Comprehensive History of India*, Vol. II, 1st ed., p. 258.

63. *JAS*, Vol. I, No. 1, 1959, pp. 41-45.

64. *Ibid.*, fig. 1.

65. *Ibid.*, fig. 2.

66. *Ibid.*, fig. 4.

67. *JAS*, Vol. IV, No. 2, 1962, pp. 44, Pl. VI, B.

68. *Ibid.*, Pl. IA.

Mallikārjuna panel, we have the *Umā-Sahitākṣa-krīḍā*[69] image where Śiva sitting on a cushion in *utkaṭikāsana*, with the *liṅga* on the right shoulder and held with the back right hand, is evidently arguing with Umā over the game. Among the six panels of the Virūpākṣa temple we have only one in which the *liṅga* is placed on the right shoulder of Śiva; but he does not hold it. The Aihole panel of Umā-Maheśvara, now in the Prince of Wales Museum, Bombay, also represents Śiva with the *liṅga* on his shoulder.[70]

Our survey will remain incomplete if we do not mention the legend how Rāvaṇa got possession of a *liṅga* from Śiva on the condition that he would always carry it. On his way south Rāvaṇa is said to have halted near the present Deoghar in Bihar to purify himself and requested Viṣṇu in the guise of a Brāhmaṇa to hold the *liṅga* for the time being; but the latter ultimately put it down on the ground and vanished. Rāvaṇa returned and saw that the *liṅga* would not move further, and it has been there ever since under the name of Mahādeva Rāvaṇeśvara of Baidyanātha.[71] We have yet a number of *liṅgas* in the south associated with this story. The famous Mahābaleśvara *liṅga* of the Pallavas, at Gokarṇa[72] in Mahābalipuram, is named after the almighty *liṅga* which refused to move in spite of the best efforts of Rāvaṇa to uproot it.[73] Rāvaṇa's attempt even to raise the mountain where Śiva carrying the *liṅga* is

69. *Ibid.*, Pl. 11.

R. Sengupta has suggested the term *Umā-sahita ākṣa-krīḍā* to indicate this particular aspect in *Gaṅgānāth Jhā Research Institute Publication* Vol. XIV, Pts. 1-2, pp. 155-58.

70. Chakravarti, S.N., *P.W. Museum: A Guide to the Antiquities of the Historic Period*, p. 21, Pl. X-a.

71. Oppert, *Original Inhabitants of India*, pp. 137, 375.

72. Gokarṇa (that is, 'Cow's ear') is mentioned in the *Rāmāyaṇa* and the *Mahābhārata*.—See *OST*, Vol. IV, p. 285.

We have a legend behind the name of this place. After a long meditation into the water when Śiva came out he became enraged and struck the earth because Brahmā, weary of the delay of former's arrival, had already done the former's task, that is, shaped the earth and filled it with life. The earth-goddess, taking the form of a cow, appeased the angry-god and Śiva ultimately rose to the surface through the ear and rose on the Gokarṇ beach (near Kerala), where a cave known as the *Rudrayoni* or 'Rudra's passage' marks the spot.

73. *Gazetteer of the Bombay Presidency*, Vol. XV, pt. II, p. 290n.

seated with Pārvatī is depicted in the sculpture of the Mukteśvara temple at Kāñcīpuram and the Kailāsa temple at Ellora. But the former specimen seems lifeless in comparison with the latter which is equated by Rene Grousset with Michael Angelo's 'Last Judgement' at Vatican.[74]

The practices of carrying the *liṅga* either on the shoulder, or on the head or suspended through strings round the neck, appear to be very old. The philosophy behind this custom was unity with the god. "Just as the larva which associates with the bee, itself in the end becomes a bee, so the man who realizes unity with Śiva through Śiva-yoga himself becomes one with Śiva."[75]

(iii) Śiva and the Liṅga in Further India

The main urge that impelled the Ancient Indians to cross the sea towards *Suvarṇadvīpa* was no doubt material, but it brought in its train the entire spiritual heritage of India. *Dvīpāntara Bhārata* or 'India of the Islands' was established by a 'gentle fusion' of immigrant Indian and non-Indian races of the colonies and the religion and culture of the 'master' permeated the life of the indigenous people.[1] While the concept of Rudra-Śiva – a grand product of the composite Aryan-non-Aryan culture—was evolving on the soil of India, the Greater India at the same time became the favourite cradle of Śiva.

The beginning of the story, that is, how Śiva got a stronghold in Indo-China and Indonesia, is lost in obscurity and we have

74. *The Sum of History*, p. 128.
Cf. Sharma, B.N., 'Rāvaṇa lifting Mount Kailāsa in Indian Art' in *East and West*, 23, 1973, pp. 327-38.

75. Danielou, Alain, *Hindu Polytheism*, London, 1964, p. 96.

1. Mukherjee, R.K., *A History of Indian Civilization*, Vol. I, 1965, Bombay, pp. 377ff.; *The Culture and Art of India*, 1st ed., p. 65.

In the preface of his monumental work (*The Art of India*, New York, 1977, p. 23) Sivaramamurti observes: "India has always loved to share its riches with others. From the earliest times Indian navigators carried men of taste and learning throughout Southeast Asia. And the fragrance of Indian art wafted through Central Asia and beyond."

only some mythical tales and traditions in this regard. In the epic and Purāṇic legends, Agastya, the archetype of Indian sage is not only mentioned as having stayed the abnormal growth of the Vindhya range, but also described in mythological language as having swallowed up the ocean in a fit of temper to stop piracy and thus got the right of access to the vast land of El-Dorado. In the Saṅgam literature, Śiva himself recruited this mythical hero Agastya for his colonizing mission and the latter composed *Śakalādhikāram*, a book on image-making. This first teacher and propagator of Śaivism in the colonies is still worshipped in Java, as *Śiva-guru*, under the Javanese name of *Valaing* (pole star) and the images of Agastya and his spouse Lopāmudrā were almost on par with Śiva and Umā in Cambodia and Java.[2] In this context it is interesting to quote an inscription from Angkar Vat[3] : "The Brāhmaṇ Agastya, born in the land of the Aryans, devoted to the worship of Śiva having come by his psychic powers to the land of the Cambodians, for the purpose of woshipping the *Śiva-liṅga*, known as Bhadreśvara, and having worshipped the god for a long time, attained to beautitude".

The Chinese annals attributed the establishment of the Hindu kingdom in Fu-nam in the first century A.D. to one Brāhmaṇa named Kauṇḍinya. We hear of another Kauṇḍinya towards the end of the fourth or the beginning of the fifth century A.D. who was elected king by the people of Fu-nan. The Kauṇḍinya tradition is interesting for more than one reason. First, how the Brāhmaṇas came to Indo-China by crossing the sea is a problem. Secondly, Kauṇḍinya's landing was at first resisted by the indigenous uncivilized people headed by the naked Nāga princess Somā whom he later married. Thirdly, he founded a royal dynasty which had a remarkable influence on all the parts of Further India and the names of his descendants, who assumed Kṣatriyahood, ended in 'Varman'. Finally, Kauṇḍinya is the harbinger and propagator of the Śiva cult in Fu-nan, and from this centre, Śaivism radiated in all directions.

Regarding the anthropomorphic representations of Śiva in colonial art we have, broadly speaking, two phases. The first

2. Mukherjee, R.K., *A History of Indian Civilization*, Vol. I, p. 377.
3. *Cf. Ibid.*, p. 378.

phase is marked by images of Śiva which are close imitations, sometimes exact copies of Indian models as if the colonists brought with them not simply the themes but even traditions and styles. The second phase exhibits the refreshing admission of the local styles on Indian themes and Śiva appears in altered dress although the impact of Indian technique is still now traceable.

In order to emphasize the dynamic character of racial fusion and cultural entity, as a result of which the Great Śiva came into existence both in India and outside, Bernet Kempers[4] used the Dutch term *Cultuurstroom*, that is, a "stream of culture" which came into being "as a result of the mingling of certain elements, which continuously absorbed elements of other cultures both in India proper and elsewhere in Asia" and necessarily changed the Indian pattern and developed into new forms of Greater Indian culture. On the mainland of Indo-China we have two powerful centres of Śaivism, Kāmboja and Campā.

Kāmboja

Kāmboja (Cambodia) was originally a vassal state of Fu-nan; but in the sixth century A.D., the latter passed into oblivion and the former took the position of supremacy and gave its name to the whole country. Our main sources of information in this respect are the Chinese accounts and the inscriptions mostly written in Sanskrit. The first batch of Hindu colonists who went over to Kāmboja and the kings of the early dynasty were followers of Śiva. In the ancient world the religion of the king was usually the religion of the people; necessarily, Śiva came to be regarded as the national god, Śaivism the state religion, and the art of the Khmer country was the handmaid of religion. That Śiva here enjoyed unique honour is proved by his multifarious names found in inscriptions, which sometimes begin with *namaś Śivāya*,[5] and representations in art, although we have not enough remains of it. Over and above his usual Indian epithets, we are to face his local names

4. *Cultural Relations between India and Java*, Calcutta, 1937, p. 17.

5. Bose, P.N., *Hindu Colony of Cambodia*, Madras, 1927, p. 265. Bhattacharya, K., 'Religious Speculations in Ancient Cambodia' in Sarkar, H.B., ed. *R.C. Majumdar Volume*, Calcutta, 1970, pp. 78-97.

and forms which prove that the great cosmopolitan god had absorbed a large number of local Khmer deities.

In the Aug Chumnik Inscription Śiva appears as the local deity *Śrī-Mrātakeśvara* and in the Prea Kev inscription he is represented as *Jalāṅgeśa.*[6] As *Śrī-Śikhareśvara* or Lord of the peak, he was represented on the hill-tops and the Liṅga—on the mountain motif, as proved by the Changgal inscription, was a favourite theme of the Khmer art.[7] The temple of Bhadreśvara Śiva, the tutelary deity of the royal family, is to be found on the peak of the Vat Phu Hill (near Bassac in Laos) also known as Liṅga-parvata.[8]

In Kāmboja, Śiva is represented both in his anthropomorphic and phallic forms. In the anthropomorphic form, the god is usually attended by Nandin and Kāla. We have a beautiful image of Hara-Pārvatī, installed in the year 613 A.D.,[9] in which the goddess is found seated on the left thigh of the god with a suggestive posture. This image is an exact replica of the Indian prototypes bearing the impact of Tāntricism since to the Tāntric worshippers the images of Devī seated on the lap of Śiva are considered as aids for the correct performance of the yoga.

The phallus was not always made of stone. We have the record of the erection of *Suvarṇa-liṅga* (golden *liṅga*) by Bhavavarman and Udayādityavarman and the *Sphaṭika-liṅga* (crystal *liṅga*) by a sage during the reign of Sūryavarman.[10] Perhaps the most popular type of representations of Śiva was in his *Caturmukha-liṅga* form. The grand pyramidal Śiva temple of Bayon of later days, which was a veritable art gallery, contained nearly forty high towers each representing four finely chiselled faces of colossal Śiva with a third eye on the forehead and rapt in

6. *Ibid.*, p. 262.

7. Bosch, F.D.K., *The Golden Germ*, Holland, 1960, p. 165.

The word 'Khmer', as the Cambodians call themselves and their languages, comes from *Kamari* (Śiva), one of the (*gotra*) class names of the Kāmbujas of India.—See Chatterji, B.R., *South-East Asia in Transition*, 1967, p. 5.

8. Majumdar, R.C., ed., *The History and Culture of the Indian People*, Vol. III (*The Classical Age*), Bombay, 1962, p. 644.

9. Majumdar, R.C., *Ancient Indian Colonies in South-East Asia*, Baroda, 1955, p. 70.

10. Bose, P.N., *op. cit.*, pp. 275-76.

meditation on the four sides. These images are also sometimes identified with Avalokiteśvara.

In Indo-China the kings were not only god's representatives on earth, but sometimes they were identified with god himself. The practice of naming both the *liṅga* and the images of Śiva, erected by them, after their own name or after the name of their ancestors, was widely prevalent in Kāmboja, Campā, Java and other areas. This practice was not unknown in India. Aśoka is said to have been a devotee of Śiva in his early life[11] and Kalhaṇa[12] notes how the great Maurya king founded two temples of Śiva-Aśokeśvara in Kashmir. Aśoka's son Jalauka erected the temple of Śiva-Jalukeśvara.[13] This early practice was followed even by the later Candella kings, namely, Pṛthivīdeva who installed the image of Śiva under the name of Pṛthivīdeveśvara,[14] and by the Cālukyas.[15] However, in Kāmboja the king Rudravarman installed his own statue as that of Śiva, known as Rudreśvara. We have near Angkor Thom a three-storied pyramid, known as Phnom Baken enshrining Yaśodeśvara *liṅga*, showing it to be Yaśovarman's shrine.[16] Again, Yaśovarman himself erected two famous images of Śiva, which bore the names of Indravarmeśvara (at the Loley temple) and Mahīpatīśvara, named respectively after the king's father Indravarman and of his maternal grandfather Mahīpativarman and interestingly enough, the face of the images was indistinguishable from those of the kings.[17]

Punnāgavarman, even during his life time, consecrates an image of Śiva 'which is made after his own likeness'.[18] In an interesting inscription from Prea Ngouk[19] we read that a

11. Smith, V.A., *Early History of India*, fourth ed., Oxford, 1924, p. 185.
12. *Rājataraṅgiṇī* I. 105-07.
13. *Ibid.*, I, 124, 148.
14. *Epigraphia Indica*, Vol. I, p. 38.
15. *Bombay Gazetteer*, Vol. I, Part II, p. 190.
16. Coomaraswamy, A.K., *History of Indian and Indonesian Art*, London, 1927, p. 190.
17. Chatterji, B.R., *Indian Cultural Influence in Cambodia*, Calcutta, 1964, pp. 223-24.
18. *Journal Asiatique*, Paris, Vol. XX, 1882, p. 145; *cf.* Chatterjee, B.R., *Indian Cultural Influence in Cambodia*, p. 224.
19. Eliot, C., *Hinduism and Buddhism*, Vol. III, London, 1962, p. 116. Over and above the anthropomorphic and phallic representations of

victorious general presented his king the booty he had captured requesting him to offer it "to your subtle ego who is Īśvara dwelling in a golden *liṅga*". In course of time there came into existence the mystic cult of Royal God or Devarāja, which was virtually a *Śivaliṅga.* Bosch[20] has shown how the *Liṅgodbhava-mūrti* of Śiva provides an adequate explanation of the 'fiery *liṅgam*' of the Devarāja cult of Kāmboja and Java, where it signifies the "fiery essence of kingship, a radiant earthly emanation of royal wisdom and dominion."

That Śaivism in Kāmboja was pantheistic is proved by the attributes lavished upon Śiva as *Vibhu, Īśa, Jagatpati,* and *Paramātman.* His commanding position over the other two deities of the Hindu Triad is clearly emphasized in the Aug Chumnik inscription[21] wherein Brahman and Viṣṇu are found standing with folded hands before Śiva. But although Śiva enjoyed a dominant position, we have here no evidence of severe hostility between Śaivism and Vaiṣṇavism; rather both religion and art showed tolerance and syncretic trend from the beginning. Like the Hari-Hara of India, we have some early examples of the composite icons, named various as, Śaṅkara-Nārāyaṇa, Hara-Acyuta, Hari-Śaṅkara, and Viṣṇu-Candreśvara.[22]

Perhaps the most interesting and original aspect of Cambodian Śaivism was the erection of *liṅgas* in the name of both Śiva and

---

the deity, the footprint of Śiva or *Śivapāda,* just like the Indian counterpart of *Viṣṇupāda* of Gayā and *Buddhapāda* on Adam's peak in Ceylon, was regarded equally sacred in Kambuja and we have heard how a famous temple was built on a hill-top in 604 A.D. to house the *Śivapāda* consecrated by a pious Brāhmin.

—See Majumdar, R.C., *Ancient Indian Colonies in South-East Asia,* Baroda, 1955, p. 60.

20. Bosch, F.D.K., *The Golden Germ,* Holland, 1960, pp. 28, 166.

In Cambodia the mystic cult of Devarāja was intimately associated with the worship of Śiva. See Das, R.R., *Art Traditions of Cambodia,* Calcutta, 1974, pp .186-87. Śiva, in Cambodia, was referred to as *Caturānana* and *Caturmukha.*

For the Harihara image in the National Museum at Phnom Penh which is 'an adaptation of an original Indian theme done in a pleasant local style' of Cambodia, see Sivaramamurti, C., *The Art of India,* p. 197.

21. Bose, P.N., *Hindu Colony of Cambodia,* Madras, 1927, p. 274.

22. Sircar, D.C., *Select Inscriptions,* Vol. I, 1965, pp. 509ff.

Viṣṇu, and thus we have the Śambhu-Viṣṇu *liṅga* erected by Īśānavarman and Śiva-Keśava *liṅga* by a potentate as found in the Vat Praptus inscription.[23] With the spread of Buddhism, there were many common traits of Śiva and the Buddha in art so that it becomes difficult to distinguish at first sight the image of the one from that of the other.

The art of Kāmboja is usually divided into two phases, the 'primitive' and 'classic',[24] and Śiva is represented in the art of both. The great Angkar monuments, which are the marvels of world art, and the Bayon temple are associated with the classic phase. The first phase, though named 'primitive', represented perhaps the best traditions of Gupta-Pallava art of India. Groslier[25] is not right when he labels this phase of Kāmboja art as the totally 'foreign' art of Fu-nan which had no influence on the indigenous art of later days as the Chen-las of the North, who were the conquerors, disdained the art of the conquered people. But it may be pointed out that, as in India, Śiva grew and developed in the religion and art of Greater India as a result of happy marriage of multifarious cultures and civilizations. Can we dream of any dynamic art or culture anywhere in the world, which has not come as a result of fusion or amalgamation ? The 'primitive' art of Fu-nan necessarily developed by natural stages of evolution into the 'classic' Khmer art.

Campā

The art and religion of Campā (Annam), on the east coast of the Indo-Chinese peninsula, were more or less identical with that of Kāmboja; rather Campā preserved the torch of the Śiva cult brightly burning, in the face of the avalanche of foreign attacks. Śrī-Māra, the first historical Hindu king who founded a dynasty and is attributed variously to a date between the second and the fifth century A.D., was a devotee of Śiva. The whole of ancient Campā was adorned with beautiful temples of

23. Bose, P.N., *Hindu Colony of Cambodia*, pp. 277-78.
24. Majumdar, R.C., *Hindu Colonies in the Far East*, Calcutta, 1944, pp. 185-86.
25. *cf.* Chatterji, B.R., *Indian Cultural Influence in Cambodia*, p. 67.

Indian type, and we have three important groups[26] of them, namely those of Myson, Dong Duong and Po-Nagar, the second being Buddhist and the other two dedicated to Śiva. Śiva was represented both in his anthropomorphic and phallic forms, and the latter was perhaps more popular.

The type and shape of the *liṅgas* in Campā were more or less the same as in India, and these *liṅgas* are usually placed on square pedestals though in some specimens the pedestal is round and *yoni* is represented therein and in some specimens several *liṅgas* are placed together on the pedestal. What distinguishes the Campā art are the extraordinary *mukha-liṅgas* in which the reigning kings, to indicate their identification with Śiva, used to depict their own figures on the *liṅga* of the deity in their peculiar Cām dress. M. Finot[27] supposes that these *mukha-liṅgas* represented the deified kings as the Cām sculptors here made a departure from all the accepted norms and lines followed in India and gave to the figure the Campā king's physiognomy, headdress and ornaments. But in the Hoa-Que Stelae inscription[28] of Bhadravarman III, the *Liṅgodbhava* legend is inscribed in which Brahman and Viṣṇu bowed before the *liṅga* and Śiva showed them his face from the middle part of the *liṅga*.

We come to know from a Sanskrit inscription (No. 2), written in chaste classical style, that Bhadravarman I (known to the Chinese as Fan-Hu-ta) founded at about 400 A.D. the sacred city of Myson and erected after his own name the famous Bhadreśvara *liṅga* or the temple of Bhadreśvarasvāmin, which became a national centre of pilgrimage and the centre of Śaivite art. The successors of Bhadravarman later on adorned Myson with beautiful sculptures of Śiva, now to be found in the Museum at Tourance. We have here the standing three-eyed figure of Śiva with a fine moustache and a smiling face.[29] Most of the specimens are very simple and less decorated and some are undoubt-

26. Majumdar, R.C., *Hindu Colonies in the Far East*, p. 149.

27. *Bulletin de l'Ecole Francaise d'Exteme Orient*, Hanoi, Tome I, p. 14; *cf.*, Bose, P.N., *The Indian Colony of Campa*, Madras, 1926, pp. 136-37.

28. Majumdar, R.C., *Ancient Indian Colonies in the Far East*, Vol. I, Lahore, 1927, p. 175.

29. *Ibid.*, p. 178.

edly "unequal in quality, the finest pieces are marvels of powerful modelling or grace of conception".[30]

According to an inscription (No. 7), it was some time in the sixth century A.D. that the great Bhadreśvara temple of Myson was burnt, and king Śambhuvarman reinstalled the *liṅga* and added his own name with that of the god called Śambhu-Bhadreśvara. Later on, a mythical origin was attributed to this presiding deity of Campā and it came to be associated with the original Hātakeśvara *liṅga* which fell from Śiva as a result of the curse of the sages of the Devadāru forest. At Dong-Duong, we have an inscription of the reign of Indravarman, which glorifies the Śambhu-Bhadreśvara *liṅga* 'filled with the essence of fire and hereditary royalty' proving perhaps the existence of the Devarāja cult or the cult of the king-god of Kambuja.[31]

During the reign of Satyavarman, as found in Inscription No. 22, the Javanese raiders burnt the Śambhu temple of Po-Nagar and carried away the famous *mukhaliṅga* established there by a legendary king Vicitrasāgara. But Satyavarman restored it and named it *Satya-mukhaliṅga*. We learn from another inscription (No. 23) how, during the reign of Indravarman, the Javanese raiders again demolished the famous shrine of Bhadrādhipatīśvara 'established there for many thousands of years'. Indravarman re-erected both the temple and image of Śiva and renamed it Indra-Bhadreśvara. The same king installed two other images of the same deity called after him, viz., Indra-Bhogeśvara and Indra-Parameśvara. Nikrāntavarman, according to another inscription (No. 30), erected three important images of Śiva by the names of Vikrānta-Rudra, Śrī Vikrānta-Rudreśvara and Śrī Vikrānta-Devādhibhaveśvara.

M. Aymonier[32] has found a fine *mukha-liṅga* in the tower of Po Klaun Garai where the face of Śiva bearing moustache and having natural grandeur is sculptured on the *liṅga* in half hunch.

We have numerous names and representations of the anthropomorphic forms of Śiva in different postures which were usually placed in the Campā temples as decorative designs. Two remarkable, though mutilated, strongly built human figures of Śiva

30. Coomaraswamy, A.K., *History of Indian and Indonesian Art*, London, 1927, p. 196.
31. *Ibid.*, p. 197.
32. *Indian Antiquary*, 1888, pp. 67-68.

standing in a defiant attitude with the head well-decorated with *jaṭāmukuṭa* are found at Tra Kieu.[33] M. Finot[34] has brought to light some early bas-reliefs of Tourance, in one of which we have a multi-armed, five-faced Śiva standing on the Nandin and holding a lance in an attitude of attack. In the second specimen we find the Naṭarāja Śiva dancing the *tāṇḍava.* The third specimen presents the seated figure of Śiva with a rosary of beads in one hand and a trident in the other. In front of the temple of Po Klaun Garai[35] there is the famous six-armed standing Śiva with two upper hands clasped behind the head, and the others holding a trident, lotus, sword and bowl respectively.

One peculiar way of representing Śiva in Campā art, particularly at Dong Duong and Tympanum, was as *dvārapāla* (doorkeeper of the temple). In this form the face of the god is almost ghostly with projecting eyes and long teeth. The *dvārapāla* is sometimes carved on his bull and brandish a sort of wedge-shaped instrument. The uncanny and terrible features are sometimes emphasized in some seated corpulent figures of Śiva as found at Yaṅ Mum and Draṅ Lai.[36] However, the tendency of representing the deity in this terrible form did not last long, and the Cām sculptors of later days, preferred the seated image of Śiva rapt in meditation, with a beautifully decorated halo behind the head. In Campā art Śiva is very often three-eyed with his Brāhmaṇical sacred thread. The serpents usually cover his body as ornaments and the mount Nandin always accompanies his master.

33. *Ars Asiatica*, Vol. IV, pl. XXII.

34. Cf. Bose, P.N., *The Indian-Colony of Campa*, Madras, 1926, pp. 138-40. Regarding similarity between the dancing Bhairava from Sumatra and the South Indian specimens, see Sivaramamurti, C., *The Art of India*, p. 198.

For the Nepalese cult of Bhairava and its image, see Lowry, J., *Tibetan Art*, HMSO, 1973, p. 39.

New researches by Soviet archaeologists at Pianjikent, in Central Asia, famous for its remarkable paintings, have yielded frescoes that have parallels in Indian art at Ajanta frescoes and Bharhut relief. See *The Sculpture and Painting of Ancient Pianjikent*, Moscow, 1959, tab. xiv.; Belenitsky, A., ('The History of Cultural Relations between Central Asia and India in the Early Medieval Period', *Ancient India*, Moscow, 1964, p. 192) has compared the blue dancer as the nīlakaṇṭha naṭarāja Śiva.

See also Pal, Pratapaditya, *The Sensuous Immortals : A Selection of Sculptures from the Pan-Asian Collection*, Los Angeles, 1978.

35. Bose, P.N., *The Indian Colony of Champa*, Madras, 1926, pp. 138-39.

36. Majumdar, R.C., *Ancient Indian Colonies in the Far East*, Vol. I, pp. 179-080.

To the Cām people, the depiction of Śiva as a normal human being was more popular than in his 'monstrous appearance'[37] and it is only in exceptional cases that the god is represented with a multiplicity of hands which ranged from four to thirty. Śiva appears sometimes with Umā, and in the Dong Phuc[38] specimen, the two coalesced into one as Ardhanārīśvara in which the male part is marked by fine moustache and third eye and the female side is indicated by the developed breast and dress. As in Kambuja, the amalgamation of the cults of Śiva and Viṣṇu is expressed in Campā by the composite figure of Śaṅkara-Nārāyaṇa, which was a favourite image to Indravarman. However, Campā cannot boast of the superb specimens of Kambuja as the Cām artists, though they followed mostly the Indian canons and forms, were not inspired by the Indian ideal in the same way as the artists of Fu-nan, and reserved a greater freedom in matters of details.[39]

Burma

In Burma, Śiva was not given the commanding position which he enjoyed in Kambuja and Campā, and we have only some stray finds of the anthropomorphic and phallic forms of the deity. Ray[40] has brought to light some coins from Arakan, bearing Śaivite symbols like trident and bull, mostly belonging to the kings of the Candra dynasty (c. 400—c. 1000 A.D.) who were evidently followers of the cult of Śiva. Regarding the phallic representations of the deity, it is interesting to quote Taw Sein Ko[41] who observed in 1924 that "no object which can certainly be identified as a *Liṅgam* has yet been discovered in Burma, and what has often been identified as a *Liṅgam* may very well be of the shape of a *Stūpa*". However, the phallic nature of the stone slab (14″ in height) discovered at Kalaganon near Hmawza[42] is not disputed today.

37. Parmentier, H., in *Indian Culture*, Calcutta, Vol. II, pp. 411-12.
38. Majumdar, R.C., *Ancient Indian Colonies in the Far East*, Vol. I, p. 189.
39. Bose, P.N., *The Indian Colony of Champa*, p. 128.
40. Kay, N.L. *Brahmanical Gods in Burma*, Calcutta, 1932, pp. 51-52.
41. *An. Rep. Arch. Sur. Burma*, 1924, p. 24; *ARASI*, 1910-11, pp. 90-92.
42. *ARASI*, 1926-27, p. 182.

We have in the Rangoon Museum an image of Śiva, discovered from Thātoñ, which on stylistic grounds may be considered as one of the earliest anthropomorphical representations of the deity in Burma.[43] Ray[44] has identified some indistinct relief slabs in one of which (No. 3) we have a seated figure of Śiva as if he was kneeling holding 'in his right hand the trident which rests on the palm of his left' and crowned with *jaṭā-mukuṭa.* But the most notable bas-relief of this group (Rangoon Museum, exhibit No. 10/6) is the Ellora-type seated Śiva-Pārvatī image, carved in bold relief on hard reddish sandstone, where the goddess is found seated between the two arms to the left of the god.[45] Considering the high *jaṭā-mukuṭa* of the deity, a halo round his head, with different popular emblems in his hands, the serpent hanging downwards from the shoulder of the god and the bull under the right foot and the total spirit of the sculpture, it is sometimes considered as 'the work of an Indian colonial artist'.[46]

Siam

Siam under the name of Dvārāvatī originally formed part of the Kambuja empire, and here also Śiva shared the same insignificant position. Śiva in his anthropomorphic form has found expression in the art of Dvārāvatī, mainly found at Lavapurī (Navapura), bearing Gupta impact. Much less interesting from the point of view of art are the large bronze statues of Śiva of later date.[47] Although *liṅgas* are still venerated in a few .temples at Wāt Pho[48] in Bangkok, we have stray finds of the *liṅgas* of early date.

Java

In Java, a part of Indonesia, the triumph of Śiva is similarly noticeable. The allusions to *Yavadvīpa* (Java) in the *Rāmāyaṇa* and Ptolemy's mention of it in the second century A. D. prove

43. Ray, N.R., op. cit., pp. 53-54.
44. *Ibid.*, pp. 55-59.
45. Coomaraswamy, A.K., *HIIA*, Pl. LV, Fig. 193.
46. Ray, N.R., *op. cit.*, pp. 57-58.
47. Coomaraswamy, A.K., *HIIA*, p. 177.
48. Eliot, C., *Hinduism and Buddhism*, Vol. III, London, 1962, p. 97.

that Java had come under the influence of India since very early times, and there also Śiva enjoyed unquestioned supremacy. An inscription of late date (732 A. D.) refers to Kuñjarakuñjadeśa which reminds us of a place of that name in South India that seems to have been the source of the Agastya cult of Java. The immigrants from the South Indian tract brought to Java a 'miraculous radiant *liṅgaṃ*'[49].

Caṇḍī is the regular name applied to a religious structure in Java. The earliest caṇḍīs are those on the Dieng plateau in Central Java, a holy city, some 6,500 ft. above the sea, dedicated to the worship of Śiva. Now we have only eight temples here although formerly the number might have been greater. The Dieng affords many notable human images of Śiva which bear the impress of the Gupta, early Cālukya and Pallava art.[50] However, considering the very sober and simple nature of the sculptures, Bernet Kempers[51] thinks it "impossible to indicate a particular school of art either in India proper or in Further India which corresponds to the Dieng temples" and, according to him, they cannot be regarded as a simple offshoot of Indian art. But we should remember that sobriety and dignity are the characteristic marks of Gupta art.

The art in the vast Śaivite complex of Lara Jonggrang in Central Java, also called caṇḍī Prambanam, containing six main temples of Śiva, Viṣṇu and Brahman and their respective *Vāhanas*, and more than two hundred minor shrines arranged in three series surrounding them, is a fitting counterpart of the art of *Caṇḍī* Sevu and the Great Borobodur and practically surpass any representation of Śiva that has been executed in ancient Indian art. "In its melting tenderness and elegance", in the words of R. K. Mukherjee,[52] "its dynamic rhythm, restlessness and poignancy Prambanam carries the plastic techniques and traditions of the Gupta and Pallava schools to perfection".

Perhaps the finest example of a 'relatively old' circular shrine

49. Coomaraswamy, A.K., *HIIA*, p. 201.
50. Mukherjee, R.K., *A History of Indian Civilization*, Vol. I, p. 393.
51. *Cultural Relations between India and Java*, Calcutta, 1937, p. 7.
52. *The Culture and Art of India*, p. 223.

of Śiva in East Java is the Caṇḍī Jabung[53] where we have some admirable images of the deity as decorative designs. A *caturmukha-liṅga* from Java is exhibited in the Indian Museum,[54] Calcutta.

As in Kāmboja, Tāntricism later on permeated Śaivism, and there was a rapproachment between the two which gave birth to a number of syncretic images. The profound tolerance and forbearance and the syncretic spirit of the Indo-Javanese Art and culture reached its climax not simply in producing the *Trimūrti* but the remarkable conjoint Śiva-Buddha image illustrated in Caṇḍī Jawī. In an old Javanese Mahāyānist text, Śiva is identified with the Buddha and in the Siṅgasari inscription, Śiva-Buddha is the national deity of Java and the Majapahit emperor Kṛtanagara was represented after his death by this composite image of Śiva-Buddha, and in Balinese theology, the Buddha is conceived as the younger brother of Śiva.[55] Thus, with the march of time Śiva appears in altered dress as a large number of native Indonesian elements were admitted and adjusted with the image. Finally, when the people became Muhammedans 'Islamic legend was grafted on Brāhmaṇical *Purāṇa*'; and we have still now Śiva, but only as a descendant of Adam.[56]

(iv) ŚIVA'S BULL IN ART

The Harappa bulls are distinguished by the primordial strength, weightiness and massiveness, coupled with noble

53. Coomaraswamy, A.K., *HIIA*, p. 208.
54. *ARASI*, 1924-25, pl. 37.

Moore, Albert C., *Iconography of Religions : An Introduction*, London, 1977, points out that among a number of customary marks of Śiva in the Javanese art the 'third eye' set vertically in his forehead, is the foremost. See p. 117.

55. Majumdar, R.C., ed., 'The Struggle for Empire', *The History and Culture of the Indian People*, Vol. V, 1957, p. 763.

The syncretic images of Buddha and Śiva are found in different forms in the art and sculpture of Further India. Nilakanta Sastri, K.A., has devoted an entire chapter 'Saivism in Ancient Ceylon' in his last book, *South India and South-East Asia : Studies in Their History and Culture*, Mysore, 1978.

56. Chatterji, S.K., *Indo-Aryan and Hindi*, 1960, p. 57.

dignity, and are, in the words of Benjamin Rowland,[1] 'among the world's greatest examples'. In fact, the 'breadth of treatment and feeling for the line and plastic form' are expressed in the bull seals of Harappa in such a unique way that is perhaps unsurpassed in world's glyptic art.

As Aśoka is said to have engraved a large number of edicts on already existing columns, it is perhaps not unreasonable to infer that the Rāmpurvā bull capital was originally dedicated to Śiva.[2] The modelling of the Rāmpurvā bull is vigorous, though not conventional, characterised by a lively naturalism and the animal stands with its 'full weight on earth in quiet and restrained dignity'.[3] In this carving, the artist, having a thorough mastery of the third dimension, expresses like the Harappa modeller, great power and strength combined with the gentleness and dignity of the bull, in such a brilliant way that it has become a great 'expressionist art'[4] bearing the legacy of the art of the bulls of the Harappa civilization both in form and modelling. But the treatment of the walking bull with accentuated muscles, veins and bones, in the celebrated Sārnāth column of Aśoka, separated from the other animals by wheels, is, unlike the Harappa and Rāmpurvā specimens, 'conventional, modelling coagulated and tension in movement over-emphasised'.[5] The archaic Sālempur and Lohanīpur bull capitals,[6] with no inscriptions, have the Mauryan polish. We have a beautiful specimen of a partially broken massive standing bull from Mainhai (Kauśāmbi) with a well-decorated necklace consisting of three threads, resembling very closely the Mauryan form, technique and polish, 'though the plastic treatment is much more summarised than that of the comparable Rāmpurvā bull' which is without the necklace.[7]

1. *The Art and Architecture of India*, Penguin, 1953, p. 07.
See also, Sankalia, H.D., *Pre-Historic Art in India*, New Delhi, 1978, pp. 46-51, 61-64.
2. *Encyclopaedia Britannica*, Vol. XII, p. 219.
3. Ray, N.R., *Maurya and Duṅga Art*, Calcutta, 1965, p. 31, pl. 9.
4. Fabri, C., in *Indo-Asian Culture*, Vol. I, 1951, p. 150.
5. Ray, N.R., *op. cit.*, p. 112, pl. 10.
6. *ASR*, Eastern Circle, 1918-19, p. 45.
7. Ray, N.R., *op. cit.*, p. 117, pl. 39.

The bull has been a favourite of Indian die-cutters and we have already described in detail the representation of bull on ancient Indian coins either as the theriomorphic representation of Śiva or as his *vāhana*. About the treatment of bull on the early punch-marked coins we should say that these coins do very little justice to the standard of plastic art that might have been reached by the indigenous artists before and after the Maurya period. Marshall[8] is not perhaps wrong when he remarks that these coins are "singularly crude and ugly, neither their form, which is unsymmetrical, nor the symbols which are stamped almost indiscriminately upon their surface, having any pretensions to artistic merit". However, the tribal mint-masters were more or less successful in delineating the figure of Śiva's bull on coins. The Audumbara coins are distinguished by the dynamic naturalism of the animal and for its 'Quiet and dignity, standing on earth with its full weight'.[9] The Ārjunāyana bull before the sacrificial altar is impressive for the 'expression of a doomed animal writ large in its face which is turned towards onlookers'.[10] On the Agra coins the hump of the bull is so prominent that it draws our attention first. The placing of the bull within a rayed circle, as on Agra and Rājanya coins, is another popular motif in art.

A fragmentary seal impression of the early Gupta period, found by Spooner at Basarh,[11] shows a roughly sketched bull 'running to right with the crescent moon above'. On the three Bhiṭā seals,[12] we find the bull standing to left with a crescent under its neck, a standing woman (perhaps Pārvatī) in front and a post or a thunderbolt behind the bull. The Saraswati collection of Calcutta contains a copper seal matrice, from Rājghāṭ, with the inscribed representation of a typical Indian bull with dynamic naturalism, conforming strictly to the Gupta plastic idiom of animal representation.[13]

8. *A Guide to Taxila*, Vol. I, Second ed., p. 24.

9. Dasgupta, K.K., *A Tribal History of Ancient India—A Numismatic Approach*, 1974, p. 250.

10. *Loc. cit.*

11. *ARASI*, 1913-14, pp. 121, 150, pl. L, N. 672.

12. *Ibid.*, 1911-12, p. 51, Nos. 26-28, pl. XVIII.

13. Majumdar, R.C., ed., *History and Culture of the Indian People*, Vol. III (*The Classical Age*), 1962, p. 558, pl. XLIII, fig. 99-100.

We have innumerable terracotta figurines of bull—either as the theriomorphic form of Śiva or as his mount—found from such widely separated sites as Kosam, Bhiṭā, Taxila, Rājghāṭ, Basarh, Pāṭaliputra, Sārnāth, Rangmahal, Balundi Bāgh and Mathurā, although it is difficult to date these specimens on stylistic ground.

In the Mathurā sculptures of the Kuṣāṇa and the Gupta periods, the animal accompanies its 'master'. The bull is seen either at the back or at the feet of the deity and some specimens show the divine couple either leaning on Nandin or seated on it.[14] The Gandhāran tradition is best reflected in a Kuṣāṇa intaglio, now in the Indian Museum, on which the three-faced and four-armed Śiva is found in the *Sukhāsana* pose on his mount Nandin.[15] In a beautiful sculpture from Orissa (Puri), the bull is found listening to its master in rapt attention with upraised head towards him when the latter played on the *Vīṇā*.[16] Gopinath Rao[17] illustrates two other south Indian bronze prototypes of the late period.

The massive image of the bull at Tanjore is perhaps universally known. The couchant bull is carved on the pedestal of Hara-Pārvatī *mūrtis* at Mahābalipuram, in the Kailāsanātha temple at Kāñcipuram and at Ellora. The vigorous expression of the vivacious bull mount at Aihole, on whose horn the right hand of Śiva rests in the *Varada* pose,[18] is a great expression in Indian art. In the outer hall of the Virūpākṣa temple at Paṭṭadakal, we have a massive bull resembling the Tanjore specimen. Even in a large number of vestibules of Śiva temple of Greater India, particularly of Campā, we notice the recumbent humped bull, with bells tied round its neck in the form of necklace, looking towards the god in the temple.[19] The 'jolly old bull'[20] of Elephanta, the colossal

14. Agrawala, V.S., *A Catalogue of the Brāhmaṇical Images in Mathura Art*, Lucknow, 1951, pp. 25ff.

15. Banerjea, J.N., *DHI*, pp. 468-69, Pl. XXXIV, Fig. 1.

16. *Ibid.*, p. 472, Pl. XXXV, Fig. 2.

17. *EHI*, Vol. II, Pls. LXXIX and LXXX.

18. Banerjea, J.N., *DHI*, p. 468, Pl. XXXIV, Fig. 3.

19. Parmentier, H., in *Indian Culture*, Calcutta, Vol. II, p. 419, Figs. 123, 036)

20. Munshi, K.M., *Saga of Indian Sculpture*, 1956, p. 38.

bulls on the Cāmuṇḍī hill, Basavangudi (near Bangalore), the 'fierce and undaunted'[21] bulls of Ajanta are some of the masterpieces of Indian art, though of later days.

21. Iyer, K.B., 'The Bull in Indian Art and Lore' in *The Times of India*, Annual, 1967, p. 26.

SELECT BIBLIOGRAPHY

Agrawala, V.S., *Studies in Indian Art*, Varanasi, 1965.

——— *A Catalogue of the Brāhmaṇical Images in Mathurā Art*, Lucknow, 1951.

——— *Śiva-Mahādeva*, Varanasi, 1966.

——— *Matsya Purāṇa—A Study*, Varanasi, 1963.

Aiyappan, A., *Society in India*, Madras, 1956.

——— 'A Siva-seal at Mohenjo Daro' in *JRASB*, Vol. V, 1939, (Letters).

Allan, J., *Catalogue of the Coins of Ancient India in the British Museum*, London, 1936.

Allan, G., *The Evolution of the Idea of God*, London, 1981.

Aston, W.G., *Shinto*, London, 1965.

Bagchi, P.C., *Pre-Aryan and Pre-Dravidian in India*, Calcutta, 1929.

Banerjee, J.N., *The Development of Hindu Iconography*, Calcutta, 1956.

——— *Paurāṇic and Tāntric Religion, Calcutta*, 1966.

——— *Religion in Art and Archaeology*, Lucknow, 1968.

Banerji, R.D., *Prehistoric, Ancient and Hindu India*, Bombay, 1934.

——— *The Age of the Imperial Guptas*, Banaras, 1933.

——— 'The Temple of Śiva at Bhumara' in *MASI*, No. 16.

——— 'Notes on Two Śiva Images' in *ARASI*, 1925-26.

Barth, A., *The Religions of India*, London, 1882.

Barrett, D., *Mukhalingam Temples*, Bombay, 1960.

——— *Early Cola Bronzes*, Bombay, 1965.

Bhandarkar, D.R., *Carmichael Lectures*, Calcutta, 1921.

——— *Some Aspects of Ancient Indian Culture*, Madras, 1940.

Bhandarkar, R.G., *Vaishṇavism, Śaivism and Minor Religious Systems*, Varanasi, 1965.

Bharatha Iyer, K., *Indian Art, A Short Introduction*, Bombay, 1958.

——— 'The Bull in Indian Art and Lore' in *The Times of India*, Annual, 1967.

Bhattacharyya, A., *Early Bengali Śaiva Poetry*, Calcutta, 1951.

Bhattacharyya, B., *The Indian Buddhist Iconography*, Calcutta, 1958.

Bhattacharyya, H., *The Foundations of Living Faiths*, Vol. I, Calcutta, 1938.

Bhattacharyya, S., *The Indian theogony; a comparative study of Indian mythology from the Vedas to the Puranas*, Cambridge, 1970.

Bhattasali, N.K., *Catalogue of Buddhist and Brāhmaṇical Sculptures in the Dacca Museum*, Dacca, 1929.

Bloch, T., *Supplementary Catalogue of the Archaeological Collection of the Indian Museum*, Calcutta, 1911.

Bloomfield, M., *The Religion of the Vedas*, New York, 1908.

Bongard-Levin, G.M., *Studies in Ancient India and Central Asia* (Soviet Indology Series No. 7), Calcutta, 1971.

Bosch, F.D.K., *The Golden Germ*, Holland, 1960.

Bose, P.N., *Hindu Colony of Cambodia*, Madras, 1927.

——— *The Indian Colony of Champa*, Madras, 1926.

Briffault, R., *The Mothers*, London, 1952.

Brion, M., *Animals in Art*, London, 1959.

Buchanan, F.H., *A Journey from Madras*, Vol. I, Madras, 1870.

Buckley, E., *Phallism in Japan*, Chicago, 1898.

Chakravarti, C., *Sex Life in Ancient India*, Calcutta, 1963.

Chakrabarti, S.K., *A Study of Ancient Indian Numismatics*, Mymensingh, 1931.

——— 'The Tribal Coins of Northern India' in *JRASB*, Vol. II, 1936.

Chanda, R.P., *Indo-Aryan Races*, Rajshahi, 1916.

——— 'Beginnings of Art in Eastern India' in *MASI*, No. 30.

——— 'Survival of the Prehistoric Civilisation of the Indus Valley' in *MASI*, No. 41.

Chandra, A.N., *The Rig-Vedic Culture and the Indus Civilisation*, Calcutta, 1980.

Chatham, Doris C., *Stylistic Sources and Relationships of the Kailasa Temple in Ellora*, Berkeley, 1977.

Chatterji, B.R., *Indian Cultural Influence in Cambodia*, Calcutta, 1967.

——— *South-East Asia in Transition*, Calcutta, 1967.

——— 'India and Java' in *JGIS*, No. 5.

Chatterji, J.C., *Kashmir Śaivism*, Srinagar, 1914.

Chatterji, S.K., *Indo-Aryan and Hindi*, Calcutta, 1960.
——— *Indianism and Indian Synthesis*, Calcutta, 1962.
Chattopadhyaya, B., *The Age of the Kushāṇas*, Calcutta, 1967.
Chattopadhyaya, D.P., *Indian Atheism*, Calcutta, 1969.
Chattopadhyaya, S., *The Evolution of Theistic Sects in Ancient India*, Calcutta, 1962.
Chennakesavan, S., *A Critical Study of Hinduism*, Delhi, 1980.
Conrad, J.R., *The Horn and the Sword*, London, 1959.
Coomaraswamy, A.K., *The Dance of Śiva*, New Delhi, 1971.
——— *History of Indian and Indonesian Art*, London, 1927.
——— *Yakṣas*, New Delhi, 1971.
——— *Archaic Indian Terracottas*, Leipzig, 1928.
Cox, G.W., *The Mythology of the Aryan Nations*, Vol. II, London, 1870.
Crooke, W., *The Popular Religion and Folklore of Northern India*, Delhi, 1968.
Cunningham, A., *Coins of Ancient India*. London, 1891.
——— *ASI Reports* made during the years 1862-63-64-65, 2 Vols., Simla, 1871.
Cutner, H., *A Short History of Sex Worship*, London, 1940.
Dalton, E.T., *Descriptive Ethnology of Bengal*, New Delhi, 1974.
Dandekar, R.N., *Vaiṣṇavism and Śaivism: A Fresh Look*, Imphal, 1977.
Das, A.C., *Ṛgvedic India*, Calcutta, 1st ed.
Das, R.R., *Art Traditions of Cambodia*, Calcutta, 1974.
Dasgupta, K.K., *A Tribal History of Ancient India—A Numismatic Approach*, Calcutta, 1974.
——— *The Audumbaras*, Calcutta, 1965.
——— *The Mālavas*, Calcutta, 1966.
Dehejia, V., *Early Stone Temples of Orissa*, New Delhi, 1979.
Dhaky, M.A., 'The Morphology of the 'Trident' Emblem' in *JAS*, Vol. XIX, Nos. 1-2, 1977.
Dikshit, K.N., *Prehistoric Civilization of the Indus Valley*, Madras, 1973.
Dikshit, S.K., *An Introduction to Archaeology*, Calcutta, 1955.
——— *The Mother Goddess*, Poona, n.d.
Diskalkar, D.B., 'Some Brāhmaṇical Sculptures in the Mathurā Museum' in *JUPHS*, January, 1932.

Dowson, J., *A Classical Dictionary of Hindu Mythology and Religion*, London, 1953.

Dubois, J.A., *Hindu manners, customs and ceremonies*, Oxford, 1953.

Dulaura, J.A., *The Gods of Generation*, New York, 1934.

Eliade, M., 'Spirit, Light, and Seed' in *History of Religions*, 11:1, 1971.

——— *Myth and Reality*, Chicago, 1964.

——— *Images and Symbols*, New York, 1952.

Eliot, C., *Hinduism and Buddhism*, 3 Vols., London, 1962.

Elliot Smith, G., *The Ancient Egyptians and their influence*, London, 1911.

Encyclopedia of World Art, Mc Graw-Hill Book, Vol. VII.

Fairservis, W.A., jr., *The Roots of Ancient India*, New York, 1971.

Farquhar, J.N., *An Outline of the Religious Literature of India*, Delhi, 1967.

Fergusson, J., *Tree and Serpent Worship in Ancient India*, London, 1868.

Fleet, J.F., *Inscriptions of the early Gupta kings and their successors* (*CII*, Vol. III), Calcutta, 1888.

Foote, R.B., *Indian Prehistoric and Protohistoric Antiquities*, Madras, 1916.

Forlong, *Rivers of Life*, Vol. I, London, 1883.

Foucher, A., *Beginnings of Buddhist Art*, London, 1918.

Franfort, H., *Cylinder Seals*, London, 1939.

Frazer, J.G., *Golden Bough*, 2 Vols. (abridged ed.), London, 1949.

Gajjar, I.N., *Ancient Indian Art and the West*, Bombay, 1971.

Ganguly, M., *Handbook to the Sculptures in the Baṅgiya Sāhitya Pariṣad Museum*, Calcutta, 1922.

Ghosh, A., 'Śiva—his pre-Aryan Origins' in *Indian Culture*, Vol. 2, April, 1936.

Ghosh, O., *The Dance of Shiva and other Tales from India*, New York, 1965.

Gardner, P., *A History of Ancient Coinage*, New Delhi, 1975.

——— *BMCCGSKI*, New Delhi, 191.

Gonda, J., *Viṣṇuism and Śivaism*, London, 1970.

——— *Change and Continuity in Indian Religion*, The Hague, 1965.

Gopinatha Rao, T.A., *Elements of Hindu Iconography*, 2 Vols., Madras, 1914-16.

Gough, R., *Comparative View of the Ancient Monuments of India*, London, 1785.

Grimal, P., ed., *Larousse World Mythology*, London, 1965.

Grousset, R., *Civilisations of the East*, Vol. II (India), Delhi, 1969.

——— *The Sum of History*, Hadleigh, Essex, 1951.

Grunwedel, A., *Buddhist Art of India*, London, 1901.

Gubernatis, A.D., *Zoological Mythology*, Vol. I, London, 1872.

Gupta, A.S., 'Eulogy of Paśupati Śiva', *Purāṇa*, 17:2, 1975.

Gupta, R.S., *Iconography of The Hindus, Buddhists and Jains*, Bombay, 1972.

Gupta, S.M., *Loves of Hindu gods and sages*, Bombay, 1973.

——— *From Daityas to Devatas in Hindu Mythology*, Bombay, 1973.

Hargreaves, H., *Handbook to the Sculptures in the Peshawar Museum*, Calcutta, 1930.

Harle, J.C., *Gupta Sculpture: Indian Sculpture of the Fourth to the Sixth centuries, A.D.*, Oxford, 1974.

Harrison, J.E., *Ancient Art and Ritual*, London, 1927.

Harland, E.S., *Primitive Paternity*, Vol. I, London, 1909.

——— *The Science of Fairy Tales: an inquiry into fairy mythology*, London, 1925.

Havell, E.B., *The Ideals of Indian Art*, London, 1911.

Hazra, R.C., *Studies in the Purāṇic Records on Hindu rites and customs*, Calcutta, 1940.

——— *Studies in the Upapurāṇas*, Vol. I (1958), Vol. II (1963), Calcutta.

——— 'Further Light on the God of the Famous Mohenzodaro Seals' in *Our Heritage*, Vol. XVII, Part I, 1969.

Heras, H., *Studies in the Proto-Indo-Mediterranean Culture*, Vol. I, Bombay, 1953.

Herbert, J., *The Hindu Mythology*, Saigon, 1952.

Hiltebeitel, A., "The Indus Valley 'Proto-Śiva' Reexamined through Reflections on the Goddess, the Buffalo and the symbolism of vāhanas" in *Anthropos*, 73, 1978.

Hodson, T.C., *The Naga Tribes of Manipur*, London, 1911.

Hopkins, E.W., *Epic Mythology*, New Delhi, 1968.

——— *Religions of India*, New Delhi, 1770.

Inman, T., *Ancient Pagan and Modern Christian Symbolism*, New York, 1903.
Jash, P., *History of Saivism*. Calcutta, 1974.
Jayaswal, K.P., *Hindu Polity*, Vol. I, Bangalore, 1943.
——— *History of India*, Lahore, 1938.
——— 'Pāṭaliputra Śiva-Pārvatī Gold Plaque' in *JISOA*, Vol. II, 1934.
——— 'Terracottas dug out at Patna' in *JISOA*, Vol. III, 1935.
Jevons, F.B., *Comparative Religion*, Cambridge, 1913.
Joshi, N.P., *Catalogue of the Brahmanical Sculptures in the State Museum, Lucknow*, Part, I, Lucknow, 1972.
——— "A Unique Figure of Śiva from Musanagar" in *Bulletin of Museums and Archaeology in Uttar Pradesh*, Vol. 3, 1969, Lucknow.
Jouveau-Dubreuil, G., *Iconography of South India*, Paris, 1937.
Kane, P.V., *History of Dharmaśāstra*, Vol. II, Poona, 1941.
Kar, C., *Classical Indian Sculpture*, London, 1950.
Karmakar, A.P., *The Religions of India*, Vol. I, Lonavla, 1950.
Keith, A.B., *Religion and Philosophy of the Veda and Upanishads*, Cambridge, 1925 (Harvard Oriental Series, Vols. 31 and 32).
——— *A History of Sanskrit Literature*, Oxford, 1920.
——— *The Mythology of All Races*, Vol. VI, London, 1917.
Kempers, B., *Cultural Relations between India and Java*, Calcutta, 1937.
Kennedy, J., *Ancient and Hindu Mythology*, London, 1831.
Kosambi, D.D., *Myth and Reality*, Bombay, 1962.
——— *The Culture and Civilisation of Ancient India*, London, 1965.
Kramrisch, Stella, *The Presence of Śiva*, Princeton University Press, 1984.
——— *The Art of India*, London, 1954.
——— *Hindu Temples*, 2 Vols., Calcutta, 1946.
——— *Indian Sculpture*, London, 1933.
——— 'Indian Terracottas' in *JISOA*, Vol. VII, 1939.
Kuiper, F.B.J., *An Austro-Asiatic myth in the Rigveda*, Amsterdam, 1950.
———*Proto-Munda words in Sanskrit*, Amsterdam, 1948.

Lannoy, Richard, *The Speaking Tree: A Study of Indian Culture and Society*, OUP (Paperback), 1975.

Leeuw, G. van der, *Sacred and Profane Beauty: The Holy in Art*, Weidenfeld and Nicolson, 1963, Part I, 'Beautiful Motion'.

Letourneau, C.J.M., *Evolution of Marriage*, London, 1911.

Long, J.G., *Visions of Terror and Bliss*, Univ. of Chicago, 1970.

——— "Siva as Promulgator of Traditional Learning and Patron Deity of the Fine Arts" in *ABORI*, 52, 1972.

Lorenzen, David N., *The Kāpālikas and Kālāmukhas: Two lost Śaivite Sects*, Berkeley, 1972.

Lowry, J., *Tibetan Art*, HMSO, 1973.

Macdonell, A.A., *Vedic Mythology*, Strassburg, 1897.

——— *A History of Sanskrit Literature*, Delhi, 1965.

Macdonell, A.A. and Keith, A.B, *Vedic Index*, 2 Vols, Varanasi, 1958.

Macnicol, N., *Indian Theism*. Delhi, 1968.

Mahalingam, T.V., *Kāñcipuram in Early South Indian History*, Madras, 1968.

Majumdar, N.G., *A Guide to the Sculptures in the Indian Museum*, Delhi, 1937.

Majumdar, R.C., *Inscriptions of Kambuja*, Calcutta, 1953.

——— *Ancient Indian Colonies in the Far East*, 2 Vols., Lahore, 1927.

——— *Hindu Colonies in the Far East*, Calcutta, 1944.

——— *Ancient Indian Colonies in South-East Asia*, Baroda, 1955.

——— *Indian Religion*, Calcutta, 1969.

——— ed. *History of Bengal*, Vol. I, Dacca, 1943.

——— ed. *History and Culture of the Indian People*, 5 Vols., Bombay, 1st ed.

Marett, R.R., *Threshold of Religion*, London, 1896.

Marr, G.S., *Sex in Religion*, London, 1936.

Marshall, J., *Mohenjo-daro & Indus Civilisation*, 3 Vols., London, 1931.

——— *A Guide to Taxila*, Calcutta, 1921.

Max Muller, *Contributions to the Science of Mythology*, Vol. I, 1897.

Mayrofer, M., *Concise Etymological Sanskrit Dictionary*, 3 Vols., Heidelberg, 1953, 1963, 1976.

Mc Crindle, J.W., *Ancient India as described by Megasthenes and Arrian*, Calcutta, 1960.

Miles, A., *The Land of the Lingam*, London, 1933.

Mitra, R.L., *Indo-Aryans*, 2 Vols., Calcutta, 1881.

——— *The Antiquities of Orissa*, Vol. I, Calcutta, 1875.

Monier-Williams, *Religious Thought and Life in India*, London, 1891.

——— *Brāhmaṇism and Hinduism*, London, 1891.

Moore, Albert C., *Iconography of Religions: An Introduction*, London, 1977.

Muir, J., *Original Sanskrit Texts*, Vol. IV, London, 1873.

Mukherji, B.L., *Atharva Veda*, Kanda XV, Calcutta, 1926.

Mukherjee, Radhakamal, *The Culture and Art of India*, London, 1959.

——— *A History of Indian Civilization*, Vol. I, Bombay, 1956.

Mookerji, Radha Kumud, *Hindu Civilization*, London, 1936.

Munshi, K.M., *Saga of Indian Sculpture*, New Delhi, 1956.

Nandimath, S.C., *Handbook of Vīraśaivism*, Dharwar, 1942.

Natarajan, B., *The City of the Cosmic Dance; Chidambaram*, New Delhi, 1974.

Nilkanta Sastri, K.A., *Cultural Contacts between Aryans and Dravidians*, Bombay, 1967.

——— *A Comprehensive History of India*, Vol. II, Bombay, 1957.

——— *South-India and South-East Asia: Studies in Their History and Culture*, Mysore, 1978.

O'Flaherty, W.D., *The Origins of Evil in Hindu Mythology*, Berkeley, 1976.

———*Asceticism and Eroticism in the mythology of Śiva*, London, 1973, Delhi, 1975.

———*Hindu Myths: A Sourcebook Translated from the Sanskrit*, Baltimore, 1975.

——— "The Hindu Symbolism of Cows, Bulls..." etc. in *AARP*. 8, 1975.

O'Malley, L.S.S., *Popular Hinduism*, Cambridge, 1935.

Oppert, G., *Original Inhabitants of India*, London, 1st ed.

Oldenberg, H., *Ancient India*; *its language and religions*, Chicago, 1898.

Pal, D.N., *Śiva and Śakti*, 2 Vols., Calcutta, 1910.

Pal, Pratapaditya, *The Sensuous Immortals: A selection of Sculptures from the Pan-Asian Collection*, Los Angeles, 1978.

Pargiter, F.E., *Ancient Indian Historical Tradition*, London, 1922.

Patil, D.R., *Cultural History from the Vāyu Purāṇa*, Poona, 1946.

Payne Knight, R., *Sexual Symbolism*, Vol. I, New York, 1957.

Philpot, *The Sacred Tree*, London, 1897.

Piggot, S., *Prehistoric India*, 1950.

——— *Phallism* (anonymous), London, 1889.

Prazyluski, J., *Pre-Aryan and Pre-Dravidian in India* (Translated from French by Bagchi, P.C.), Calcutta, 1929.

Radhakrishnan, S., *Indian Philosophy*, Vol. I, London, 1958.

Raffles, *History of Java*, 2 Vols., London, 1830.

Ramachandra Dikshitar, V.R., *The Matsya Purāṇa—A Study*, Madras, 1935.

Rapson, E.J., *Indian Coins*, Strassburg, 1897.

——— ed. *CHI*, Vol. I, Delhi, 1962.

——— *CCAWKTB*, London, 1907.

Rao, S.R., *Lothal and the Indus Civilization*, 1973.

Rao, T.A. Gopinatha, *Elements of Hindu Iconography* (2 Vols)., Madras, 1914 and 1916.

Ramanujan, A.K., *Speaking of Śiva*, Penguin, 1973.

Ramakrishnan, V., *Perspectives in Saivism*, Madras, 1978.

Rau, Heimo, *Reflections on Indian Art*, Bombay, 1976.

Ray, N.R., *Brāhmaṇical Gods in Burma*, Calcutta, 1932.

——— *Maurya and Śuṅga Art*, Calcutta, 1965.

Raychaudhuri, H.C., *Political History of Ancient India*, Calcutta, 1938.

——— *Studies in Indian Antiquities*, Calcutta, 1958.

Renou, L., *Religions of Ancient India*, London, 1953.

Rice, B.L., *Mysore*, Vol. I, London, 1897.

Risley, H.H., *Tribes and Castes of Bengal*, 2 Vols., Calcutta, 1891.

Rivers, W.H.R., *The Todas*, London, 1906.

Rocco Sha, *The Masculine Cross and Ancient Sex Worship*, London, 1898.

Rowland, B., *The Art and Architecture of India*, Middlesex, Penguin, 1967.

Sadasivaiah, H.M., *A comparative Study of two Vīraśaiva monasteries, a study in Sociology of Religion*, Mysore, 1967.

Sahai, B., *Iconography of Minor Hindu and Buddhist Deities*, New Delhi, 1975.

Sahoo, A.C., "Śaivism as Reflected on the Gold Coins of the Nalas" in *JNSI*, Vol. XLII, 1980, Parts I-II.

Sakhare, M.R., *History and Philosophy of Liṅgāyata Religion*, Belgaum, 1942.

Sankalia, H.D., *Pre-Historic Art in India*, New Delhi, 1978.

——— *Prehistory of India*, 1977.

——— *Prehistory and proto-history of India and Pakistan*, Poona, 1974.

Saraswati, S.K., *A Survey of Indian Sculpture*, Calcutta, 1957.

Sarker, H.B., ed. *R.C. Majumdar Volume*, Calcutta, 1970.

Sastri, K.N., *New Light on the Indus Civilization*, Delhi, 1957.

Scott, G.R., *Phallic Worship*, London, 1941.

Sharma, B.N., *Iconography of Sadāśiva*, New Delhi, 1976.

——— "Rāvaṇa Lifting Mount Kailāsa in Indian Art" in *East and West*, 23, 1973.

Sherring, M.A., *The Sacred City of the Hindus*, London, 1868.

Shivpadasundaram, P., *The Śaiva School of Hinduism*, London, 1934.

Siddhantashastree, R.K., *Śaivism Through the Ages*, Delhi, 1975.

Singh, S.B., *Brāhmaṇical Icons in Northern India*, New Delhi, 1977.

Sinha, B.P., *Archaeology and Art of India*, Delhi, 1979.

Sircar, D.C., *The Śākta Pīṭhas*, Calcutta, 1948.

——— *Studies in the Religious Life of Ancient and Medieval India*, Delhi, 1971.

——— *Indian Epigraphy*, Delhi, 1965.

——— *Select Inscriptions*, Vol. I, Calcutta, 1965.

Sivaraman, K., *Saivism in Philosophical Perspective*, Delhi, 1973.

Sivaramamurti, C., *Naṭarāja in Art, Thought and Literature*, New Delhi, 1976.

——— *The Art of India*, New York, 1977.

——— *Śatarudriya: Vibhūti of Śiva's Iconography*, New Delhi, 1976.

——— *The Painter in Ancient India*, New Delhi, 1978.

——— *Royal Conquests and Cultural Migration in South India and the Deccan*, Calcutta, 1955.

——— "Parallels and Opposites in Indian Iconography" in *JAS*, Letters, Vol. XXI, No. 2, 1955.

Slater, G., *Dravidian Element in Indian Culture*, New Delhi, 1976.

Smith, V.A., *Early History of India*, Oxford, 1924.

——— *History of Fine Arts in India and Ceylon*, Bombay, 1962.

——— *CCIM*, Calcutta, 1906.

Smith, W.R., *Religion of the Semites*, Edinburgh, 1889.

Spencer, H., *Principles of Sociology*, Vol. I, London, 1877.

Srinivasa Aiyanger, P.T., *Pre-Aryan Tamil Culture*, Madras, 1930.

Srinivasan, Doris, "The so-called Proto-Śiva Seal from Mohenjodaro: An Iconological Assessment." in *Archives of Asian Art*, 29, 1975-76.

Srinivasan, T.N., *A Handbook of South Indian Images*, Tiripati, 1954.

Stack, E., *The Mikirs*, London, 1908.

Subramanian, K.R., *Origin of Śaivism and its history in Tamilland*, Madras, 1925.

Suddhananda Bharati, *The grand epic of Śaivism*, Madras, 1970.

Shukla, L.K., *A Study of Hindu Art and Architecture*, The Chowkhambą Sanskrit Studies, Vol. LXXXII, Varanasi, 1972.

Tarn, W.W., *Greeks in Bactria and India*, Cambridge, 1938.

Theobald, W., *On certain Symbols or Devices on the Gold Coins of the Guptas*, Calcutta, 1885.

——— 'Notes on some symbols found on the punchmarked coins' in *JASB*, 1890, Nos. III and IV.

Thomas, E., *Essays on Indian Antiquities of James Prinsep*, 2 Vols. London, 1858.

Thomas, P., *Epics, Myths and Legends of India*, Bombay, 1961.

Thurston, *Castes and Tribes of Southern India*, Madras, 1909, Vols. I-III.

Taylor, E.B., *Primitive Culture*, London, 1891.

Upadhyaya, P., *Female Images in the Museums of U.P. and their Social Background*, Varanasi, 1978.

Vats, M.S., *Excavations at Harappa*, 2 Vols., Delhi, 1940.

Venkataramanayya, N., *Rudra-Śiva*, Madras, 1941.

Vettam Mani, *Purāṇic Encyclopaedia*, Delhi, 1979.

Vitsaxis, Vassilis G., *Hindu Epics, Myths and Legends in Popular Illustrations*, OUP, New Delhi, 1977.

Vogel, J. Ph., *The Influences of Indian Art*, 1925.

——— *Catalogue of the Archaeological Museum at Mathurā*, 1910.

Wake, C.S., and Westropp, H.M., *Phallism in Ancient Worships*, New Delhi, 1970.

Wall, O.A., *Sex and Sex Worship*, Kimpton, 1920.

Watters, T., *On Yuan Chwang*, Vol. I, Delhi, 1961.

Weber, A.F., *The History of Indian Literature*, Varanasi, 1961.

Werner Stark, *The Sociology of Religion*, Vol. II, 'Sectarian Religion', Routledge and Kegan Paul, 1967.

Westermack, *History of Human Marriage*, London, 1891.

Wheeler, R.E.M., *Civilizations of the Indus Valley and Beyond*, London, 1966.

Whitehead, R.B., *Catalogue of Coins in the Punjab Museum*, Lahore, 3 Pts., 1914-1934.

Whitney, W.D., *Oriental & Linguistic Studies*, 2 Vols., London, 1875.

Wilkins, W.J., *Hindu Mythology*, Delhi, 1972.

Wilson, H.H., *Hindu Religion*, Calcutta, 1899.

——— *Works*, Vols. I-X, London, 1786-1860.

Wilson, H.H., *Rig-Veda-Sanhita*, 6 Vols., Bangalore, 1946.

——— *Religious sects of the Hindus*, Calcutta, 1958.

Winternitz, M., *A History of Indian Literature*, Vols. I and II, Calcutta, 1959.

Zimmer, H., *Myths & Symbols in Indian Art & Civilization*, New York, 1962.

——— *The Art of Indian Asia*, 2 Vols., New York, 1955.

INDEX

B

I

J

Q

R

S

W

Y

ADDENDA AND CORRIGENDA

(p = page; l = line)

	Read	*For*
p. 8, para 4, l.2	explained in	explained n
p. 13, Para 2, l. 12	regarding	ragarding
p. 15, para 2 (last line)	name'!	name'.
p. 16, para 3 (last line)	another	anotner
p. 29, f.n. 11	A. N. Chandra	A. K. Chandra
p. 29, f.n. 11	or rather anti-sacrificial	or anti-sacrificial
p. 36, para 1, l. 3	rapprochement	rapproachement
p. 40, para 3, l. 2	Girijā	irijā
p. 42, para 1, l. 6	sanctify	sancitfy
p. 49, para 1, l. 5	built,	built
p. 51, f.n. 190	III.33.1	III.83.1
p. 53, para 2, l.19	term	terms
p. 54, para 3, l.1	rapprochement	rapproachement
p. 59, f.n. 265	Venkatara-manayya, H.	Venkatara-mayya, H.
p. 60, f.n. 272	Vol. XXIX	Vol. XXIV
p. 62, l.6	instrument,	instrument
p. 75, para 2, l. 10	identified	idedtified
p. 77, f.n. 22	A. S.	A. S:
p. 79, f.n. 33	Theobald, W.,	Theobold, W.,
p. 80, f.n. 45	p. 13	p. 18
p. 87, para 4, l. 12	that then,	that,
p. 89, f.n. 31	Vol. XVII,	Vol. XVIII,
p. 95, f.n. 4	Generation	Generations
p. 96, para 2, l. 3	just an	just on
p. 98, f.n. 20	p. 890	p. 980
p. 100, f.n. 3	DHI, 1956	DHI, 1965
p. 103, f.n. 31	Vṛṣéhi	Vṛṣ hi
p. 104, f.n. 32	pp. 455-58	pp. 455-48
p. 105, f.n. 37	"The Indus	'The Indus

	Valley 'Proto-Siva'	Valley' 'Proto-Siva'
p. 105, f.n. 37	Vahanas"	Vahanas
p. 106, para 2, l. 2	alluded to, in the Ṛgveda,[3]	alluded in the Ṛgveda[3]
p. 107, para 1, l. 4	Zorastrian	Zoraostrian
p. 109, para 2 (last but two lines)	tribe,[23]	tribe.[23]
p. 111, f.n. 41	1888	1889
p. 112, f.n. 49	1965,	1965
p. 113, para 2, l. 9	resurrector	resurrectors
p. 120, f.n. 119	1897,	1879
p. 126, para 3, l. 7	of Śiva.	of Śiva
p. 131, para 3, l. 1	by Banerji	by Benerji
p. 131, f.n. 47, l. 6	102:4)	102:4
p. 131, f.n. 47, l. 8	innermost	inermost
p. 133, f.n. 55, l. 3	less	ess
p. 134, para 1 (last line)	Viśvadevas.	Viśvedevas.
p. 141, f.n. 61 (last para)	(Ramanujan's... 1973)	'Ramanujan's... 1973,
p. 144, para 2, l. 3	Curtius	Curtias
p. 146, para 2 (last but one line)	level	lavel
p. 150, f.n. 46	Deogarh'	Deograh'
p. 156, para 3, l. 3	representations	representation
p. 156, f.n. 83	Doris C.,	Doris, C.,
p. 156, f.n. 83 (last line)	77-80	77-78
p. 157, para 2, l. 12	groove	grove
p. 163, f.n. 35	pp. 109-11	pp. 109-01
p. 165, para 2, l. 7	In the art	In art
p. 166, f.n. 53	53	S3
p. 174, f.n. 19 (last line)	p. 70	p. 60
p. 176, para 1 (first line)	groups[26];	groups[26]
p. 177, para 3, l. 12	Vikrāntavarman,	Nikrāntavarman
p. 178, f.n. 35	Campa	Champa
p. 178, f.n. 36	pp. 179-80	pp. 179-080
p. 179, f.n. 39	Campa	Champa
p. 179, f.n. 40	Ray, N. R.,	Kay, N. L.
p. 182, l. 6	rapprochement	rapproachment
p. 183, f.n. 1	p. 17.	p. 07.

p. 183, f.n. 3	Śuṅga	Duṅga
p. 183, f.n. 4	p. 151	p. 150
p. 185, para 2 (last but one line)	Gopinatha	Gopinath
p. 185, f.n. 19	136.	036)
p. 185, f.n. 20	p. 33.	p. 38.
p. 187, 1. 11	1931	1981
p. 187, 1. 12	1905.	1965.
p. 187, 1. 14	Banerjea, J. N.,	Banerjee, J. N.,
p. 188, 1. 17	Campa,	Champa,
p. 190, 1. 5	Dulaure,	Dulaura,
p. 191, 1. 4	1885.	1785.
p. 191 (last line)	1970.	1770.
p. 192, 1. 5	1933.	1938.
p. 192, 1. 31	1981.	1984.

PLATE I

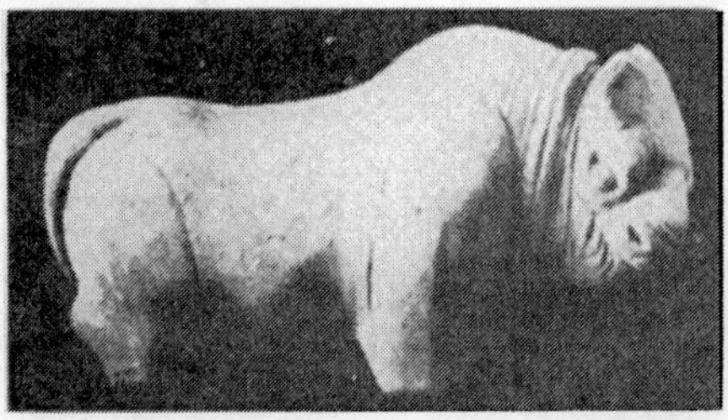

The Harappa Bulls
(See p. 183)

The Proto-Śiva with the animals (See pp. 143, 164)

PLATE II

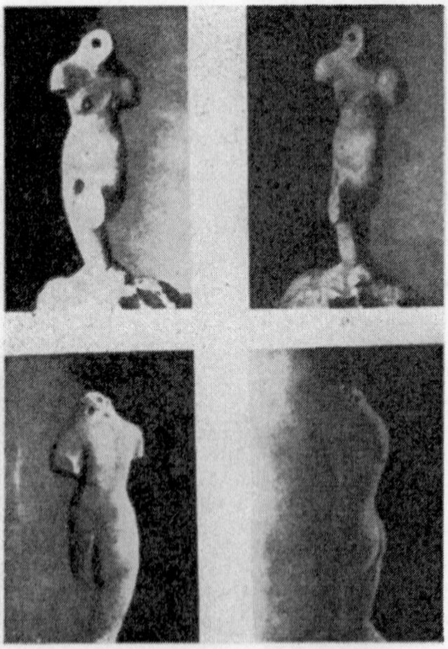

Dancing Figure of Harappa (prototype of Naṭarāja ?) (See pp. 61ff., 143-44)

Guḍimallam Liṅga (See pp. 128, 154, 157, 164-65)

Rāmpurvā Bull (See p. 183)

Śiva-heads of the Mathurā School
(See pp. 148, 151)

Bull on the Rājghāt Copper Seal-matrix
(See p. 184)

PLATE IV

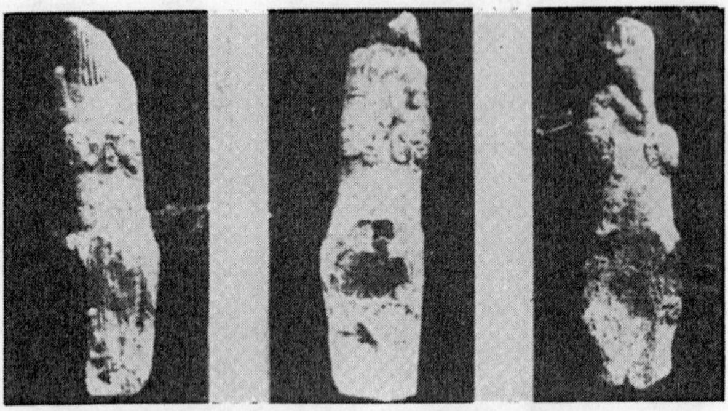

Mukhaliṅgas : Khoh Specimens (See pp. 159-60)

Sārnāth : Śiva head
(See p. 145)

Khoh : Mukhaliṅga
(See p. 160)

Śiva-Liṅgin, Mathurā Specimens (See pp. 160-62)

PLATE V

Heads of syncretic Harihara, Mathurā Museum (See p. 152)

Hara-Gaurī in the Mathurā Museum (See pp. 151-52, 165)

Hara-Gaurī in the Mathurā Museum (Side view)

PLATE VI

Devī Carrying the *liṅga* over her head, Mathurā Museum (See p. 166)

Trimūrti in the Peshawar Museum
(See pp. 54ff.)

Śiva-Pārvatī relief from Kosam
(See pp. 151-52)

Liṅgoḍbhavamūrti (Tanjore)
(See pp. 163-64)

Śiva on Nandin, Indian Museum
(See p. 148)

A Pañcamukha type Śivaliṅga (See pp. 161-62)

Terracotta Relief of Siva-Pārvatī (See p. 144)

Vaṭuka Bhairava (See p. 67)

Vṛṣavāhana, Aihole (See pp. 155, 185)

PLATE IX

Kalyāṇasundara, Vākāṭaka period, Elephanta. (See pp. 42ff.)

PLATE X

Rāvaṇānugraha showing Śiva as *Liṅgin*, Mukteśvara Temple, Kāñcipuram (See pp. 168-69)

Vīrabhadra (See pp. 68ff.)

Gaṅgādhara Vākāṭaka period, Elephanta (See pp. 58ff.)

Ardhanārīśvaramūrti, Chola Specimen (See pp. 43ff.)

Umā-Sahita Akṣa-Krīḍāmūrti, Mallikārjuna Temple, Paṭṭadakal (See pp. 167-68)

PLATE XII

Śiva as *Liṅgin*

(a) Virūpākṣa temple, Paṭṭadakal
(See p. 167)

(b) Kailāsa temple, Ellora (See p. 167)

(c) *Vīṇādhara*, Saṅgameśvara temple, Paṭṭadakal (See p. 167)

(d) Śiva with Umā, Virūpākṣa temple, Paṭṭadakal (See p. 167)